HOW TO BE A POP IDOL

HOW TO BE A POP IDOL

JEFF CLARK-MEADS

metro

Published by Metro Publishing Ltd,
3, Bramber Court, 2 Bramber Road,
London W14 9PB, England

First published in paperback in 2003

ISBN 1 84358 048 9

All rights reserved. No part of this publication may be reproduced, stored in a retrieval system, or in any form or by any means, without the prior permission in writing of the publisher, nor be otherwise circulated in any form of binding or cover other than that in which it is published and without a similar condition including this condition being imposed on the subsequent publisher.

British Library Cataloguing-in-Publication Data:

A catalogue record for this book is available from the British Library.

Design by ENVY

Printed in Great Britain by Bookmarque

1 3 5 7 9 10 8 6 4 2

© Text copyright Jeff Clark-Meads

Papers used by Metro Publishing are natural, recyclable products made from wood grown in sustainable forests. The manufacturing processes conform to the environmental regulations of the country of origin.

Every attempt has been made to contact the relevant copyright-holders, but some were unobtainable. We would be grateful if the appropriate people could contact us.

Contents

ACKNOWLEDGEMENTS		7
Chapter 1	THE THREE Rs	9
Chapter 2	R IS FOR RECORDS	23
Chapter 3	R IS FOR RETAIL	39
Chapter 4	R IS FOR RIGHTS	51
Chapter 5	THE TWILIGHT ZONE – A&R	65
Chapter 6	MAKING A STAR	83
Chapter 7	BROAD HORIZONS	99
Chapter 8	ONLINE	115
Chapter 9	THE LAW	123
Chapter 10	THE INDUSTRY ORGANISATIONS	135
Chapter 11	THE PEOPLE	149

Chapter 12	THE CHARTS	165
Chapter 13	GOVERNMENTS AND POLITICS	181
Chapter 14	MAJORS AND INDIES	195
Chapter 15	THE AWARDS SHOWS	209
Chapter 16	THE TRADE FAIRS	219
Chapter 17	THE MEDIA	233
Chapter 18	TOURING	245
Chapter 19	THE RIGHTS AND RESPONSIBILITIES OF BEING A STAR	259
Chapter 20	THE GLOBAL BUSINESS	271
Chapter 21	AND A FINAL WORD ON NEW TECHNOLOGY	287

Acknowledgements

In grateful thanks for the greatest gifts the music industry has to offer: Rachel Sylvie Lellouche, Janet and Michael Berridge, Pete Cronin, Debbie Gregson, Gem Howard, Colleen Hue, Maurice Jones, John Love, Iain McNay, Ralf Plaschke, Dominic Pride, David Redfern and Rich Zahradnik.

Plus, of course, Mam and Dad, Jenny Fraser, John and Pat Clark, Adrian Baron, Andrew Robinson, Howard Snape, Ian Whitehead and Nick Wright.

Chapter 1

THE THREE Rs

THERE IS ONE INDUSTRY that is very familiar to us all. It is full of people seeking attention, people who will do anything and everything to advance their own careers, self-seeking egotists and, of course, the good guys who want to do an excellent job and assist those around them to the limits of their ability.

That industry is called insurance. Or banking. Or shipbuilding. Or, indeed, music.

There is a general and very, very popular view that the business of music is somehow different to other industries. Well, in my experience of several commercial sectors, music has just the same proportion of good guys and bad guys as any other. It also has exactly the same motivations as any other: to make a decent profit by selling goods that people want to buy at a price the market is prepared to pay.

In short, the music industry is alarmingly similar in motivations, outlook and *modus operandi* to virtually every other legitimate profit-making business on the planet. This is an important – perhaps the most important – concept to grasp about this industry. When we realise music has the same headaches and the same drives and the same legal and commercial framework as any other business, it makes it seem a lot less remote and esoteric. In fact, there are few reasons why the music industry should be in any way impenetrable to the outside observer. Perhaps the only reason is the way it is portrayed in the popular media.

Television and radio programmes looking for ratings and magazines fighting for sales are pretty much interested only in the glitzy, glamorous end of the business. It's not hard to see the sense of that: a sexy person singing a song people enjoy or chatting about a lifestyle that is both interesting and attractive will bring in a lot more viewers than a tedious but worthy middle-aged gentleman explaining what impact the Copyright Directive might have on mechanical royalty rates. (Believe me, I've been there and done that. People just think: He's boring and ugly, and turn over.)

But mechanical royalties are the bedrock of the whole business. Stars come and go – the majority just flit through the public consciousness like an infatuation – yet 'mechanicals' have been the basis of money made from music for the past hundred years. Thus, if you really want to make a living out of music as a performer, an entrepreneur or an executive, it's far more important to know what a mechanical royalty is than who is top of the charts this week and whether he's having a do with the lead actress from your favourite soap opera.

In truth, then, there are only two things that set the music industry apart from other businesses:

1. It and its products are constantly in the public eye. This is a prerequisite of the business. Nobody needs to buy music – it is not food or fuel – so it has to stay public and popular to survive. It must, by the correct marketing of the correct product, make people want what it produces.

2. Its product is invisible. Yes, records are round, tangible pieces of plastic. But nobody pays a decent sum of good money just for a round, tangible piece of plastic. What people are buying is the sounds it contains – an invisible, intangible commodity.

THE THREE Rs

That second element, though hidden from public view, is nonetheless the vast, unseen heart of the music industry. This is the rights sector – the area of the business that deals with copyrights, music, royalties and other invisible, intangible matters – and it is the bulk of the industry. Though the other two Rs – records and retail – are far more obvious, rights underpins and overarches all else.

Let's take a look at what these three Rs do and how they relate to one another, starting with the most obvious R – records.

When people think of the music industry, they tend to think first, and generally only, of record companies. That's not surprising since, out of every area of the business, only record companies are ever portrayed in the media; it is also because these companies, or labels, are the only part of the business that produces something you can buy and take home.

So what, then, do record companies do exactly? Simplistically put, they find talented people, develop their abilities, record their songs and make records with them, then market those records – and in the process try to make a profit.

Let's take that one step at a time. How do record companies find talent? Firstly, they look at what's under their noses, namely at all the thousands of tapes and demo discs that turn up in the post every day. That's pretty much a full-time job but, to ensure they are missing nothing – and, remember, they are highly motivated in this; the music industry is predicated on music – A&R scouts scour the country watching dozens of gigs every day to see who's out there.

In addition record companies talk to other sectors of the industry – publishers, promoters, managers, retailers, everybody they know – to keep connected to whatever the word is about any hot new act emerging.

Record companies can also create their own acts. If a label believes it needs, say, a boy band on its roster, it need not wait for one to emerge. Rather, by taking three, four or five appropriate young men, it can put them together, give them the songs it wants sung, create an appropriate image, market them appropriately and, hey presto, have exactly the kind of hit it wants – if the label is both bright and lucky.

Once an act, of whatever style or nature, has been signed, the record company then sets about developing the talent that attracted its attention in the first place. If the label has signed, say, a four-piece mainstream rock band who write their own material, the first thing it is likely to do is help them develop that material. That means putting them in a rehearsal room or studio or whatever is needed to get the best out of them.

Sometimes, though, developing talent means touring – and pretty much nothing else. When Chris Blackwell, founder and long-time top dog at Island Records, signed U2, he put the band on the road for two years to learn their trade. History tells us that was a wise decision.

But, whatever route is taken to bring the band to their full potential, once the process is complete the record company begins the recording process. That means ensuring the band have the right songs – their own or somebody else's – then putting them in the studio with the right creative people around them. It's a very important step to ensure the act feels comfortable with both their environment and support because musicians find it virtually impossible to create to the best of their ability when they're not happy

When the album is finished, then begins the task of selling it. In this process, selling it to the industry is top of the list of priorities. If an album isn't in Virgin and HMV and Woolworths, it can't get into the chart – and without chart exposure, a new act can never enter the mainstream.

So, a record company's first job is to ensure the retail chains are interested in the new product. Persuading them to be interested is, however, enormously difficult because, in the UK alone, there are around twenty-five thousand new releases – albums and singles – each year. With space in retailers' racks finite and often tiny (how many non-chart albums can you find in the average Woolworths?) the competition just to get the album past the shop's doorstep is overwhelmingly enormous. Add to that the fact the label is trying to sell the album to the retailer and that the record store has to hand over good money in return for taking it into its premises and you can see the kind of pressure labels' sales departments are under.

But, assuming that the retailers are suitably enthused about the album, the label can then begin marketing it to the public. The easy way of doing that is to buy advertising – easy, yes, but expensive. The more advertising the label buys, the more chance the album has and, of course, the more expensive the process gets.

The other aspect that goes hand in hand with advertising is promotion. This is a broad term covering every public exposure of the album and the band. It ranges from public appearances – signing sessions and suchlike – to concert tours to having the singles from the album played on the radio and the band appearing on television.

These last two areas are by far the trickiest and achieving them is the core function of the label's promotion department – people who spend all their time urging radio and television producers to give airtime to the new band they are handling. However, every other record company is doing exactly the same thing and TV and radio producers are utterly inundated with requests for exposure for new acts. And not only are the new acts competing with all the other new acts for airtime, they are also competing with all the established artists. There is not a huge amount of music on television (even when the dedicated music channels are included) and if a label wants to secure just three minutes of it, it has to have something that stands out from its peers and holds up against Madonna and the Rolling Stones and every other top act with a video in the vaults.

It is a truism of the record industry that its core function is to make people famous. Once the performer is famous, half the job of marketing and promotion is done before their album is even released. Making people famous in the first place is, then, both the defining principle of the business and its greatest challenge.

That, in a nutshell, was our first R - records. Let's move on to the second, retail. This is the public face of the record industry, the one that everybody sees on the high street. Retailers range from the small to the huge, the dedicated to the non-specialist, the indie to the corporate.

A disappearing breed is the indie store, the one-off operation run by a fan or a family. In the US, they call them 'mom-and-pop stores', which is a lovely, quaint way of describing such home-grown operations. They tend to be quirky or specialist or both; that's because there's no point being mainstream if you have an HMV or Virgin or Woolworths nearby. If, as an indie, you compete with such majors on their ground, you will lose; they have more power to advertise, more power to sell at lower prices and more power to promote than the indie.

Instead, successful indies offer something the major retail chains don't, be it a specialised stocking policy or specialist knowledge from the staff. The only way to survive in that tough high-street market is to offer things other people aren't. There's no point in indies trying to out-HMV HMV because that's an eminently suicidal business strategy.

Even so, due to a number of factors, not least the success of the major chains, indies have been declining in number since the end of the eighties. From a peak of around two thousand stores, there are now about five hundred left in the UK. At least, though, the ones that remain are fairly well established and this country can claim to actually have an indie retail sector; in some other countries they have been pretty much totally eradicated.

France, for instance, has seen its indie retail sector decline

THE THREE Rs

to virtually nothing in the past ten years because of the policies of the hypermarkets. Anybody who's been to France will be familiar with these huge, out-of-town retailers like Carrefour and E. Leclerc. Both these chains, and the others operating in this sector, carry a huge range of goods from food and clothes to televisions and computers. One minor line for them is music; I say 'minor' because in terms of their turnover, music hardly shows up.

But those chains have used music as a loss-leader to attract people into the stores. Carrefour and Leclerc and the rest have sold music and videos very cheaply – often below cost price – to give customers a reason to take the time and trouble to leave the town centre and come to them. Once in one of these vast retail palaces, people tend to buy a lot of other goods, too, so the policy is an effective one from the companies' perspective. However, because they sell mainstream chart product far, far cheaper than an indie could ever afford to, the 'mère-et-père' stores in France have gone to the wall in huge numbers.

When the indies disappear, what are we left with? In essence, the chains. There are dedicated chains – HMV and Virgin prime among them – and those other retail groups for whom music forms a part of their overall mix, most notably Woolworths and WH Smith and, in Scotland, John Menzies.

The big difference between a dedicated retailer and a more general one is the depth of their stock, that is, the number of titles they carry. If the Rolling Stones have a new album released, the average HMV and Virgin store will carry both the new release and all the band's earlier albums. Less committed retailers, like Woolworths and WH Smith, are likely to take just the new one and maybe one or two of the earlier ones.

So, not only do dedicated retailers carry stock in more depth than more general stores, they also stock in much greater breadth. Woolworths and WH Smith may have some albums in store from a non-mainstream act – say, a heavy-metal or garage or techno band – but a dedicated retailer will have dozens or hundreds or, in extreme cases, thousands.

All music retailers, of course, operate in conjunction with the other elements of the music industry, and their closest colleagues in that enterprise are the record companies. The relationship between the two aspects of that business liaison is one of dynamic equilibrium; each side is constantly pushing and jockeying the other to gain greater commercial advantage. Don't forget that buying a record from the label to put in store represents a significant financial commitment from a retailer and, if it doesn't sell, often the retailer can be stuck with it and lose money. Because music, as we noted, is not food or fuel, stocking is a high-risk business. Certainly the Beatles and the Stones and Sir Elton John and Pink Floyd are likely to remain popular for the foreseeable future and a copy of *Dark Side Of The Moon* probably won't stay on a retailer's racks for too long. But is a retailer going to risk money on a new album by a new band? Would you?

The retailer-record company dynamic has been greatly affected in recent years by the fact that major retail chains have advanced at the expense of the indies, a situation that has both advantages and disadvantages for the whole music industry. The disadvantage is that the number and scope of outlets is diminished. Say a label has a hot new non-mainstream act – a thrash-metal band, perhaps. If there was an indie store in every town dealing in non-mainstream material, the label would have a chance of giving the band a national sales base by selling to all those indie stores. But if most towns and cities are served only by a Woolworths and a small HMV, where are a new, hardcore-thrash band going to find their way into the stores?

The other side of the coin is this. HMV and Virgin are a presence for music on the high street. Amid all the other consumer commodities – the shoe shops and clothing stores and everything else – just by being in the town centre, the dedicated retail chains put music on a level playing field with all the other competitors for our punter's pound. On top of that, big companies like HMV and Virgin have slick marketing and advertising operations that spend plenty of money and work hard and effectively to attract people into their stores. Additionally, the stores themselves are designed to be just as alluring, both externally and internally, as all the other shops around them. All this means that music is packaged and presented in the most attractive manner possible and is placed right in the middle of the places where people go to shop.

This presence of music retailers in the main shopping areas opens major opportunities to the record companies. If a label can do a deal with HMV so that each HMV store across the country has as its window display the new Stones or Madonna or whoever's album, that is a massive presence on the high street for that album and is going to give a major boost to its sales.

But the downside of such retail power being in relatively few hands is, once more, that, for every album HMV puts in its windows, there were thousands that it chose not to place there. An indie store in a town would at least have provided one more alternative for exposure.

OK, now the third R – Rights. This is the tricky one to describe because, by its nature, it involves nothing that can be seen. In comparison, record companies' and retailers' trade is more readily understood because they deal in pieces of plastic. Those involved in rights deal only in the manifestation of ideas and the royalties that arise from them.

The basis of rights is 'intellectual property'. But don't worry – this is not some abstruse legal concept. It simply means that those people who make things own the things they make, no matter whether those things can be touched and felt or not. In this term the word 'intellectual' is just an adjective. The only word that matters is 'property' – and the legal principle applying to intellectual property is exactly the same as the concepts we are used to in the physical world.

Thus, in the world we are familiar with, if a man uses his hands to make guitars, he owns each of the guitars he makes and can sell them or rent them out – or not; it's his choice, depending on whether the money being offered for it is acceptable to him. It's important to understand that exactly the same is true of musical compositions. They are the sole property of the person who created them and that person may sell them or rent them out – or not; the choice is entirely that of the creator. But if the creator chooses to rent out the songs for use, the level of rent – that is, the royalty the creator receives – has to be acceptable.

The people and organisations who administer such royalty payments are the rights sector and, as we noted, that sector is huge, the vast bulk of the music industry. There is a simple reason why it is so large: every time – yes, every time – music is used, somebody is paying a bill and all those payments have to be collected, collated and distributed to their rightful owners. The sources of income are legion – records are a large one, but there's also airplay on radio and television (broadcasters pay big sums each year for the right to play music to an audience), music played in public places like shops, football grounds and restaurants, music in clubs and pubs, music in film soundtracks and computer games. There are so many places we hear music that we tend not to be conscious of its presence. But each time it's played, other than when a busker hammers out a tune in the street, somebody, somewhere is handing over money for the right to play it to you.

That's because, yes, music is property. Somebody invented it from nothing and, in Western society, inventors are always paid when people want to use their invention. We expect James Dyson to get money every time somebody buys one of the revolutionary vacuum cleaners he invented; the exact same principle applies when somebody wants to use music that a creative person invented.

And because people are creating property when they create music, it means that possibly the best living to be had from the music industry is by being a songwriter. A successful writer sells his work to recording artists, filmmakers, advertising agencies and the rest and never has to go through the slog of going out on the road on tour or getting out of bed at some unreasonable hour to appear on breakfast television.

Another bonus is that a successful songwriter – as opposed to someone who is both songwriter and performer – has a wonderful cloak of anonymity. It means that they can do their shopping without being mobbed but, should they choose to garner a little respect in the pub, they can just drop into the conversation that they wrote such-and-such a number-one hit (even if it was only number one in Albania).

The purpose and defining principle of the rights sector is to look after the interests of songwriters and ensure they get the money they are due. None of these people in the business of rights does it for love, however, and each takes their due cut of the income. But this is how all business works: your insurance broker doesn't shop around to get the best deal for you because he thinks you're a wonderful human being; he shops around to get you the best deal because that's the job he is paid to do.

And so it is with the whole rights sector. This enormous grouping of people, the majority of whom work for companies called music publishers, protects songwriters and administers the monies that change hands on their behalf. Now, the sums publishers take as their cut are a proportion of the songwriter's earnings and that proportion is decided by the individual contract each composer has. But, whether that proportion is 1% or 50% of the songwriter's total earnings, it has helped some publishers become very big companies and has created thousands of employment opportunities for people who want to work in the music industry and thousands more openings for people who want to start their own company.

The publishers' business is, though, broadly based. A few current hits are very nice, but what every publisher wants in the catalogue of songs it administers are timeless classics. For instance, if you are the publisher administering the rights to Cole Porter's work or Noël Coward's or Sir Paul McCartney's, you know those compositions are going to be used again and again and again in a thousand different areas of business. In many ways, once a song becomes a classic – or a standard, as they are often known – the publisher need do little else except sit back and count the money.

But, as we noted with the record sector, a big aspect of a publisher's work is making a song into a standard in the first place. That requires time, effort, money and talent – and a large slice of luck. We'll look more closely at how publishers achieve that in Chapter 4.

Good publishers are very active in helping raw, talented youngsters become big stars. Just as with record companies, it's in everybody's interests that the new talent they sign should become as big as possible. Finding and developing such talent, and administering the (hopefully) immortal classics those people write, makes publishers strong. The best and most successful publishers are the ones that have been doing this for many years and now have a mixture of the old and the new on their books: that is, the old, established set of writers and the hottest new property in the business who's going to write half the chart singles for the next five years.

But the challenge publishers face is making that happen; it isn't as easy as it sounds. Failure is a way of life in the music industry. We general consumers of music hear only of hits (of one degree or another). We never even see the thousands upon thousands of singles and albums that never made it into the chart or even into the racks in a significant number of retailers' stores. Nor are most people aware when a project is a hit but required so much cash to make it such that nobody involved made any money.

It is a sobering fact – and one that counters all those arguments about the music industry being made up of fat cats – that only one album in ten released makes a profit. That's a result of the intense competition within the business and the external competition the industry faces from all those other people who want to take the consumer's leisure spending.

The rest of this book will deal with how the industry is geared to meeting those profound challenges.

Chapter 2

R IS FOR RECORDS

THE BIGGEST PART OF the music industry may be rights, but the beating heart of the business is the record companies, or labels – a term that goes back to the days when the company's name appeared on the paper label in the centre of a 78rpm record. Record companies are the most aggressive, most active, most obvious part of the business, and how they perform tends to be how the industry as a whole is perceived. They play by far the largest role in finding, developing and bringing to public attention new talent – and all of them have their part in that, no matter what their size.

The biggest record companies are called 'majors' and these are Universal, Sony, EMI, BMG and Warner. If those names don't look particularly familiar, it's because they are the names of the overall company. Many labels make up a big company. For instance, 'Universal' doesn't appear as the main name on a record; that honour goes to Mercury or MCA or Polydor or whichever of the labels Universal owns that happens to have put out the record.

Confusingly, the name 'label' can be used to describe either the whole group of companies or the constituent company that has its name on the record. I'll try to keep the confusion to a minimum here.

All the biggest labels – and by that I mean label as in an operation that directly puts out records – tend to be structured in broadly the same way and generally comprise these departments:

A&R
Marketing
Legal/Business affairs
Finance
Operations
Sales
International
The Big Boss
Stuff

Let's put 'Stuff' to one side first. This is all the areas nobody (except the people in those professions) really cares about: things like human resources, security, office services and business information. Vital elements though they are, life's too short for such matters and we won't be dealing with them.

We'll go into A&R in more detail in Chapter 5, so, putting that to one side for a moment, too, let's look at the other areas of the record company operation, areas which regularly fail to get the credit they deserve.

Marketing is the department that actually brings new acts to the public. A&R may find and develop new acts, but without marketing to present them to the target audience, no matter how talented the new signings are, nobody would ever know they existed.

And if that sounds like one department in all this is more important than the others, it shouldn't. Each department depends on all the others around it – including 'Stuff', without which nothing would get done. Only by working together are all the departments an effective commercial unit.

R IS FOR RECORDS

So, marketing brings acts and records to the public attention. Let's take two examples of what these people do, to see the diversity of the decisions they make. First, let's look at what a UK label would do if it were marketing Sir Elton John's new album. Sir Elton is a big star with an established fanbase and a certain amount of absolutely guaranteed sales. The first thing the label will do in dealing with his new release is look at sales of the past one, two or three albums and see what kind of scale of operation can be contemplated. Once the company has worked out how much it can reasonably commit to an artist of Elton John's stature and still make a profit, the marketing department will set about spending the money it has been allocated.

A major act like this justifies pulling out all the stops, and the biggest, most expensive stop of all is television advertising. Sir Elton sells enough, though, to justify such alarming expense and it is likely the label will buy TV ads for him. And because he is a mainstream act with mainstream fans, it makes most sense, though it costs most money, to buy ads in mainstream programmes such as the news and the soap operas or a big film.

The price of TV ads depends on two things: the length of the ad and the number of people watching when it is broadcast. A thirty-second ad during *Coronation Street* costs a damn sight more than a thirty-second slot at four in the morning during 'Pro-Am Sheep Wrestling' (and if nobody's patented that format for a TV show, I lay my claim here and now). The label will have to think very hard about whether the expense of taking time during *Coronation Street* is justified but, for an artist of Sir Elton's size, is highly likely to decide that it is.

The label's decision will be swayed by the fact that it knows it is going to sell a lot of copies of his new album. It will also know that just making a lot of people aware of its release will stimulate sales. Committed fans simply need to know the new album is out; slightly less committed ones need to know only it is available and to hear as much music as the ad can cram into thirty seconds.

The record company also has another valuable tool when deciding whether to take that *Coronation Street* slot – Sir Elton's track record. It will have done plenty of market research to establish just what happened last time it TV-advertised one of his albums. It will know precisely – very precisely – what ads lead to what sales; executives will have researched extensively the relationship between the amount of money they spend and the amount of profit they can expect in return. They will leave as little as possible to guesswork and intuition.

So, the label commits itself to advertising Sir Elton's new album on television. Though that is the 'nuclear option', it still won't suffice on its own. Other advertising strategies have to be employed in conjunction with it.

The most obvious of those are ads in the press. Print ads will undoubtedly include space in the music magazines Sir Elton's fans are most likely to read – *Mojo*, *Q* and the rest of the adult music press – plus, most probably, ads in the other music publications such as *NME*. In addition, because Sir Elton appeals to older, mainstream fans, it is also likely that ads will be taken in the mainstream press; the magazines that go out with the *Daily Mail*, the *Daily Express* and the broadsheet newspapers seem fairly ideal for the purpose.

On top of that will come poster ads on billboards around our towns and cities and, as a final cherry on the pie, any other medium the marketing department can think of and believes is appropriate and worth the cost.

A marketing department will go to such lengths and such expense for an artist of Sir Elton's size and durability because he virtually guarantees a healthy return on such marketing investment.

Sadly, the exact reverse is true for the new, young band on their debut album. Such an act – let's say they're a straight-down-the-middle pop-rock four-piece called the Miracle

Trees – is virtually guaranteed to lose money for a major record company.

Because they are almost certainly a loss-maker, the record company has to think hard about how much money it is prepared to lose. Now, this is a tricky decision to make.

Remember that the record industry is predicated on making acts famous – this is its largest and most difficult task and the only way it can secure a reasonable future for itself – so labels have to decide whether the band's later career will reward the record company's initial spending.

So, a label can decide that the Miracle Trees' debut is so stunning and has such a broad-based appeal that it is worth spending the money on TV advertising. The marketing department then decides to spend £500,000 on a fairly modest TV ad campaign (half-a-million quid doesn't go that far in televisionland) but, sadly, very few people agree with the label's assessment that the album is stunning and has a broad appeal; on the contrary, most people think it's crap and virtually nobody buys it. The label has invested £500,000 and has nothing to show in return.

A wasted half a million is not going to bankrupt a major label, although it would still show up as a fair-sized hole in the profits. It would, though, break the back of the vast majority of indies. Many, many of them have gone to the wall through their misplaced belief in the sales potential of their main act.

You may ask why executives have such misplaced belief. Well, contrary to much of the popular portrayal, people who work at record companies (and here I mean both the majors and indies) love music and get excited when they hear music that they believe in.

As we noted, nine times out of ten such belief is misplaced. But I think the greatest compliment that can be paid to the music industry is that it continues to put out albums knowing it is almost certain to lose money on them – and each of those albums released adds to the sum total of music available and is giving pleasure to somebody somewhere. (I suspect I am one of the few people who have Budgie's *If Swallowed Do Not Induce Vomiting* on their shelf and I greatly doubt that the label involved made a profit on it. But it's giving me and the handful of others who bought it significant pleasure; and the same is true of all those relatively obscure albums you have lying around at the back of your collection. Each one represents an investment by the record company and each one has added to the totality of music we consumers can choose from.)

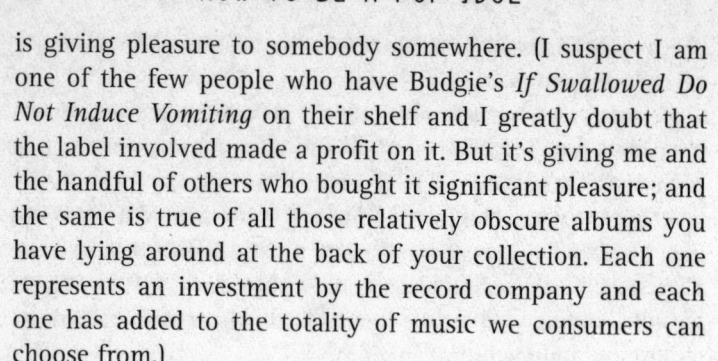

If money is a factor in marketing a new band – as it certainly is – just what can the label do? Well, in terms of advertising, its options are relatively limited. If it spends a more reasonable and normal budget rather than that fanciful £500,000 we were talking about, the advertising it would get is probably a few ads in the relevant magazines and perhaps some flyposting (although such things are illegal in many cities).

But, thankfully, there are other ways of breaking a band (and 'breaking' is the term the music industry uses to mean making a band famous rather than anything destructive). However, these other ways require a lot of outside assistance.

A vital part of the marketing department is the promotions people, often referred to, not always charitably, as 'pluggers'. It is their job to 'plug', or promote, the label's acts to television and radio producers. 'We have an act we would like you to put on your programme,' the promotions staff say. Once more, though, there are huge contrasts in the way they go about this. Sir Elton John can pretty much pick and choose which programme he wants to be on. All the plugger has to do is turn up at the BBC and chat for a while with somebody senior about where and how they both want to do it.

But if that same plugger goes to the BBC representing the Miracle Trees, the task is much, much harder. Producers tend to be fairly cynical about new acts on the basis that, as they are all too painfully aware, most of those acts are going to sink without leaving a trace on the public consciousness. Precious airtime can't be wasted on a band that are going to die a death, and, more particularly, it can't be wasted on a band that aren't going to appeal to that show's audience.

So, the first thing a TV or radio producer wants to know when confronted with the Miracle Trees is what they sound like: yes, music remains at the core of the music industry. The plugger will then hand over an album and/or a demo or sampler, along with a little written material on the band: a biography and suchlike.

The plugger will also put up an argument for why the producer should play the Miracle Trees' music on his or her show. The arguments will include things like:

'This band are the hottest thing since the Tree Miracles.'

'They're perfect for your audience.'

'The label really believes in them.'

'I sent a copy to your boss and he/she really likes it.'

This last contention tends to be the reserve of the rogue or the cheeky. Cheek is often an advantage in promotion (no, correction, it is always an advantage) but rogues rarely prosper over the long term in the industry.

The producer will always take the material to listen to, no matter what the plugger says, but, because there are so many new acts and new albums, it is extraordinarily difficult to penetrate that producer's consciousness. The best way of doing so is to offer music that is going to make the producer jump up and down and/or weep in excitement, but not all music is inspired enough to achieve this effect.

So, assuming that the Miracle Trees are a decent, talented, somewhat innovative act and that the debut album is attractive and interesting rather than truly exceptional, what else can the promotion person do to attract the producer's attention? Well, the plugger can invite the producer to a gig (bands always come over best on stage, I think) or to a launch party.

The launch party is a tried and trusted weapon in the

label's armoury and entails all the elements you would expect in a party. It will be held at an attractive venue – a lavish and plush location for Sir Elton, merely a comfortable and nice one for the Miracle Trees – and there will be some food and plenty of beer and other drinks. During the party the band's music will feature heavily, either as the album which is played over and over or in a short set played by the band at some point.

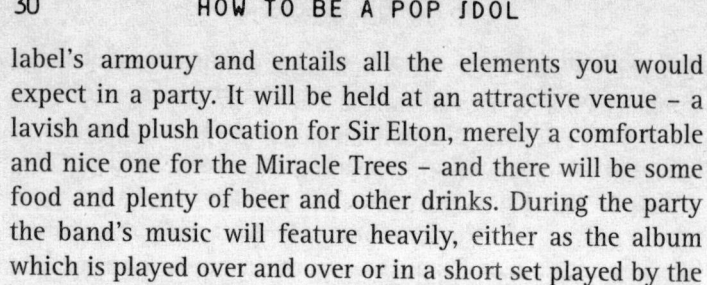

Bright labels and good, working musicians will also make themselves available to go round the room and make sure all the guests – all important people from the media and the industry, remember – feel welcome and happy and suitably enthused. The best example of doing this properly I ever saw was an East West Records showcase (as these things are often called) for Tori Amos early in her career.

Normally a showcase attracts between fifty and five hundred people and such big events are not always an exciting evening's entertainment. Like many other folk in the music industry, I have called into showcases on dozens and dozens of occasions just to eat their food and save me cooking when I got home (and/or because it was on my way to the pub or football match). Trust me, after your first couple of hundred launch parties and showcases, the novelty wears off significantly.

But the Tori Amos showcase was different – far, far more subtle and civilised than normal. Firstly, the invitation wasn't the usual, mass-produced card that turns up in the post. This time it came in the form of a discreet phone call from the chairman of the company.

At the event itself there was another big difference to the norm – just twenty-five people were present. Instead of the usual scrum for the buffet, we were given a very nice dinner at a posh London club and, while we ate, Tori wandered round the room talking to people – and she knew everybody's name and job!

Now, what East West had done was to go for quality over

quantity. While there were only a handful of people in the room compared with a more usual showcase, each of those twenty-five was a decision-maker, a man or woman in a position to have a significant influence on Tori's career and therefore on East West's profits.

At some point before the event, Tori had sat down and learned the names and positions of two dozen people – impressive in itself, and I can't tell you the impact it had. We all felt very flattered. Then, after dinner, Tori played a little set, perhaps five or six songs, and, in the intimate atmosphere of that small gathering in that small room, the impression this made was enormous. Her career took off from that point. In one evening's effort she had won over the hearts of all the most significant retailers and industry people. Such are the rewards for musicians working unceasingly at the beginning of their career; when they're famous, then they can relax a little.

Back now to the Miracle Trees. Their launch party is likely to be in a nice restaurant with decent food, nice wine and beer. Such a party will attract media people if the event is not competing with too many others at the same time. If Sir Elton is having his on the same night in the next street, attendance will necessarily be reduced. But, if the date and location are chosen wisely, media people will call in for a variety of reasons. If that reason happens to be a free pint and an opportunity to chat to their mates, well, at least they're there within earshot of the Miracle Trees' music.

A launch party/showcase/whatever-you-want-to-call-it is always a valuable tool. But, if that fails, the marketing people have one more weapon in their armoury: the stunt. This is a manufactured, ridiculous, possibly scandalous event designed purely to attract attention.

It has never been done better than with the Sex Pistols' seminal first album for Virgin Records, *Never Mind The Bollocks, Here's The Sex Pistols*. A retailer in Nottingham, Selectadisc, put up a poster in its window in the city centre with the title, and therefore the word 'Bollocks', prominently displayed. Shortly afterwards there was a complaint to the police that displaying this word in such an obvious place was an affront to public decency and broke the Obscene Displays Act. The police prosecuted and Selectadisc pleaded not guilty on the basis that 'bollocks' is not rude and is a venerable and decent part of the English language. Selectadisc's denial of any wrongdoing meant there had to be a trial and a trial is a public forum which the media can report in its entirety without fear of prosecution for libel or anything else. The media now had licence to use the word 'bollocks' with utter impunity.

Once it got to court, the case consisted largely of very learned, very worthy academics arguing the toss over whether 'bollocks' is a rude word or not. Understandably, the media loved it: for the red-top tabloids it was titillating and naughty; for the broadsheets it was a serious and learned discussion of etymology (and it was titillating and naughty). Either way the Sex Pistols got massive publicity from it. The band were plastered across every newspaper and TV and radio news broadcast for a week. When the court decided that 'bollocks' is not an obscenity, they got even more famous and their album became a *cause célèbre*.

So how was this a stunt? The person who made the complaint to the police claiming to be offended by the word 'bollocks' was an employee of Virgin Records. A triumph of the marketing department's art.

Finally in our look at marketing, another part of the department's operations, and often a department in its own right, is the press office. In the same way that promotions deals with broadcast media, the press office deals with print media. The press office's tactics and attitudes are broadly similar to the promotions department's, as are the challenges it faces. For instance, if Sir Elton decides to do a series of interviews in connection with his new album, the press office can place those pretty much anywhere; just about every credible magazine in the country would like an interview with him. And when the press office comes to deal with the Miracle Trees, it faces exactly the same difficulty as the promotions people.

A bright journalist might help, though. If the same press office is dealing with Sir Elton and the Miracle Trees – and every major label in the world has big and not-so-big acts on its books – a wise editor will give a little space to the Miracle Trees in return for some assistance when the interviews with Sir Elton are being handed out. Nonetheless, just like its colleagues in promotions, the press office always faces an uphill battle when handling new acts.

Now let's move on to the role of the legal department, often called business affairs. This is another essential department in that industry always needs lawyers. (I pass no comment on whether this is a good thing.) It is the lawyers' job to make sure all the contracts are watertight. So, if the managing director signs an act and wants them to make three albums, the contract must hold the act to that. The paperwork can't allow the act to walk away after the first album.

The contract must also ensure the record company owns all the rights. None of us can see what new technology is going to emerge next, but whatever is coming the record company needs to protect its investment. If CD is overtaken by MFI or QPR or BSE (or whatever it is that's in the pipeline), the record company needs to know that it will still own the band's recordings, no matter on what format they are released.

As in all businesses, the legal framework is the support for the whole operation. The record company's rights must be protected under the law and the band's rights must be protected. The lawyers are there to see that they are. Though the label's and the band's agenda will often differ and their respective lawyers will lock horns from time to time, if somebody is making illegal copies of an album, both the act and the record company are losing out. It is those people the lawyers will pursue most vigorously and it is essential that they do. (See Chapters 10 and 20 for more on this.)

Just like the legal stuff, finance is also vital. The people in this department may be looked upon disdainfully as mere accountants, but they are the folks who keep record companies in business. If a label spends more on marketing than it gets in profits for every act on the roster, it won't be a record company for very long. It will simply be another bankrupt ex-label (and the world has seen far too many of those).

The financial people keep close tabs on what's coming in and what's going out, then they tell everybody else how much money there is in the pot to spend on finding, nurturing and breaking new talent and keeping current big stars big. Without them, nothing would get done.

Now to the sharp end of any record company: the operations department. This can be summed up as 'the bits of plastic department', as it is responsible for making, storing and then distributing the records that are the lifeblood of the company. It is an awesome task. Operations starts with bags of unexciting, raw polymer powder and only ends when the finished record is safely in the consumer's hands.

The central point of this process is the manufacturing facility. All the major labels have their own, a pressing plant where their CDs are made. Some indies also have their own, but smaller labels tend not to be able to afford their own factory, and they use custom pressers. These are separate businesses which do nothing but make discs for their customers.

Major record companies, though, are big enough to do the job for themselves and, for them, making the discs is a very large operation. A major label tends to release its biggest albums globally; that is, throughout North and South America, Europe, Asia and Australasia at the same time, and that means an enormous amount of co-ordination for the operations department to handle. The discs must be pressed on time and must leave the factory on time to reach their destination when required by the retailer. Because the majors tend to press all their CDs for the whole of Europe in one place, it means that sometimes the retailer can be several countries away from the manufacturing plant. This results in discs being transported halfway across the continent on a regular basis, a process which, again, must be done on time. Operations is obviously not a simple business and, just to add further spice, it is also the ultimate in unforgiving.

Consider: if I'm buying a new bed, I'm fairly relaxed about whether it's delivered next week or the week after that. If I'm buying a chart record, I want it now. Next week there'll be other records around and I might have forgotten all about the first one I was after; and, what's more, the retailers will certainly have lost interest in a record that has started to drop down the charts. Thus, if there is demand for a record and a big batch of discs intended to meet that demand is late by a week or even a day, that can make the difference between a record rising in the chart and falling. And, in the fast-moving world of pop music, a world based on a chart released each week, a falling disc is history. There is, then, no opportunity for an operations manager to say, 'Sorry, your order won't be with you for another couple of weeks. Is that OK?'

(There is a music industry joke, generally told by retailers frustrated by orders not turning up, that has been used about every major record company at some point in its history when its operations department is going through a particularly difficult time. It goes like this: Did you know Dead Dog Records have found a cure for the common cold? Yes, they press it, give it a catalogue number, then nobody can get it.)

Keeping those retailers happy and supplied with records when they want them is operations' big challenge. Getting the stores interested in the first place is the responsibility of the sales department.

Sales people sell records – not to the public, but to retailers. As we saw in the previous chapter, if a record isn't in the shops, customers can't buy it – or at least not in significant numbers, despite the Internet and mail order and suchlike systems.

So, the sales department liaises closely with retailers. Its first priority is, of course, the big chains. Why is that the first priority? Because one big chain buys more records than all the indie stores put together. In addition, the chains buy centrally. HMV, say, will buy all its Beatles albums in one deal. That's big business for the Beatles' record label, EMI.

But the relationship between the sales department and the retailers has many facets. For instance, the sales department is responsible both for making sure that HMV's normal monthly requirements for Beatles albums are met and then trying to beat that level. Pressure is always on sales to sell more. Sometimes that's tough; if *Sergeant Pepper* hasn't been promoted for five years there's not a lot the sales department can say to a retailer to boost his interest. However, if Sir Paul McCartney decides to tour and play just songs from this classic album, the department has good reason for urging HMV and the other chains to a bigger order.

In addition to keeping sales of older albums at a reasonable level and selling the big new releases from top acts, sales staff must also shoulder their share of the burden of that perennial difficulty for labels – how to break a new act. If the sales rep is trying to persuade HMV to take the Miracle Trees' new album in store, he or she has to give the retailer a good reason why the album will sell. Points sales reps tend to suggest are:

'It's brilliant music that people will love.'

'We are buying ads in national magazines that will create demand.'

'The band are playing a national tour and will be in twenty venues that are close to your stores.'

The first of these arguments isn't likely to get very far because: a) the rep would say that, wouldn't he? and b) the retail chain buyer has heard it several thousand times about several thousand albums that nobody can remember any more. The second, though, is likely to produce some impact. By spending the cash to buy ads, the label shows that it really is putting its money where its mouth is and is getting behind the band. In addition, the retailer knows that the more ads that are taken, the more likely the album is to sell – and if an album is likely to pass from his racks to his till, he's happy. It's the ones that are set to lie in the racks until doomsday that he wants to avoid.

The last of these arguments is also likely to carry some sway. Gigs means interest and if only ten new punters come out of the local venue looking for the Miracle Trees' debut album, that's ten sales the retailer can garner if he has it in store. Furthermore, and following on from this last gambit, the sales department can always invite the retailer to a gig (and, generally, to the party afterwards). That serves two functions: it makes the retailer feel as though a fuss is being made of him and it exposes him to the band's music.

We'll see a little more about the workings of the sales department, and its relationship with the label's customers, in the next chapter, on retailers. Similarly, the international department is dealt with in Chapters 6, 7 and 16, leaving us with the Big Boss.

Every record company has a man – and, with two exceptions, the person at the head of the major labels in the UK has always been a man – who is in overall charge. This man, be he known as managing director, chief executive, chairman or president, has to make sure all the other departments are doing what they should be doing.

The first thing he has to take care of is to ensure they are working as a team. The Big Boss will chair a meeting each week, traditionally at 11am on Mondays, where all the departments will be represented. There he has to check that each department knows exactly what its counterparts are doing and is in step with them. In short, the company must be playing as a team, not a collection of talented individuals.

In addition, the Big Boss is responsible for creating policy. If he decides the company is going entirely heavy metal or jazz or something else, he has to communicate that policy to the staff and make sure it is put into place. More on Big Bosses in Chapter 11.

For the moment, though, let's just note that the Big Boss affects everything that happens in a record company. He affects the mood and morale of the employees; he affects A&R, marketing and sales policy; he helps or hinders the process of playing as a team. And when the company is working together, just like a football club, the team will reflect the Big Boss's philosophies and be aggressive, flamboyant, conservative, innovative or any combination of the above.

Chapter 3

R IS FOR RETAIL

RETAILERS SELL RECORDS TO people who want to buy them. Sounds simple, doesn't it? But, as with all commercial enterprises and, in particular, as with everything in the music industry, it ain't as easy as it sounds. If it was, everybody would be doing it and getting rich by it.

There are three key issues that make life a challenge for a retailer:

1. Location, location, location. There is no point having the world's greatest record shop if the only way to get to it is a two-hour drive in an off-road vehicle.

2. The right stock. There is no point being in the right place if the only records you carry are ones that nobody – not even the artist's mum – has any interest in.

3. The right price. There is even less point in carrying exactly the same stock as the record shop next door but selling it at a 20% higher price.

On top of that are the additional challenges and, regularly, irritations of the retailer's relationship with the record companies – or the suppliers, as retailers rather soullessly describe them – and with all the stores round about. First, though, let's look at that tricky concept of location.

The stores that do best are the ones in the most prominent positions in the main retail centres. That means the store has to be in the high street or the shopping mall, whichever people go to most in any given town. The advantage of such a high-profile setting is that the busier the street outside, the more people pass your door and are likely to be interested in your goods. If the store is on a busy street that a million people a month walk along, it is better to have 2% of their total consumer spending than to be on a quiet street with a thousand people a month on it and have 2% of that trade. But the retailer pays a price for this – often a very big one. Rent for prime retail sites is a lot more than for ones on that quiet street, and the retailer has to justify that position on the busy high street by selling enough records to make a profit there.

However, as we saw in Chapter 1, the whole music industry benefits when a retailer is in a prime site because that makes music a prime consumer good alongside everything else an average shopper is likely to spend money on. At least if the retailer is in the main shopping area, music is in a fair fight in the battle for cash.

Music retailers know, though, that because they are there among the premier league of stores – Boots, Debenhams, Tesco and the other multi-billion-pound groups – they have to fight very, very hard to compete with them. That means spending money on attractive exteriors and interiors and on staff who don't make you feel like a monkey because you want that song you heard on television the other day and don't know what it's called or who it's by.

After that difficult decision on location (should the retailer spend top dollar on a top site or a lesser amount on a lesser site?) comes the equally tricky matter of the right stock. The reason why it is so problematic is that there is no single answer as to what constitutes the right stock; the solution to the conundrum varies enormously, depending on what type of retailer is making the decision. Let's look at some of the different answers, starting with the biggest players first.

Woolworths, with around seven hundred outlets selling music, is Britain's widest-spread record retailer, the one people are most likely to have in their local high street. To Woolworths, the right stock is, by and large, chart material. If you want a single that's in this week's Top Twenty, you know that your local Woolworths will have it. If you want an album that's in this week's Top Twenty, Woolworths will probably have it, depending on what the album is.

But, outside this week's Top Twenty, Woolies starts getting scratchy. The company devotes only a modest proportion of its stores to music and that finite amount of space will not accommodate much beyond this week's most popular records. This is purely chart-oriented retailing. It is not Woolworths' intention that you spend five hours in the store browsing through their vast range of titles and choosing your music. Generally, people go in knowing exactly what they want, find it, buy it and leave.

The advantage to the music industry of Woolworths' approach is that they are making music available in a lot of places – seven hundred or so across the UK, which is more than HMV, Virgin, Andys Records and several other dedicated music operations put together. They are also putting music under the noses of people who may not have had music in mind when they went into the shop. Just as Woolies suggests in its advertising, somebody may have gone in for a mug or a garden hose or any number of other things and decided to buy a record simply because it was there in front of them while they were in buying mode – an impulse buy, as it's known.

In contrast, a dedicated music retailer such as Virgin or HMV has a vastly different stocking philosophy. With their large stores in central locations, they want customers to come in and wander, drift and browse. To encourage them to do so, Virgin and HMV stock the widest possible range and depth of music.

Their two flagship operations in Oxford Street in London

exemplify what the companies are trying to do. In each of those stores the music goes from Beethoven through Billie Piper to Black Sabbath. The idea is that, whatever the customer's taste, there is plenty to pore over. Even if the customer only popped in for a chart album or single, there will be lots more from the same act to consider.

This is an important issue as there have been many notable occasions when a band which have worked for years in relative obscurity suddenly have one hit single that gets people interested in the totality of their work. If a big retailer carries all the albums the band have made – the band's catalogue, as it's called – then this demand can be met and everybody from artist to record company to retailer is happy.

But here we are into the big, dedicated retailer's biggest dilemma. Just which catalogues does it stock in its racks? There are literally millions of albums available to choose from and the store neither can nor wants to buy them all. (And, remember, a retailer must purchase an album from the label before it goes in store; the stores have to invest a lot of hard cash in their business decisions.)

Of course, there are some catalogues that every big retailer will have – the Beatles, Rolling Stones, Michael Jackson, Madonna, Pink Floyd and so on, never mind whether those acts have had a hit in the past ten years or not. They have all produced classic albums that will sell steadily and without promotion for the foreseeable future.

Then comes the more difficult decision. Does the retailer carry the Budgie catalogue? This Welsh power trio are venerated by hard-rock fans and still loved today in the denim-and-leather fraternity, but most other people haven't heard of them and wouldn't care about them even if they had. So, if the retailer decides that Budgie can still sell a few, which catalogue does it leave out to make room for their music?

Well, in this day and age, a retailer has a lot of electronic devices to help him make such decisions. Every time a bar code is scanned at the till, that information is gathered and used. In this way the store group knows where the album was sold, when and, if the buyer used a credit or debit card, to whom. Furthermore, if the buyer paid with a card, the store will also be able to see if the same person has bought four other Budgie albums in the past month or if this is a departure after a lifetime diet of seventies disco.

Using all this information, Virgin and HMV make many decisions on which catalogues they should continue to carry. If those Budgie albums haven't moved from any of the stores in two months, that will be the end of Budgie's presence in the major retailers' outlets.

So a big retailer carries chart material because that's the sharp end of the business, and it carries catalogues it knows will do OK, too, because that's nice, steady turnover. But what else should it stock?

Well, the national chains regionalise. Even though HMV and Virgin buy most of their stock centrally – one office in London puts in a big order on behalf of all the stores across the country – tastes differ from one region to the next and the chains seek to recognise that. For instance, a band from the north of Scotland will probably have a bigger fanbase in Aberdeen than in Penzance, so the HMV in Aberdeen is likely to stock the band's new album whereas the Penzance branch is much less likely to do so. Even more specifically, if Liverpool Football Club release a single, Virgin in Liverpool is certain to have it in store. But will Virgin just down the road in Manchester, where there aren't many Liverpool fans and the local football followers have a strong antipathy to their near neighbours? Quite possibly not.

The other element in a big retailer's stocking mix is new product from unknown acts, but we'll return to that once we've had a look at how the indies go about filling their shelves.

As we have seen, there is no point in an indie trying to out-HMV HMV. If an indie takes on the majors head to head, it will lose. The majors have more money, more power, more space to carry stock in store and more power to advertise it — that's why we call them majors.

To survive, an indie must do something that the majors are not. It must be in a place the major chains are not, or sell something the major chains do not, or offer something the major chains do not.

Ian Duffell, who in his time has been boss at both HMV and Virgin, reckoned there were around 250 high streets in the UK worth being represented in — from HMV or Virgin's point of view, of course. So, if you're an indie prepared to open premises in one of those high streets not in the 250, you may have the market to yourself — or at least you can expect an easier time than if HMV or Virgin was just over the road.

Now we come on to the second survival technique for indies and the one which involves that core issue of stock. Simply, an indie must specialise in what it carries. Though a big HMV or Virgin will have plenty of jazz and garage and techno and everything else, a good indie specialist in any of those genres will have more, and must have more to attract business.

And that leads us on to the third point. If an indie is specialising in, say, folk and traditional music, its range of stock has to be broader and deeper than HMV's or Virgin's folk and traditional department on the other side of the city centre, otherwise buyers will just stay on the other side of the city. Then, following on from the question of better stock, the quality of service should be better, too.

It is not possible for any person to be clued up on all releases in all genres all the time. With twenty-five thousand records put out in the UK alone each year, nobody can follow what's happening everywhere in the musical pantheon. So an assistant in HMV or Virgin, while bright, connected and helpful, will probably know less about any given genre (bar the one they have in bucketfuls at home) than the assistant in a specialist store who, during his or her working life, deals only with one area of music. And a good assistant in that specialist store will be helpful in guiding consumers who do not yet have – or have no intention of acquiring – that level of knowledge.

The most successful indie retailer in the country is Andy Gray. His chain, Andys Records, has stores in around thirty towns and cities in the east and north of England and he's taken elements of each of those indie strategies to achieve that. He's obviously doing something right as every other indie chain in the country has come and gone while Andys Records has been steadily growing. Exemplifying what indies can do when they plough their own furrow rather than hanging on the coat-tails of the major chains, Andy has stores in towns where the majors would fear to tread. Many of these are not in the 250 prime high streets that Ian Duffell once defined. No harm in that; Andy and his brother Billy – the two men who own and run the imaginatively named chain – are not short of a bob or two.

OK, now on to the thorny issue of how retailers deal with new releases by new acts, possibly the most delicate and political of issues they have to face.

For Woolies, the issue is simple. They don't bother. Woolies is chart-oriented and, if you're not in the chart, you're generally not in Woolies. As you might imagine, the record companies have some problems with this black-and-white philosophy. They argue, how do new, young acts get in the chart in the first place if the retailers like Woolworths won't stock their records? And without new generations of talent coming through constantly, what future is there for pop music?

Such arguments fall on deaf ears at Woolworths but find more sympathy among the dedicated music retailers, who have a greater stake in the continued health of the record business. Should the music market ever collapse completely, Woolworths would fill the space music now occupies in store with garden products or something else. However, HMV and Virgin, even though they also sell videos, games and magazines, would find the bulk of their business eradicated. So, without those exciting new acts emerging, the labels feel, what reason will people have for coming into HMV, Virgin, Andys and the like in the first place? To a very large extent the dedicated retailers agree.

So who does what in the process of bringing through those young acts? As we've seen, record companies try to persuade the media to take an interest in their new artists and once the media has done so, retailers are almost guaranteed to follow suit. For instance, if the label's sales rep says to the retailer that next week the Miracle Trees are on two youth shows, on BBC1 and ITV1, the retailer knows that is bound to result in sales and will take the new single, album and video in store.

However, if the sales rep says of the Miracle Trees, 'The band are touring at the moment and are building up a real buzz and a fanbase. We're going to put out the first single next month and the album the month after. We're confident that Radio X will play the single a lot,' that's a very different story.

The retailer hears this: 'The band are out there gigging to learn their trade, they may or may not be attracting big audiences and there's virtually no chance of them being on the radio or television.'

So, to do everything possible to make the retailer interested, the sales rep will give the retailer a disc to listen to and will invite the store owner, or relevant executive from one of the chains, to a show by the band. The retailer may think, after seeing the gig, that their music is interesting and innovative in its way and is likely to have some appeal. But the retailer may also conclude it is nothing out of the ordinary and there are twenty other bands with a debut single and album all equally deserving of the store's shelf space.

So what does the retailer do? He wants to help bring through the next generation of bands – that's as much in his interest as in the label's – but space in store is, as we have noted, extremely limited. For every new title he puts in, he has to take one out. Which goes in, which comes out? That is a decision that is taken many, many times each week – and for every new act the retailer elects to stock, there are ten or a hundred he ignores and chooses not to get behind.

This decision is not only crucial for the retailer, it is life-changing for a band. That's because, if the record is in store, they have a profile and if it isn't, they haven't. It is too true for musicians that out of sight is out of mind. Secondly, if the record is not sold through recognised retail outlets, it can't get into the chart. More about that in Chapter 12.

The key point here is that competition for all concerned is tough – very, very tough. Even if the Miracle Trees are signed to a major label with a big advertising campaign behind them, there is still no guarantee that HMV or Virgin will take the record and even less of one that Woolworths, WH Smith and John Menzies will. It's easy to see that to succeed in the music industry requires a great deal of fighting and a great deal of luck and, often, plenty of money, too.

So, if a retailer chooses not to stock a particular record, it hurts everybody involved, not least the retailer itself. Store owners know that the more records they have in their racks, the more they will sell. But, until each store is infinitely large and the retailer has infinite amounts of money to commit to his stock, those difficult stocking decisions will always have to be made.

Moving on to look at the other, more positive side of the coin, what happens when a retailer decides he does want to stock a particular record? Well, any number of deals between label and retailer might be done, and the agreement finally reached will depend on the three variable factors of record company, record store and the record itself.

Let's look at a straightforward example – say that Virgin wants the new Beatles hits compilation in its stores. Everybody knows such an album is going to sell well, so there is no question of not stocking it. All Virgin wants to know is how much money the record company is going to spend on

TV advertising and suchlike other promotion. The more EMI spends on ads, the more copies Virgin is likely to buy.

The higher the number of copies Virgin decides to take, the more interesting becomes the question of the price it will pay, because, as in any other business, there are discounts for bulk buying. With an album like a Beatles hits compilation, Virgin and HMV and the other big retailers will obviously want a lot, and though it may say in the EMI catalogue that this new release costs £x, if you're buying fifty thousand or a hundred thousand copies, you will have no intention whatever of paying that list price. But how big that discount should be has been the subject of the hugest and loudest of arguments. On more than one famous and verifiable occasion, blows have been traded between retailer and record company during the negotiation of this amount.

These discounts – file discounts, as they are known – have also been the subject of friction between different retailers. Of course, the intense competition between Virgin and HMV means both chains want to think they are getting a better deal than the other, but only the record company knows which one actually is (though if I were running the label I'd tell both of them that they were coming out ahead). Further than that, though, smaller retailers have been hugely upset by not being able to garner the same level of discounts. But though they complain bitterly about the fact, they really can't expect any different. If a one-off indie retailer is ordering twenty copies of an album and HMV is ordering ten thousand, it is logical, reasonable and usual that HMV should get a much better price.

The indies have always argued, however, that the labels are digging their own hole by favouring the major chains. It has always been the contention of the smaller stores that if they are forced out of business because they can't match the prices the big stores can offer, the opportunities for breaking new acts will diminish. With two thousand or so indies in the mix – as there were at the end of the eighties – there were that many more chances that a store was going to take a punt on the Miracle Trees' debut album, they point out.

Their words have become a self-fulfilling prophecy in that, for whatever reason, there are now about a quarter of the number of indie stores that there used to be. And for those that remain, their single biggest complaint continues to be that they always come second to the major chains in the discount stakes. In fact, one indie famously used to buy all his chart stock from the local Woolies because Woolies retailed chart records cheaper than he could buy them wholesale.

OK, back to the major chains. Once a big music retailer has decided to stock a record and a price has been agreed, what can they do in conjunction with the record company to help it sell? Well, the ultimate liaison is the co-op ad campaign. This is a campaign that connects retailer and record company and whose cost is shared by both of them. A typical one would be a TV ad that said: 'Buy Cliff Richard's new album at Woolworths.' I think we've all seen this kind of promotion.

On a smaller scale, stores can choose to back an album within the confines of their premises. Most prominently and effectively, they can dedicate their window display to that album – such an honour, of course, is a service they will sell to a record company. Further, a retailer can put up posters and stickers in store, stock the album in a prominent place and, as is increasingly done, play it to consumers via in-store radio or whatever other sound system they use.

In return, a label can send the band to appear in the chain's stores – either to play or just to smile and sign things – and can generally co-operate as fully as possible. Though it is true to say that, on occasion, retailers and record companies can't agree what day of the week it is, they both know that this kind of mutual assistance helps both of them to sell more records and make more of a profit.

The same is true with the indies, but, of course, it tends to be on a smaller scale. If a label and an indie retailer decide to get together to promote a record, it tends to be a non-mainstream release (there's no point in a label promoting that new Beatles hits compilation exclusively through a company with two shops). But the principles are the same.

If, then, a label is releasing, say, a new classical album, it can work with a classical chain such as MDC to promote the release. The label and retailer might work together to share the cost of advertising, and the conductor or principal musician could visit stores to promote the work.

The fact that such label-retailer liaisons can take place at all levels of business is important. Through it, retailers and record companies can see clearly that such working together brings results for both of them. And, even though it is often difficult for them to do so, given the pressures of business and their conflicting interests, nonetheless they manage it on a regular basis. In fact, without such co-operation, there would be a much bleaker future for the industry.

Chapter 4

R IS FOR RIGHTS

RIGHTS IS THE HARDEST area of the music industry to comprehend because there is nothing to see. Indeed, if there is something tangible – a CD, for example – the issue isn't rights, it's something else.

Yet the question of rights is, in essence, a simple one. It becomes so when you think of rights as property, in exactly the same way as your house, your car or the things you make are property. As we saw in Chapter 1, rights are often called 'intellectual property', meaning simply that they are property created by brainwork rather than manual labour. If we substitute the word 'invisible' for 'intellectual' and call this 'invisible property', that may make things clearer. To make it plainer still, let's drop the adjective altogether and just call it 'property'.

The core of the issue is this: if you make something, you own that thing you made. If, as we saw, a craftsman makes guitars, provided he has paid for his raw materials, the statement that he owns what he made is true in law. If a songwriter makes original music, the same statement is true in law. If a performing artist makes a recording, again that statement is true in law.

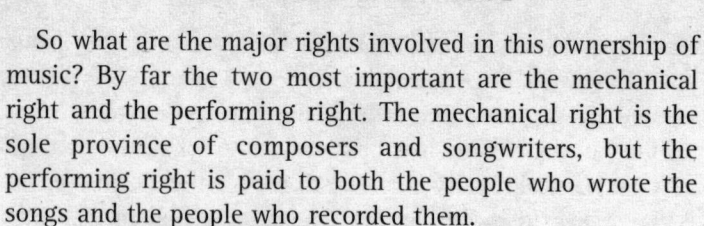

So what are the major rights involved in this ownership of music? By far the two most important are the mechanical right and the performing right. The mechanical right is the sole province of composers and songwriters, but the performing right is paid to both the people who wrote the songs and the people who recorded them.

We'll get to the performing right a little later, but let's look first at the mechanical right. The mechanical right is owned by composers and it is paid every time a song is made into a record. Its name goes back to the days of player-pianos, which reproduced a tune mechanically according to instructions given to their mechanisms on metal cylinders. The composer of each tune put on to those metal cylinders got a royalty – that is, a payment – for each cylinder that was sold.

The principle remains in operation today. For each record pressed, the composer gets a set amount of the price as a mechanical royalty. That amount is set out in law and it is a wonderful thing for a composer to have because it means he or she must get paid at a certain level – no arguments, no messing. If the composer's songs are popular, it's guaranteed income. (And if the composer's songs aren't popular, it's still guaranteed income, though at a vastly reduced level.)

Let's go a little further into what this mechanical royalty is. It applies each time music is reproduced on a physical carrier. The ultimate example is a record and, as we noted, the principle is exactly the same as it has been for more than a century. In legal terms, it doesn't matter if the composer's song is on a metal cylinder for a player-piano or a compact disc: the songwriter still gets an amount of the selling price for this mechanical reproduction of his work. This is only fair in that, when people buy a CD, they aren't handing over money for a small piece of plastic, they are buying the music it contains. The creator of that music should, then, be justly rewarded.

So a mechanical royalty applies to any form of mechanical reproduction of music. Until the digital age, that was simple to define. However, new and emerging technologies have already caused huge arguments about what is or is not a mechanical reproduction. More about that in Chapter 9.

But, no matter how it is applied and to what, the concept of a mechanical royalty is unquestionably an enduring one. It is fixed in British, European, US, Japanese and many other countries' law. And, having been invented under Napoleon as the *droit d'auteur* (author's right), it ain't likely to go away now. Indeed, if it were to go away, there would be no music industry because it is this concept that makes music somebody's property and means that it is possible to make a living from selling it. If there were no such right, all music would be as free as air and nobody would be able to turn a reasonable profit from writing it, performing it or selling it.

Thankfully, as things are, music is property and in law (and, yes, I'm saying this again because it's important) it has exactly the same rights as tangible property. None of us would expect to take away somebody else's tangible property without paying for it and, because of Napoleon, the same is now true of intangible, invisible, intellectual property. So, given that music is property, how much does a concept from nineteenth-century France earn for songwriters alive today?

Well, at the time of writing, a mechanical royalty in the UK is set at 8.5% of published price to dealer (PPD) and in continental Europe it's worth just a whisker more than 9% of PPD. And what is PPD exactly? Published price to dealer is the price of a record as it appears in the relevant record company's catalogue; that is, the list of its products and their associated prices that each label produces and issues to retailers. In that list each record has a specific price. This list price is the published price to dealer, or PPD.

Now, as we saw in the previous chapter, if HMV is buying a hundred thousand copies of an album it is most certainly not going to pay the price that is stated in the catalogue. But the law offers built-in safeguards for the composer in this system: no matter what price a major chain ends up paying for a record – even if, as occasionally happens, the chain pays nothing at all (see Chapter 12) – the songwriter's income is not affected in any way because the mechanical royalty is based on the list price (the PPD), not the price actually paid. In this way – and this is a theme that you'll see repeated again and again – the composer's rights are much more secure than the performer's rights.

We'll look at how those rights and royalties are administered in a moment, but first let's examine the other right – the performing right.

So, the mechanical royalty goes to the person who wrote the song but the performance royalty goes to the writer, the recording artist and the record company. Don't panic, though, that's not as tricky as it sounds. Let me try to simplify. As a first step, let me say again that a mechanical royalty goes only to the person or persons who wrote the song. A mechanical royalty is paid when music is reproduced in a physical medium. Now, a performance royalty is paid when a song is reproduced without the sale of a piece of plastic being involved – that is, when it is heard by an audience simply as vibrations in the air. This performance royalty is paid to the writer, the record company and the recording artist.

Let me break down this idea into its component parts by using the analogy of the guitar-maker again. Think of a three-man company, Tom, Dick & Harry Instruments Limited, which makes guitars. Tom makes fretboards, Dick makes the body and Harry specialises in strings and machine heads. Between them they make the total package. When a consumer buys the total package, the finished guitar, he or she would expect Tom, Dick and Harry to get a share of the money. And that is exactly the way it works with performance royalties; it is no more complex. The person who wrote the song, the person who recorded it and the company which facilitated the recording – the three elements which go to make up the total package of the finished record – each get their share.

When a song is performed, say, for example, on a BBC

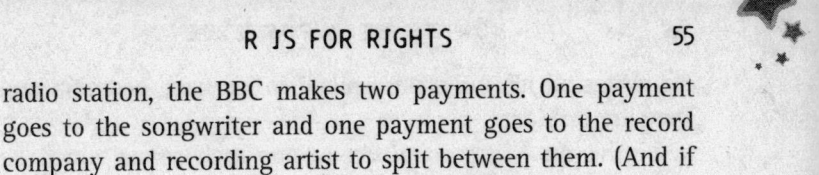

radio station, the BBC makes two payments. One payment goes to the songwriter and one payment goes to the record company and recording artist to split between them. (And if this seems an unfair distribution of money, it is; it is yet another example of the author of a work having a more solid and beneficial right than the recording artist.)

The amount the radio station pays depends on the size of its listenership: simplistically, the more people listening, the more it has to pay. But, whatever the amount, the songwriter gets his or her share with no questions asked – and, in contrast, the label and artist have to fight each other for who gets what percentage of their payment.

The reason that there has been debate over this artist-label split is that the performer's share is based on the law which says the recording artist must get 'reasonable remuneration'. But what's 'reasonable'? Discuss.

Thankfully, at the end of the nineties, before the lawyers got into abstruse and expensive arguments over just what this word means, representatives from the record companies and the performers agreed that 'reasonable' means a fifty-fifty split. That is, of whatever the radio station pays to the recording side, half goes to the record company and half goes to the one, four or twenty people who were in the act that recorded the song.

Now, before we go any further, let's just take a moment to look more closely at this division of labour between the writing side and the performing side. In law and in practice these are separate entities. But confusion often arises because, in reality, they tend to be the same person. Let's look at both sides of the coin to illustrate what I mean. Let's assume Beethoven is a twenty-five-year-old, slightly reclusive composer alive and well today and living in a small village near Nottingham. The lad is a brilliant songwriter and can write in any style. But, since arriving from Germany, he now hates to travel, so doesn't leave his village, doesn't perform, never goes near a recording studio and won't appear in public.

He writes all his tunes on a piano in his back bedroom and they are brilliant.

Beethoven writes some classy pop-rock songs which he sends to the Miracle Trees. Excited by what they see on paper (the composer has sent out the songs as sheet music), they record the stuff and have a number-one single. When that single is played on the radio, the royalty structure means that Beethoven gets his payment and the Miracle Trees and the label they are signed to get a separate payment. Of the money coming in to those who made the record (the record company and the band), the label takes half the payment, then hands over the other half to the Miracle Trees. The band then split the money between them as they see fit. There are no rules about who gets what among the musicians; the only obligation in law is that half the recording royalty goes to the band. Once the band receive it, how they divide it up is entirely their decision. But, as they're a four-piece, the logical thing is to split it into four equal amounts. If they choose not to, we can only hope that all members – including the one who gets the smallest amount – agree to that system, otherwise the row, both legal and emotional, will be huge.

Assuming the radio station has made a total payment of £100 for playing the Miracle Trees' new number-one single – written by Beethoven and only recorded by the Miracle Trees, remember – here's how that money would break down under this system (and assuming the band split the cash equally between them):

Beethoven (as composer)	£50
The recording interests	£50
The recording side's share then breaks down as:	
Label	£25
The Miracle Trees	£25

With four members in the band and an equal split, each musician gets £6.25.

R IS FOR RIGHTS

I think you can now see how much more lucrative it is to be just a composer rather than just a performer.

Right, that was one side of the coin, where the songwriter and performer are entirely separate people. But very, very often they are the same person.

Let's look at Sting's 'Englishman in New York', a song both written and performed by Sting. A £100 performance royalty payment for that would break down as:

Sting (as composer)   £50
The recording interests   £50
The recording side's share then breaks down as:
Label   £25
Sting (as performer)   £25

– meaning that Sting walks away from this deal with £75, compared with the Miracle Trees' £6.25 each.

Sting's sole financial obligation from this – apart from what he owes to the taxman – is to ensure the other musicians on the record are suitably rewarded. He could have done this in two ways. When hiring them to work, he could have said either:

1. I will give you x amount to play on this record; it's a flat fee and I'll owe you nothing more at any point;

or:

2. I will pay you the lower amount, y, and I'll give you such and such percentage of the performance royalties which come in.

Now, Sting is not offering the musicians a proportion of his composer's income; he wrote the song alone and takes all the money that it accrues. But, of the £25 he earns as the recording artist, he may hand over an amount to the other people who appeared on the record.

To avoid confusion, let's just run through that again. But now let's assume that the Miracle Trees follow up the hit that Beethoven wrote for them with a song they've penned themselves. They record the song using no other musicians. Now it breaks down like this:

The Miracle Trees (as composers)	£50
The recording interests	£50
The recording side's share then breaks down as:	
Label	£25
The Miracle Trees (as performers)	£25

So, assuming an even split between the band on both writing and recording royalties, each of the four musicians now gets a quarter of the £50 and a quarter of the £25 – a total of £18.75.

This basic principle doesn't just concern airplay. It applies whenever music is heard in a public place. Apart from buskers in the street, every time music is played, somebody is paying a bill in the form of performance royalties. To illustrate this, here's a few examples of the kind of areas that generate performance royalties. Now, this is by no means an exhaustive list, but it gives an idea of the uses to which music is put, something of which we are not always aware because there is so much of it about. So, each time you hear music in one of these ways, somebody is paying a bill and that money is going to both the composer and the recording artist. In no particular order, these uses are:

1. Music on TV and radio – whether upfront music in a music-based programme like *Top Of The Pops* or something that's in the background in a drama or comedy show
2. TV and radio ads
3. Concerts
4. Theatre shows, particularly musicals
5. Public performances in places like football grounds, public spaces, pubs and shops
6. Film soundtracks
7. Clubs

8. Muzak
9. Computer games/CD-Roms
10. Telephone hold music
11. Health clubs and gyms
12. Samples and remixes
13. Internet sites
14. Sheet music

Please note that most of the things on this list don't involve mechanical or physical reproduction of music. For the bulk of that list, the person hearing music gets it just as those wonderful vibrations in the air and nothing else. For the rest, computers games and CD-Roms, film soundtracks and sheet music, mechanical royalties can apply but not at the rate of 8·5% of PPD as they do on a pure audio CD. I'm not going to complicate matters here by going into the different rates those different items pay at, but I will simply repeat that, because they reproduce music physically, some money is due to the composer as a mechanical royalty. But, let me say once more, in each case above when the music is reproduced just as vibrations in the air, everybody involved in making the relevant recording gets their performance royalty.

OK, so when mechanical royalties and performance royalties from whatever source are paid to a composer, to whom does the money go in the first instance? Answer: to a music publisher. And what does a music publisher do?

Well, a music publisher is a company that administers the rights in music and which works on behalf of the songwriters it represents. The company operates on exactly the same principles as the people publishing this book; the only difference being that you can't see or feel or touch the wares of a music publisher. However, if you want to use them, you have to buy them, just like – bless you – you bought this book.

Let's continue that analogy to demonstrate once again that intangible property and tangible property are both still property and both can be bought, sold and traded. So, music publishers handle the rights involved in compositions in just the same way that the book publisher is handling the rights to this book. As the author, I have turned over all my rights to the book publisher and the company is doing the best it can to maximise my – and its own – income by selling as many copies as possible of this book. The company does that by marketing and promotion and professional sales techniques. It also protects my rights by making sure nobody is copying this book in illuminated manuscript and selling unlicensed copies from a warehouse in Prague. For those services, the book publisher takes a percentage of all income generated by this book and sends the rest to me in a regular cheque.

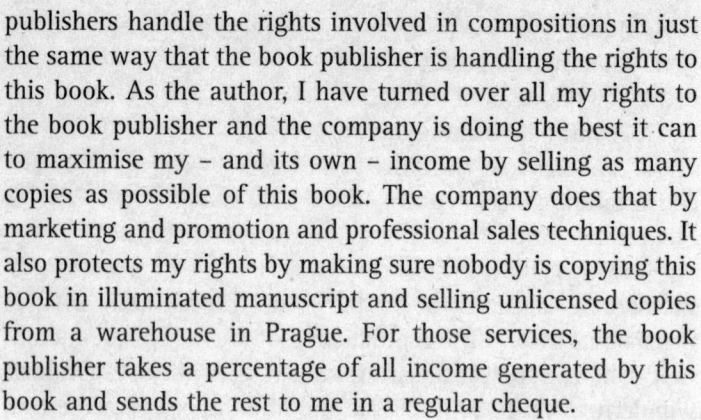

Such a relationship between book author and book publisher is exactly mirrored in the relationship between song author and song publisher. The songwriter composes his or her works then hands them to the publisher to promote and to sell in any and all places the publisher can think of. The music publisher takes a cut for such national and, hopefully, international promotion and protection, then sends the rest of the money to the composer. (Oh, and I should add that, in law, lyricists count just as much as songwriters as people who write music. If they are two people – as in Sir Elton John and Bernie Taupin or Andrew Lloyd Webber and Tim Rice – how they split the money between them is entirely down to them.)

Now, having said what a publisher does, let's just look again at what a publisher does not do. A music publisher works on behalf of songwriters only. Publishers handle music and are not involved in or directly concerned with making records. Music and a record are not the same thing. One is an original composition; the other is a mechanical reproduction of that original composition. In law and in practice, they are separate issues and concerns. Just to emphasise the separateness of these commodities, let's note that a record can exist without music and music can exist without a record. There are CDs of birdsong, whale song, waves crashing on the shore, trains pulling away into the distance – all records with no (human) music on them. And performed music, made by a live musician, is the antithesis of a record.

Please keep in mind how isolated from each other the act of writing and recording are as I say again: a publisher represents only the songwriter – even if the songwriter is Sting, who also records the works he writes. Recordings are the province of the record company; publishers handle only the music itself. Sorry to labour the point, but it's an important one.

Now let's see how publishers work in practice by looking once more at that Beethoven-written hit single by the Miracle Trees. When the BBC radio station plays the record on air and hands over the sum it owes to the composer – our youthful Beethoven in his village near Nottingham, remember – it doesn't send a cheque to his house. Such a thing would be administratively formidable in that, with the thousands of records the BBC plays every day, it would need to employ thousands more people just to handle the royalties that arise.

Instead, the BBC hands over a cheque to Beethoven's publisher. That is, a company, say EMI Music Publishing, which looks after his rights on his behalf. This is an excellent arrangement in that Beethoven is a composer and has not the time, the inclination or the means to chase every radio and TV station across Europe, America and Japan to make sure he's getting his money.

Instead, a big publishing company with offices across the world does the job for him. And what does EMI Music Publishing get out of this? Well, as we noted earlier, its profits come from taking a cut of Beethoven's earnings at a rate which it has agreed with him. In return, EMI makes sure the people using Beethoven's work pay their bills and, on top of that and more pro-actively, the company markets his talents to potential customers, the kind of people who use music on the list given earlier in the chapter. For example, if an advertising agency is looking for music for a new car ad, EMI will say, 'Use Beethoven's stuff; it's brilliant and just what you're looking for.' Of course, EMI is in fierce competition with all the other publishers who are also saying to the ad agencies, film companies and so on, 'Use our stuff.'

So the BBC and other users of music pay their cheques to Beethoven's publisher, yes? Well, very nearly.

All the publishers working together own the two operations that are the front door for payments – the Mechanical Copyright Protection Society (MCPS), which handles mechanical royalty payments, and the Performing Right Society (PRS), which administers performance royalties. So, in terms of performance royalties, the BBC – as do all the other broadcasters – logs each record that it plays, both on its national networks and its local radio and TV stations, then totals up the amount it owes and sends a cheque to the PRS, along with that list of the records it has played, so that the royalties due can be checked.

It's rather like eating in a restaurant. You choose items from the menu, consume them, then settle up at the end of the meal, paying for the items you chose. Though you may have eaten many different things, it is not for the diner to send money directly to the farmer who produced the meat and the baker who baked the bread and the dairy which made the ice cream; that's the restaurant's job. In the same way, the BBC consumes music and settles up for what it has consumed with the PRS. The PRS then passes on the relevant sums to each of the publishers who belong to the society as members.

The PRS administers all performing rights, and, remember, the performing right applies whenever music is delivered to consumers as vibrations in the air rather than as a record. When records are involved in the process, there is mechanical reproduction of music, so the mechanical royalty applies.

So who pays mechanical royalties to the MCPS then? Answer: the record companies.

It is vital to remember that record companies do not own the music on the records they put out. The record company owns the recording but not the music itself. Because music is property, the label has to pay the owner of that property for each use of it.

And, of course, the owner of that property is the songwriter. But, once more, the cheque for the single Beethoven wrote for the Miracle Trees will not go straight to Beethoven's house. Record companies pay all their mechanical royalties to the MCPS, which then passes on what each publisher is due in exactly the same way that the PRS does. This is because record companies press thousands of titles a year and it is simpler for them, just as it is for the BBC, to settle up in one go and in one place rather than deal with potentially thousands of different composers individually.

That, I hope, summarises what songwriters are due and how they get it. Now, what about those who record rather than those who write. What happens to their performance royalties? Those who record – that is, the band and the record company – do not have to have a structure in place to handle mechanical royalties because, remember, as they didn't write the song they don't get any. Yes, of course, the band may well have written the song but, as we have seen earlier in this chapter, the composer and the recording artist are dealt with entirely separately even if they occupy the same skin. It's like being Clark Kent and Superman – and I leave you to decide whether the composer or performer is Superman. So, it is true to say that record companies and recording artists receive only performance royalties, paid each time the record they made is used.

When the recording side's proportion of all these royalties is paid, it goes to the record companies' equivalent of the PRS – Phonographic Performance Limited (PPL).

The principles involved are exactly the same as with the PRS in that PPL collects all the money from all the places using recorded music and then divides it up appropriately and distributes it to its members, the labels. They then take their share and hand on the rest to the performers.

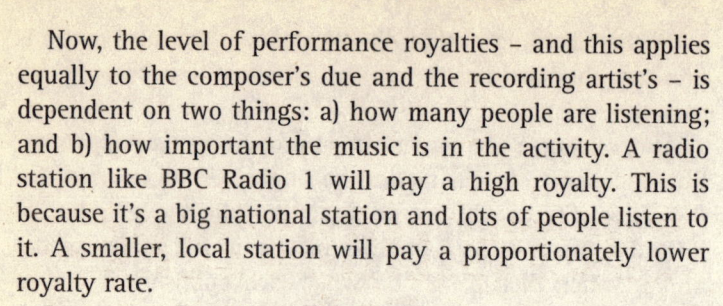

Now, the level of performance royalties – and this applies equally to the composer's due and the recording artist's – is dependent on two things: a) how many people are listening; and b) how important the music is in the activity. A radio station like BBC Radio 1 will pay a high royalty. This is because it's a big national station and lots of people listen to it. A smaller, local station will pay a proportionately lower royalty rate.

In terms of public performance, the other factor is the activity itself. An aerobics club with fifty people in it will pay a higher rate than a hotel playing music in its lifts. This is because music is essential to the aerobics session whereas music in a lift is just a pain in the arse for everybody. (Ever heard anybody say, 'NO! I'm not getting in that lift. There's no music in it!' Of course not. Nobody has.)

Such are the wonderful vagaries of the rights sector, a sector without which the industry would crumble to nothing. We'll be revisiting many of the issues the rights sector addresses later in the book. For the time being, though, I'd advocate a nice cup of tea to allow all this stuff time to sink in.

Chapter 5

THE TWILIGHT ZONE – A&R

LET'S START WITH THE A&R JOKE.

A rabbit and a snake are both rushing through the woods when they bump into each other. Picking himself up, the rabbit says, 'So sorry I didn't see you, but I'm blind.'

The snake replies, 'No need to apologise. So am I.'

After a moment's pause, the rabbit says, 'Do you know, I've never found out what kind of animal I am. Do you mind having a feel and telling me?'

Says the snake, 'Sure. Then after that you can feel me and tell me what I am.'

'OK,' agrees the rabbit.

The snake feels his new friend for a while before concluding, 'Well, you've got long ears, a small, fluffy tail and you're covered in fur. I think you must be a rabbit.'

'Brilliant,' says the rabbit. 'Now let me try.'

After feeling the snake for a while, he says, 'Well, you're slimy, you've got very little backbone and no ears. Are you in A&R?'

Poor old A&R people. Nobody understands them yet everybody wants to criticise them and demean them.

Why does nobody understand them? Firstly, because, as we

noted at the start of the book, nothing has ever been written or broadcast which accurately depicts how these people think and behave and how they go about their day-to-day work. That puts them into, yes, their own mysterious Twilight Zone, dark and impenetrable to the outside world. In fact, the only time A&R people are exposed to public gaze is when something truly bizarre happens, and I don't believe any of us would feel an accurate portrayal of our lives and personalities was being given if observers looked only at the highly infrequent bizarre things we do rather than the routine daily graft.

The second reason why A&R people get such a hard time is that their job is purely subjective. There is no single right and wrong answer in what they do. Consequently, they are treated like football managers and their decisions held in similar regard: that is, everybody – and I mean everybody – thinks they have better judgement, insights and ears than the A&R person they are dealing with/talking about/slagging off (and, sadly, those three things tend to happen simultaneously).

What is A&R exactly? Its full name gives us the answer: A&R stands for 'Artists and Repertoire' and it means that the A&R staff are responsible for – either in whole or in part – every creative decision a record company makes. Let me do that again: A&R people have a role in every creative decision a label makes. We'll look more closely at the ramifications of that later in the chapter.

For now, let's go a little further into what A&R people do and how they manage to upset so many people doing it. Sadly, upsetting folks is inevitable and unavoidable simply because so many people want to be professional musos and so few are capable of doing so. Let me illustrate the point.

The outpouring of desire to access the glamorous high life of a star results in a tide of music that swamps through each label's letterbox every day. A major label will, in each post, receive several hundred demos – a demo being a disc or a tape containing a sample of a would-be superstar's work. But, my, what a toxic tide it tends to be.

Now, it is not my desire to belittle the efforts of those who send in demo tapes. Their passion for and love of music is what makes this business commercially viable and emotionally exciting. And, as a man who thinks perfect pitch is somewhere good to play football and a semi-quaver is a new pub snack, let me tell you that you have more talent than I do. But, just like my youthful desires to be a professional footballer, often enthusiasm and self-belief outstrip talent by a very long way.

Some years ago I asked a couple of my mates in major-label A&R departments to give me a random sample of one day's rejections. Though I asked for just a sample from just one day, that still ran to around a hundred or more demos – and, Lordy, I can tell you it was desperate. Everything – and, once more, I mean that word literally – was at best derivative, tedious and alarming inasmuch as the perpetrators believed a major label might be interested in such acts of audio terrorism. I certainly don't have ears ('ears' being the standard term for somebody with an ability to recognise talent when he or she hears it) but I have heard hundreds of successful albums and thousands of unsuccessful ones and I have come to know the difference. That audio flow which oozes through the labels' letterboxes every day is, I regret to say, generally not even within the same parsec as the worst of the unsuccessful albums I have heard.

I genuinely mean here that I regret to say this. It is a tragedy that music which carries its creator's heart, soul, love and aspirations is not held in suitably high esteem by dispassionate observers. But, I really, truly, genuinely regret, in virtually every case it ain't.

This, then, is the cause of all the upset that the A&R people create. If somebody has put everything into making a sound that embodies the spirit which moves them (or just creates a loud racket which they adore), they absolutely do not want to hear that it has been turned down by the label. Further, they find it almost impossible to accept that a rational human being would have been capable of turning it down.

So, not only are all those people who have their work rejected upset, but they also act as a grapevine on which the reputation of A&R staff is hung out to dry. Every person who is turned down is likely to stand in his local pub saying, 'The A&R people didn't understand me/don't know what they're doing/etc.' (And they are highly unlikely to say, 'Yes, I think the A&R department made a good decision on my demo. Really, I think I'm not up to the job.') Because there is no objective measure of who is right and wrong in such matters, when the rejectee complains loudly about A&R incompetence, his mates tend to be influenced by what their friend is saying and down another notch goes the already tarnished reputation of A&R people. The sad truth is, though, that, while A&R people are not above making errors in the same way that fish are not above birds, it is likely they understood the rejectee all too well. But, with several hundred rejectees every day, that is a lot of folk going around saying A&R people wouldn't know successful music from a hole in the ground.

Such statements are, though, in the final analysis, merely a distraction, and I don't worry unduly about A&R people's emotional well-being because you don't get to be successful in that business without having a skin as thick as your wallet.

Let's look, then, at the more positive aspects of the role. As we saw in Chapter 1, A&R people's prime, first and best function is to seek out new talent and new musical forms (and if that involves boldly going where no one has gone before, they can always put it on their expenses). Somewhere within each day's incoming tide of demos may be that exciting, enthralling, epoch-changing thing the A&R person seeks. But where is it? The only way to find out is to listen to every single disc and tape.

This means that, contrary to some popular perceptions, every demo gets listened to. Yes, every demo. Why? Because the pressure on A&R staff to find the next big thing is enormous and unrelenting; it amounts to a fire burning beneath them, driving them to extreme lengths to gain the cooling relief that only success brings – and they do not know if success lies in that tape over there, or the next one or the next one or the next one. They do know, however, that if a rival label signs an act that this A&R person failed to listen to through lack of time or sheer ennui, this A&R person is going to get the mother of all bollockings and probably a P45 to go with it. If A&R people do not have the most precarious careers in all of capitalism, I don't know who does. (And if it's you, I wish you well.)

Now, we have all heard the amusing stories about blank tapes that have been sent in to a label and returned to their owner with a letter saying, 'We have listened to this most carefully and do not believe the style is something for us.'

All this indicates is that the junior A&R person who listened to it just pulled it out of the machine and, under pressure of moving on to the next tape, threw it into the pile marked for return to sender. The department's secretary then simply puts a corporate, computer-generated letter in the envelope with the tape (and I hope nobody thinks the department is going to write an individual letter to the several hundred people it rejects each day) and, *voilà*, through the return of a blank tape to whichever jovial prankster sent it, the legend of more A&R daftness is born.

It is only fair, though, to acknowledge that A&R people are easily capable of mistakes. They are as human, as fallible and as flawed as the rest of us (particularly when we're under pressure) and can make almighty cock-ups. The mightiest was, by general consensus, that of Dick Rowe. Never heard of him? He's the guy who turned down the Beatles. Ah, I sense some degree of recognition now. I wrote his obituary when he died at the end of the eighties and I remember his son ringing me as I was about to put pen to paper asking me not to mention the fact that he had shown John, Paul, George and Ringo the door. But poor old Dick, despite signing the Rolling Stones, was forever known as the man who turned down the Beatles. Undiminished by his massive success with the Stones and other sixties and seventies heroes, Dick carried that Beatles decision like a millstone round his neck and, sadly and unwittingly, with it he made another massive contribution to the legend of A&R stupidity. And although somebody in the A&R profession was bright enough to sign the Fab Four, as with so much in life, the negative makes a much deeper impression than the positive.

Yes, A&R people can get it wrong. They can also get it very right a very large number of times – hence the massive volume of adored music in all styles that exists in the world today. Every act that you, your mates, your parents, your children and that mad bloke at the bus station enjoys has been found, developed and brought to fruition by A&R people. A&R people are responsible for every brilliant album on your shelves (and also all the shite ones you gave to the Oxfam shop under cover of darkness, but let's not dwell on that).

It is, then, the burden of the A&R department to find and then to nurture each new generation of talent. A&R staff must be able to recognise not only what will do well in the current climate but also to identify what the record-buying public is going to want long before the public knows itself. This kind of clairvoyance is based on the fact that a band signed today won't have their first album in the stores until a year from now. In a world where most of us don't know what's for tea tomorrow, understanding where tastes are going to be twelve months on is very impressive.

I say it is the burden of the A&R department to carry out this task because the life and death of a record company hangs on their success. That's a heavy load to bear. Certainly, a major label and a big indie can survive for a while on repackaging and remarketing its catalogue albums, but without new hits, it will, sooner rather than later, wither and fail.

And on top of the A&R department's challenge of finding

and developing new talent is another exacting task – doing the job in the white heat of global publicity. Whether the A&R staff are succeeding in their mission to locate and break young bands is not just obvious, it is a fact that is broadcast to millions of people every week. The measure of success in the music industry is the charts (more on them in Chapter 12) and, unlike a football league table, where there is a conspicuous end to the season and everybody starts with a clean slate at the beginning of each new term, the charts are published relentlessly, week after week after week. In the fast-moving world of pop, having a hit two months ago means less than bugger all; you are only as good as your standing in this week's listings. While a major label can go one week or even two without having a Top Ten album or single, if that sequence gets to three weeks, the UK boss will want to know why – as will his boss in New York or Los Angeles.

The pressure on the A&R department is, then, unremitting and terrible. It is even worse than on a football manager because at least a football club gets the close season to put its house in order. There ain't no close season in the music business and next Sunday's chart will expose you for what you are.

How, then, do A&R departments create the musical and commercial triumphs that are required of them? As we noted, the process begins with that daily trawl through the demo tapes. And who does this? Well, though titles vary from company to company, the bottom rung of the A&R ladder is somebody likely to be called something like an A&R assistant. This person, probably the youngest member of the department and certainly the most junior, listens to everything that comes in – and that means everything. As we noted, nothing can be ignored because it is impossible to tell without listening just which demo will contain the next Westlife or Elton John or, indeed, Beatles.

The assistant gets his or her ears round each demo that turns up. The tiny, tiny fraction of tapes and, increasingly, discs that the assistant deems worth that important second listen will be passed on to his or her boss, a person with a title along the lines of A&R scout. The scout will give his (or her, but we're going to keep this simple and use just his) second opinion to the demo. Then, just like the A&R assistant, the scout will discard the overwhelming majority of demos that arrive on his desk. But, if he does find one worthy of even further attention, he will do one or both of two things with it. The scout will take the demos he believes interesting to either the company's weekly A&R meeting and/or to his boss, an A&R manager.

The weekly meeting, a gathering of all the more senior A&R people, will discuss everything on the table. That is, they will listen to and talk about all the demos that each of the A&R scouts has brought to the meeting. Then, once more, having rejected the vast bulk of what was up for consideration, the remainder will be considered further by the A&R director – the head of the department – and the best of that rump will finally go to the head of the company, the managing director or chairman or whatever he calls himself.

You can see, then, that there are four or five layers of filters. At each layer the majority of demos up for consideration are rejected. At that first layer, the initial listening, the rejection rate is around 98%, meaning that of every hundred demos that arrive at the company, only around two get a second listen. That still adds up to plenty of demos that go upstairs to the A&R scouts, but it also means an awful lot never get that far.

Of those that do, the A&R scouts reject most of them before sending on the rest to their boss, so maybe 70–80% fall at this hurdle. Even more are turned down at the A&R meeting and by the A&R managers, so it's a pretty optimistic assumption to think that even one demo in a thousand makes it on to the A&R director's desk.

OK, so what happens with those demos that the A&R department does think have some potential? The first stage, of course, is to contact the people who made the music. The second stage is to have a look at them live and A&R scouts travel monstrous distances to do this. For most London-based record companies, a junior A&R scout has a patch that runs from the south coast to Leeds – and is expected to be at a gig at least five nights a week.

I defy any human to drive from London to Leeds, watch a gig, drive home, get to bed around three, then be at the office at nine on the dot the following morning (or ten o'clock, as nine o'clock sharp is known in the music industry). Hence the A&R person's reputation for being slug-a-beds who only come out after dark. They're knackered after driving round the country for most of the previous evening, and the evening before that and the evening before that. (And, as you can imagine, stable relationships are not particularly prevalent in the early stages of this profession.)

Assuming, then, that the A&R staff have heard the tape and seen the gig and remain suitably enthused, they then set about signing the band to the label. This, though, is often not as simple as it seems. Although the A&R department want to sign the act and the act want to be signed – they wouldn't have sent the demo in the first place if that wasn't the case – there are a number of things that can get in the way. One of them is the act deciding they don't like the company's policies and methods once they see them up close. Another is the act's management issuing all sorts of stupid demands that make the label think the whole project is more trouble than it's worth. A third is another label coming in with a better offer.

The first two can be overcome, and generally are, as both sides are well motivated to do so. Young bands close to their first record deal tend to be prepared to do anything to get on the label, and labels either don't want an act at all or want it desperately. So, if the label expresses an interest, it's a big interest. By the time both these passionate would-be partners get round a table, they tend to be salivating over each other – in a business sense, of course. And such commercial salivation means that both sides are eager to find a way around any difficulties that may lie between them and, despite the occasional spat, tend to do so.

The record company's last problem, that of another label coming in with a better offer, is an unavoidable function of a competitive market. It tends to be that a band are wanted by nobody or everybody, so there is regularly competition for a signature. This is a product of the industry grapevine. People talk, not always wisely and not always profitably (see Chapter 11 for more on this) but they talk nonetheless, which means that if an A&R guy goes to a gig by the Miracle Trees he will be seen and somebody will report it to a rival label. The rival label then becomes determined not to lose out on this potentially hot new act and makes sure it knows what the band are about. Thus, if the Miracle Trees do have something to offer, everybody knows about it and wants it.

Ultimately, which label gets the band's signature on its contract depends on a number of factors. Money is a very big influence, of course, but there are other, often more powerful ones all playing a part – such as the nature of the company, its A&R philosophy, the personalities of the people involved, all sorts of things, including luck.

Some years ago a label which shall be nameless (mainly because I can't remember which one it was) was courting Irish songstress Enya. They loved her music, liked her as a human being and were in the process of wooing her into a deal. This label was the envy of its rivals because of Enya's obvious talent and potential, something that, due to the gossip network I mentioned, everybody was aware of. So, this label was ahead of the game in getting Enya on its roster and, mindful of the competition it faced for her signature, was on a serious charm offensive to persuade her to sign. Part of that commercial seduction involved taking her to one of the big, glossy industry functions, in this case the Brit Awards, and Enya was invited to join the label on their table for dinner and then see the show. But the label execs she was due to meet were late and she ended up sitting alone for a considerable while. Spotting her rather bored solitude (there are only so many times you can read a menu before tedium sets in), Rob Dickins, then head of Warner Music in the UK, went over to her and, telling her she shouldn't be sitting there alone and fed up, invited her over to the Warner table. They talked a lot, Rob suggested she come to his office the following day and a deal was done very rapidly after that. Enya's huge international success on Warner since then is a matter of record and records, both sold and broken.

(And, by way of digression, Rob Dickins is one of only two record company execs I am aware of who have been mentioned in a popular song. He ended up in Enya's first hit single, 'Orinoco Flow', in the line 'something, something, something, with Rob Dickins at the wheel'. The other exec immortalised in lyrics is Claude Nobs, former gaffer at Warner in Switzerland, who is in Deep Purple's classic 'Smoke On The Water' as 'Funky Claude was running in an' out, pulling kids out the ground.')

Assuming a label wants to sign an act and that act wants to be signed and that they have reached agreement in principle, what happens next? Well, after that, the lawyers then put that agreement in principle into the kind of language they like (so no other bugger can understand it), then lay that document on the table for the other side's lawyers to discuss – again at length. It's all alarmingly long-winded, if you ask me, but it's a system we're stuck with.

Once it's out of the way, though, the A&R department can get on with doing what it does best: bringing the act to its full potential. This is the bulk of the A&R department's job. Finding the talent was only the tip of the iceberg that the outside world sees; down there in the Twilight Zone, under the surface, much activity ensues. It is in those uncharted deeps of the real business, away from the public gaze, that the Herculean task of turning a young band's potential into real, countable sales and measurable success gets under way.

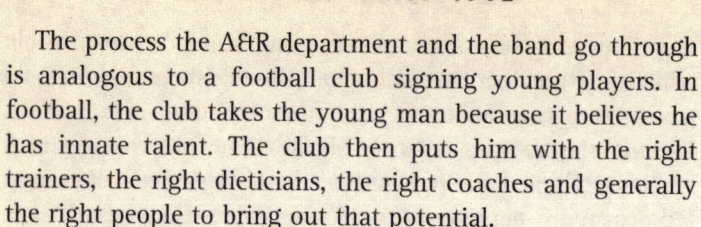

The process the A&R department and the band go through is analogous to a football club signing young players. In football, the club takes the young man because it believes he has innate talent. The club then puts him with the right trainers, the right dieticians, the right coaches and generally the right people to bring out that potential.

So it is with a record company. Now, it may be that the label has spent millions on signing the finished article – just as Virgin did with the Rolling Stones in the early nineties – and has a set of polished pros on the blocks and ready to run. But, just as in football, buying established talent is hugely expensive and it is far more likely that the A&R department will be dealing in the first instance with an act on their first deal.

This, then, involves a lot of human as well as professional skills. It may be that this new band need a few raw edges in their style smoothing out. That's a lot more difficult than demonstrating improved technique to a young footballer. Show a young player how to better control his body and move his feet and so on, and the ball will go where he wants it more often. Show a band something new and there is always the possibility that they will say, 'This is the way we've always done it and we're not going to compromise our style.' The problem is, of course, that, unlike football, there is that perennial difficulty for the A&R people: there is no objective measure of what is better style. The A&R person will then have to tactfully, carefully and respectfully discuss his ideas with the band and aim to take that discussion in the direction he wants them to go.

The A&R person's tact is also greatly taxed at all subsequent stages of this process. It is likely that a young band may never have worked with a producer before, so the A&R person has to both find the right producer and ensure the producer's relationship with the act runs smoothly. Similarly, if the band do not write their own material or need a couple of songs from outside sources, the A&R person must ensure the right songwriters are chosen and the outside work is seamlessly melded into the band's own style and desires (which is a task akin to trying to fold blancmange). And, because the A&R person's work is never done, the same applies to finding the right engineer, the right crew, the right location and equipment and support staff – including somebody who cooks like the young musos' mums.

All these elements – and not least the last of them – are important because the act were signed as creative people and, in my experience, as we noted in Chapter 1, nobody creates well unless they are relaxed and happy. It is the A&R person's job to make sure this is the case – by putting the act in a studio they are happy with, by surrounding them with people they are happy with and by making them as happy as possible as human beings. This final element is the particularly tricky one, and it may involve even more tact when trying to point out, say, a better and more conducive lifestyle. It will also take a good measure of genuine sympathy and empathy when dealing with the problems that young men face in the world and life and love, along with plenty of patience when they're throwing a tantrum (not if, but when; it's inevitable) and a shoulder to cry on when they miss their girlfriend, dog, football team or whatever it happens to be.

It also, of course, requires a great deal of financial commitment. While a young act is in the studio recording their first album or in the rehearsal rooms writing it, they are simply eating up money and earning nothing for the label. Even without all the cost of designing, pressing, marketing and promoting the album further down the line, already the band are a huge drain on the resources of the label. The record company, then, needs to have been convinced at the outset that the band were worth this multi-thousand-pound commitment – which is precisely why the A&R process is so rigorous.

So, the band are having all this money spent on them and a lot of effort expended on their behalf. What is their responsibility in return? Well, simply to provide the record company with a product it can sell. What the label does not want is for a band to get into the studio for the first time and suddenly decide that, having got a record deal on the strength of their catchy three-minute pop songs, they would like to do a fifty-minute, one-track concept piece. It is unlikely that a band on their first album would make such a commercially mad decision, but older, more experienced acts have been known to take such radical directions.

It is, then, a large part of the A&R process to monitor what the band are producing. With a young act, this involves advice, guidance, cajoling, whatever is required to bring out their potential. With some older acts, it can involve bellowing, 'Give me a sodding single, you pointless pillock!'

Bellowing between A&R people and bands is not unknown (in much the same way as cold winter days are not unknown) and there are any number of things that can set it off. Singles (or the absence thereof) is a big and common one because A&R people and the whole record company want singles. Hit singles are what sell albums and label execs lust after them.

Why? Well, singles are analogous to film trailers. In fact, a major-label single will rarely make a profit in its own right – recording, packaging and marketing costs are too high for that – but, like a film trailer, it is hugely important in getting people to partake of the main feature, the album. It is an introduction and invitation to the band's music. A good working band will give the label at least one single on the album, and preferably three – this being the magic number to ensure that the album stays in the charts and the public consciousness for the maximum amount of time.

Some bands' music does not lend itself to singles, of course, but the A&R department obviously were aware of that at the outset. When Virgin signed Mike Oldfield, it knew *Tubular Bells* was never going to provide any easily digestible three-minute songs for *Top Of The Pops*.

However, some bands, seemingly eager to bite the record

company hand that is trying to feed (and feed off) them, consciously try to resist the idea of singles being lifted from their album, either as a point of principle or out of some notion that it compromises their artistic integrity. Often this makes it much more difficult for them to have a career, although Led Zeppelin, Genesis and Yes are prime examples of bands who did manage to prosper through this tactic. I can't give you the massively longer list of bands who failed to succeed by getting on their soapbox in this manner because, of course, we never heard of any of them.

So, the A&R department watches what is happening in the recording studio like a nervous expectant father. Will the band give birth to a handsome commercial and artistic masterpiece or some misshapen, unloved musical lump? The A&R department has put all the conditions in place for the former, has advised, assisted and nurtured, but can now only sit back and wait. It will, though, want regular updates and somebody from the department will call into the studio regularly and/or take away rough tapes to see what is happening and where things are going.

If the direction being taken is one that both the band and the label are happy with, then the birth goes smoothly. If, however, there are differences of opinion – over the absence of singles, style of music, lyrics or anything else – that's where the trouble begins.

I think this is the appropriate point to go back to those people who claim they are misunderstood by A&R departments. While everybody who has failed to make an impact on the music industry complains that this is the case, for some people it is actually true.

There have been classic instances where the A&R people and the band had radically different ideas. In some of those cases the band were right but the A&R staff couldn't see it, so artist and label had no option but to go their separate ways. In those circumstances a few of the artists were able to prove they were right by signing to other labels – for example, the

Sex Pistols and George Michael (er, but not together); in many more of those cases, though, the band just went to the great hit parade in the sky.

I am going to say again this fact that there is no measurable, black-and-white answer to many A&R questions and it is solely for that reason that there can be these serious and divisive creative differences between band and label.

Let me give you an example of how such differences between people of good conscience can occur and how labels and musos can see the same thing in utterly different ways – though I hasten to add that this particular difference of opinion was conducted calmly and with a lot of mutual respect. PolyGram in France found a splendid French band called Niagara, a kind of rocky Eurythmics with a good, broad appeal. They begged Niagara to sing in English. The band declined, arguing that if they abandoned their lyrics in their native French, they would no longer be Niagara. John Waller, a senior figure at PolyGram UK, brought them over to London, made a fuss of them and told them about all the hits they could have in the big, wide world outside France if they would only sing in English. Niagara again declined to do so, arguing strongly once more that if they did sing in English they would no longer be Niagara and nobody would buy their stuff and their large and solid fanbase back home in France would melt like dew.

Who was right? Discuss.

Oh, and one more example of such things. Madness, them good old nutty boys, came to Dave Robinson, founder and gaffer at indie label Stiff, with their demo. Dave liked the sound of the band immediately. Now, in addition to the fully fledged tracks on the demo, there was also a tiny, few-seconds-long snippet of a song. Dave loved this in particular and wanted the band to record it full length as a single. The band refused, saying that it was nothing and should be ignored. Dave, never a man to take no for an answer (he was the guy who taught me how to fight with a baseball bat), took the snippet, cut it and pasted it, and created 'One Step Beyond', the song that launched the band's illustrious career. Was he right to do so? Was he right to risk pissing off the talent he was courting? Was he right to risk losing this potential goldmine of an act for the sake of a single? Or was he right to trust his instincts and kick-start Madness's career with a song that is still massively popular today? Discuss. Or, rather, don't; we have business to attend to.

And our business is looking at the A&R process and how it works with our young band in the studio (sorry, it's been a while since we thought about them, but I'm sure you remember who they are). But what happens after the album is recorded, and what does the A&R department do in that? Well, the A&R department – and, most specifically, the A&R manager who has been assigned to the band – will have an involvement at every point down the line. While he may not have much say – or even interest – in where the disc is pressed and packaged, every creative aspect is within his remit.

The A&R manager will, then, talk to the art department, the designers, everybody with an impact on the sound of the record and its physical appearance, to discuss what is right for that particular act. Whether the A&R manager's wishes are always adhered to is another matter, but certainly they will be part of the discussion.

As the A&R manager prepares the act for the release of the debut album, he will also talk to the performers about image, presentation and all those important matters which will, hopefully, create a strong impression in the public mind. Everything the band do, from their music to what they say in interviews, should be consistent if the maximum impact is to be made. It is the A&R manager's and the A&R department's job to co-ordinate that and, in conjunction with the band, decide what the message is in the first place.

When everything goes well, this process is a happy and relaxed one and band and A&R people end up having a healthy professional relationship that often crosses over into friendship. Indeed, there are bands that feel comfortable working only with certain A&R people.

Witness Clive Davis, founder and long-time head of Arista Records, who went on to set up his own label, J Records. Clive is essentially an A&R man and musicians want to work with him just as young footballers want to work with managers whose style they enjoy. When Rod Stewart left Warner Music in 2002 after a twenty-six-year relationship, he could have gone anywhere he liked. But, instead of going with a major, he chose to go with J Records. Now, I am sure the deal had plenty of financial inducements for Rod, but I am also certain that he also simply wanted to work with Clive and that, had he been offered a similar deal or even a slightly better one in financial terms by another label (which he almost certainly was), he would still have gone with Clive because he knows his reputation and likes his style.

Chapter 6

⭐

MAKING A STAR

WE HAVE NOTED BEFORE – and I'm damn sure we'll do it again – that the *raison d'être* of the music industry is to make people famous. Once they are household names, at least half the job is done.

We will see in Chapter 12 that there are lots of regulations about what record companies can and cannot do to get their acts in the charts, but when it comes to just making an act famous, the ferocity of the contest makes the law of the jungle look like the rules of bridge.

Lots of people will do anything to be famous and lots of powerful companies will do anything to help them. There are few practical limits to what either of these sets of people are prepared to do.

But by far the best way to be famous in the music industry is the simple one: to have remarkable, innovative, popular music. That's the longest way into the business but also the longest way out. Having got to Chapter 6 without making up a rule, here's my first: the longer it takes to get into the music industry as a creative artist, the longer it takes to stop being famous. There, that's a good generalisation for history to test. We'll talk again in twenty years to see if I was right.

For now, let's look at the practicalities, the day-to-day routine, of making musicians famous.

Remember first, though, that only one album in ten makes a profit for the record company. That is, despite all the efforts, expertise and money that goes into promoting an album and the musicians behind it, nine times out of ten the project fails in commercial terms.

This shows us that there are no specific sets of buttons to push. There is no one single right answer to the question: how do we make this act famous?

So what are the options? Let's take a classical route – and by 'classical' I mean tried and tested rather than orchestral. A classical route goes like this:

1. The record company signs a hot new act, the Miracle Trees.

2. The band make an interesting first album, a record that is highly regarded in its field (let's say mainstream pop-rock).

3. The label works hard to get the Miracle Trees on TV and radio and, because of the quality of the music, a mainstream national radio station plays the first single extensively. In addition, a national terrestrial TV channel gives the band a slot on Saturday morning TV.

4. The music press carries a couple of interviews – now a little momentum is building up.

5. The band go on tour to support the new album. That is, they gig from Penzance to Inverness, playing loads of material from the first record as well as featuring prominently the current single and the next two songs that will be released as singles.

6. Everywhere they go on tour, the band make sure they do an interview with the local paper and the local radio station.

7. The single continues to get radio play, it rises up the chart and the band are invited to play it on *Top Of The Pops*. The record company pays for them to take a

private jet from Manchester to record the song for *TOTP*, then back for that night's gig.
8. The single reaches number eight, where it peaks.
9. The record company releases the second single from the album.
10. The band continue to play concerts every night and do interviews every day. A genuine national fanbase is now building.
11. On the strength of the UK success, the record company persuades its sister label in Germany and France to release the album and the single.
12. The band continue to tour the UK and to do interviews with anybody willing to interview them. Now, though, the single is also doing OK in the chart in Germany, so they start doing interviews with the German media.
13. Interest grows and the Miracle Trees go on tour in Germany, where a fanbase begins to develop. They are invited to play on a national TV music programme.
14. The UK record company's sister labels around the world become conscious of the band's success and ask if they, too, can release the singles and the album.
15. The UK label is delighted to do so and the band are prepared to go to a number of countries to tour, appear on TV and do interviews. They are now on the way to a global fanbase.
16. Repeat steps 2–15 for the second and third albums.

That's the plan. It's a great plan but, as with any plan, it's just a theory of how things will go and there are significant obstacles to it working. The biggest of these is that the music must be right; secondly, the media must be enthusiastic about it; thirdly, the fans must like it. The hard fact is, only the smallest percentage of people who want to be stars actually make it.

The key – and the difference between making it and not –

is, as with everything else in the music industry, the music. The quality and popularity of this commodity is the foundation stone for all else that happens. If people don't like what a musician does, that musician will never make a living from his creativity.

In this chapter, though, we are proceeding on the basis that the Miracle Trees' music is at least moderately attractive and popular. If it is attractive and popular enough – and it gets a following wind of good fortune – steps 2–15 above will go like a dream. There are, though, about a billion things that can, and often do, go wrong. Let's take a look at some of them and what can be done about it.

Step 1
We'll skip this; just assume the Miracle Trees have been signed.

Step 2
Like much else, this is not as simple as it seems. Bands have ideas about the kind of album they want to make. The record company has ideas about the kind of album it wants the band to make. These two sets of notions may or may not marry and live happily ever after.

However, contrary to popular perception, record companies tend not to try to force bands into anything. Such an attempt would be hugely self-defeating for the simple reason that nobody would get what they want. Bands and recording artists are creative people and creative people do not create well unless they are relaxed and happy (and I know I've said that before, but I promise you it's true and it's a matter that definitely has to be addressed). Even tortured artists writing emotion-jangling music need happier times when they can function well enough to actually commit their material to paper or tape or whatever it is they use.

So, as we saw in the previous chapter, record companies do their utmost to keep their artists happy, particularly when they are creating. That means not arguing with them and, particularly, it means not trying to convert a folk band into a heavy metal outfit. (Besides, what would they do for a big stage finale? Burn their cardigans?)

Record companies sign a band in the first place because they like that band's style and what they do. They are not about to try to change that style – though, of course, they will suggest, advise and try to bring out the best, in the manner that we discussed in Chapter 5.

Assuming, then, that the Miracle Trees play mainstream pop-rock and the record company likes their sound, everybody is happy so far. If the band produce work that contains one, two or the magical three singles, then everything continues to go smoothly.

Hopefully, with a good, working band and helpful A&R people and each side listening to the other, the Miracle Trees will make an album that is better than their wildest dreams and the record company will get a product of which it is proud and which lends itself to good marketing.

And herein lies the inseparable, mutually dependent relationship between band and record company that we have touched on several times. Neither can do this without the other. The band need the record company to do the marketing and promotion task well; the record company needs a record it can actually market and promote. Chickens and eggs.

Step 3

Here's where the record company is truly tested. Assuming, as we are, that the Miracle Trees' debut album is innovative, interesting and attractive, with a broad-based appeal, now the label has to prove it can do what it exists to do: break new acts.

The first step the label will take along this road is to have a meeting – product meetings, they call them. In attendance will be everybody with a stake in the record: the A&R people, the marketing people (including promotions), sales and, possibly, the Big Boss and the international department.

They will discuss the plan for the record – which, of course, is finished, pressed and packaged by now – and, specifically, how it is to be marketed and promoted. The classical timing for these things is that the debut single is released to coincide with the start of the band's tour (see Step 4) and the album is issued a little later. However, there are no rules about this and these timings will be adjusted to suit individual plans and ideas.

It is important, though, to remember that, as we saw in Chapter 2, no matter what the plan is, it is a co-ordinated project through which all departments are pulling in the same direction rather than doing things that counter and contradict each other. But, whatever the plan, at its core will be the Miracle Trees' music. This will determine both where the album is advertised and where it is plugged. If the Miracle Trees were a pure dance band, there would be no point promoting them to the rock media, and vice versa.

So, the record company decides where and how it is going to market – including plugging – the Miracle Trees. The decision is taken that the band's mainstream pop-rock has appeal to a broad range of mainstream buyers, so ads are taken in the – yes, you guessed it – mainstream music press. In addition, the promotions people feel that the band would be acceptable to a range of broadcast media ranging from Saturday morning children's TV, through daytime radio, to some of the later, more adult shows. A plan is drawn up on which producers to hit first.

TV and radio producers are targeted, of course, because they are the people who actually make the decisions about what is going to be broadcast on the show. The producers the record company wants to hit first are the ones with the biggest audiences, and that means daytime radio and Saturday morning TV. Once that list is drawn up and prioritised, the staff then go about making sure the relevant producers are plugged.

The promotions staff can do no more than lead their horse to their water. Once they have exposed the producer to the Miracle Trees' music, there is not much else they can do if the producer feels that the whole project has been a waste of plastic.

And if things are not going well, in addition to the most attractive environments in which to present the music – that is, the gigs and launch parties we looked at in Chapter 2 – the promotions department still has the stunt tactic. When I was news editor at *Music Week*, the professional magazine for the UK music industry, I was working in a building full of music mags: *Music Week, Sounds, Record Mirror, Kerrang!* and, er, *What Hi Fi*. More than one act got a feature in one magazine or another simply by turning up at our office and singing to us and/or buying a few people a pint.

This was a relatively successful tactic because seeing a musician performing in the flesh just adds elements that can never be captured on record. However, as always, there has to be something in the music as a band ain't going to be written about if they have nothing to offer.

(There was one glorious occasion when somebody had told this aspiring young band of the success of this tactic and that they should come and play outside our office building, which had obviously been described to these young musos as the biggest one in Camden. Now, our office building was big, but they ended up playing a set to the Post Office.)

Don't think, though, that the stunt tactic is a life-saver. Over the years virtually every variety, type and species of stunt has been pulled; experienced TV and radio producers, the most plugged and stunted people on the planet, have seen them all and are pretty much immune to them. It is far, far better for a band's career to concentrate on having the music the world and its media will admire. A band may create the best stunt in the world, but if the music associated with it is tedious, derivative and poorly executed, no media person on the planet is going to get excited enough about it to give them airtime or column inches.

Let's assume, though, for the purposes of making a star that the Miracle Trees have passed this hurdle and that the media is actually interested in them.

Step 4

So, if now the media decides the Miracle Trees have enough to offer to make them worth interviewing, then comes the tricky business of actually conducting the interview. Young bands interviewed for the first time can do any number of unhelpful things, the two most common being either freezing and talking nonsense they regret later or letting this first trapping of fame seduce them and talking nonsense they regret later. Handling this delicate situation is something I discuss more in Chapter 17.

Assuming, though, that the band come through with flying colours – half-mast, at least – and that they say things that are both interesting and human, a head of steam is now building up and they can truly claim to have taken a step on the road to success.

Step 5

Now comes the sheer hard graft part of being a working musician: going on the road and doing the publicity along the way. Every musician I've ever met likes being on stage, but the price they pay for that is the tedium and travail of covering the miles between gigs, doing the soundchecks, the yet-another-hotel syndrome and the simple tension of just being away from home. (See Chapter 18 for more on this.) But, if you want to be famous, there is no option and no choice. Nobody ever made it to the top without working for it and fighting harder than those around them. If there are two bands of equal talent and equal attractiveness, the one that works hardest will have more success than its rival.

So, the Miracle Trees are on the road and are performing

MAKING A STAR

at mid-size venues across the country. How is this going to help album and single sales? Well, there is a very clear and long-established correlation between the number of people who see a band live and the number of people who subsequently go out and buy their records.

The band, of course, are not on their own in this enterprise. The record company and the concert promoter will both be doing everything they can to publicise the tour. The record company may add the tour dates to the album artwork and the concert promoter (again, see Chapter 18 for who these people are) will buy media advertising and posters. Both will also seek to publicise the dates through their public relations activities with the media. These things are important because the Miracle Trees' career development is directly related to – and may well be measured by – how many bums they can put on seats.

Assuming, then, reasonable publicity and a fair attendance, provided that the show itself is a good one and the reviews of it are positive, this debut tour will be the vehicle for the Miracle Trees' music and, in particular, the current single which will be played to many thousands of people. These people are now far more likely to go out and buy the single and the album than they would have been had the band played no gigs.

While the first single will already be out by the time the tour begins, the second two tracks to be taken as singles from the debut album may be undecided. Audience reaction to the various songs the band play will make an important contribution to the process of deciding which tunes will be the second and third singles.

Because the show will also feature, of course, both the singles and many other tracks from the first album, demand for the album, too, is being built even before the record is in the shops. The same is also true of the next two singles: the people who have heard these tunes and like them can't wait to own them; again, demand for them is being created before the records are even released.

Step 6

Here comes more sheer hard graft. Everywhere the band go, they must do the interview with the local media. Often bands baulk at this idea. Generally, the *Hull Daily Mail* or the *Grimsby Evening Telegraph* don't sound very exciting to them.

Well, here's a fact that should sweeten the pill a little. Between them, the *Derby Evening Telegraph*, the *Leicester Mercury* and the *Nottingham Evening Post* sell as many copies as the *Guardian*. Now, a band would be happy to do an interview with the *Guardian*; by putting in a little more effort – doing three interviews instead of one – they get a readership equivalent to the *Guardian's* but without the kind of competition for space there is in the *Guardian*. Besides, if the band are playing Nottingham, Derby and Leicester, they will pretty much give the same interview to all three papers, so the task isn't too intellectually demanding. In fact, dealing with the regional press is generally a lot easier than dealing with the national media and is deeply rewarding in commercial terms. More about this in Chapter 17.

Suffice it to say, though, that the band must talk to each paper and radio station wherever they go. While it may seem a real chore to do yet another interview and be asked pretty much exactly the same questions all over again, these interviews all add up. They all contribute to the publicity momentum building up behind the band. They put bums on seats at gigs and add to the total number of people likely to see the band and/or take an interest in their music.

Besides which, the alternative is too terrible to contemplate. When the day comes when the *Hull Daily Mail* doesn't think the Miracle Trees are worth interviewing, the band's career is truly over.

Step 7

But, assuming regional press and local and national radio are behind the band, things really begin to move. Every play of the single on the various radio stations boosts its chances of success and helps the Miracle Trees gain access to the real rocket launcher to stardom: *Top Of The Pops*.

Appearing on this show is a guarantee of success. Every song ever featured on *TOTP* has done better – or at least no worse – in the week after the show compared with the week before. Ah, but did I say every song? I meant, every song except one ...

An Australian heavy-metal singer called Angry Anderson was given the job of singing the love theme from *Neighbours*. Now, this was a guaranteed winner. *Neighbours* was and is a huge soap opera around the world; there was a wedding involving Kylie Minogue and Jason Donovan and the theme written for it was a classic love song. If anything in the uncertain world of the music industry was going to be a hit, this was. And, just as expected, it raced to number one or thereabouts in many of the countries in which *Neighbours* is seen. So, after he had promoted and plugged this thing across the world, Angry Anderson finally came to the UK to perform on *Top Of The Pops*. Normally, this is a brilliant career move. In Angry's case, it wasn't. The problem was that Angry Anderson, helluva singer though he is, is also as ugly as sin. The record-buying public were expecting some tanned Adonis to be doing the crooning on this sweet record and when they saw a bald, short, tattooed, fang-toothed (no, I'm not making this up) metal man instead, sales actually went down – a first for *TOTP* and another triumph for the metalmen's art.

Back with the Miracle Trees: assuming that they are not some kind of mutants (though that's not always a handicap), *Top Of The Pops* will do their career a power of good. In fact, so influential is the show on the nation's record-buying habits that, no matter where the band are playing on the day the programme is recorded, the distance should not be too far to stop them coming to London to record their performance of their single. Even if they are in Manchester or Edinburgh or Aberdeen, it certainly makes commercial sense for the record company to hire a jet to fly them down for the gig. No, this isn't being flash; it's just the only way to do the show and play the gig. In fact, it makes a lot of financial sense. By going to the expense of hiring the jet, the label and the band will still be showing a profit because of all the extra record sales a *TOTP* performance can generate. On top of that, if you turn down the show once, you never know if they will ever ask you again. Commercially and in terms of career development, an appearance on *TOTP* justifies virtually any expense and effort it entails.

Step 8

Bolstered by the *TOTP* slot, the Miracle Trees' single has reached the Top Ten, an exceptional achievement for a band's debut release. By getting to, let's say, number eight, the single – along with the album it comes from and, of course, the band – is firmly in the media spotlight both in the UK and internationally. This produces two effects. Firstly, it puts the band into the consciousness of the record-buying public: the Miracle Trees becomes a name we recognise; we know who they are, what their music is about and what style they play in. Secondly, a hit single gives the band credibility within the industry – retailers are more likely to take their records; record companies outside the UK are more likely to get behind them and generally executives are more likely to take them more seriously. This is what is known in the business, in a desperately overused but nonetheless accurate phrase, as 'moving up to another level'.

Steps 9 and 10

The work goes on. If you're a muso there is absolutely no point in having one hit single, deciding you've made the big time and resting on your laurels. The phrase 'one-hit wonder' is an ugly term of abuse in the music industry. Bright musos understand that once that first single is a hit, the door is unlocked but it is not yet open, and it can only be forced wide with more effort – a lot more effort. That means more gigs, more interviews, more public appearances – oh, and a damn-good follow-up single that is going to keep the public interested and remind everybody that, above and beyond all else, the music industry is about music.

Step 11

Now, in company with the Miracle Trees, let's take our first tremulous step into the big, wide world. It is at this point that the band's career begins to take on a cross-border dimension, so it is an appropriate moment to look closely for the first time at the work of a record company's international department.

Let's start that process from the beginning. Every major record company has an international department. So what do these people do? Well, as their name suggests, they handle all record company interests outside the home territory. And why is that important? Simply because it's a big world out there, with lots of potential record buyers, and to ignore them would be utter folly and commercial suicide.

Let's assume the Miracle Trees are signed to the world's biggest record company, Universal. Now Universal has its headquarters in the States and it also has dozens of semi-autonomous, so-called affiliate, companies operating around the world – Universal UK, Universal France, Universal Germany, Universal Japan and so on.

These companies are bound together under the same corporate umbrella and all obey the rules and guidelines laid down by the Big Boss in Los Angeles, but they also operate in accordance with their own judgement and in keeping with local market conditions and tastes. That is, they each pursue their own A&R and marketing policies within budgets agreed with the Big Boss. This, obviously, makes a lot of sense. Musical tastes in Japan are a lot different to what they are in France, so the A&R policy has to reflect this; Japan is also a lot bigger than, say, Belgium, so marketing policies also have to be tailored to the revenues generated by the various countries across the world.

Each country produces its own local heroes – acts who are stars in their own backyard but who wouldn't be recognised in a crowd of two anywhere else – but the very top echelon of artists can become truly international stars. The biggest number of these cross-border, trans-oceanic, intercontinental acts are American but, after that, the largest contingent is British. In fact, the only substantial numbers of international acts are either American or British; despite the hits that have come out of the West Indies, France, Spain, Germany, Africa and Latin America, the US and UK are in a league all of their own when it comes to having global success. So, every time a major record company in the UK signs an act, it has at least one eye on how that act will sell overseas.

Making sure an act sells outside these shores is the job of the UK label's international department. The people tasked with making the Miracle Trees global stars are Universal UK's international department. How does this department do that? Well, its first move is to liaise with its colleagues around the world in an effort to persuade them to give the Miracle Trees' record a release in their country.

Now, persuasion is the only tactic the UK international department has. It cannot force its sister companies into action. And, of course, its colleagues around the world are going to be wary of releasing any record by a new act because such a release means a significant commitment of time, resources and money.

It helps the international department's arguments enormously if it can show that the act is already a hit at home; that number-eight single we looked at in Step 8 is going to go a long, long way towards achieving that. Indeed, if Universal UK goes to Universal Germany and asks it to put out a Miracle Trees album that has failed to make the charts in its home country, the German company will ask, 'If you can't have a hit with this in the UK, how do you expect us to have a hit with it in Germany?' Thus, having had a hit single and, let's say, chart success with the associated album, the Miracle Trees won't yet be a hot property worldwide but at least they are beginning to defrost.

For the sake of our example, we'll say now that Universal companies across Europe and in Japan are so convinced the band can be a hit in their countries, too, that they agree to put out the singles and albums in their respective territories.

Steps 12 and 13
But, just like in the UK, nothing good is going to happen to the record unless it gets a healthy promotional push. This means doing exactly the same things as were done in the home market: the record must be marketed with advertising and that must be backed by solid graft – more interviews, more appearances, more gigs and a performance on the local version of *Top Of The Pops* if the local TV people can be persuaded to take the band.

Steps 14 and 15
Assuming things go well in France and Germany, other territories will soon become aware that the Miracle Trees can sell records. Hits outside the home country will prove international credibility and, prompted by the UK international department, Universal affiliate companies across the world (including the US, where one in three of all records are sold) should start sitting up. If they can be persuaded, either by sales they see in other countries or by direct lobbying by Universal UK (and, in truth, probably both) they will release the Miracle Trees' records. But, wherever that happens, the band must go to support the label's effort, just as in Steps 12 and 13. That means a year or possibly more of non-stop touring, being interviewed, showing a smiling face, etc. etc. It's a long

way to the top if you wanna rock 'n' roll, and it ain't no place for the faint-hearted.

Step 16
Do it all again for the next twenty-five years.

Chapter 7

BROAD HORIZONS

MUSIC ISN'T ONLY THE stuff that's in the chart this week. The world isn't only the country you see around you.

Two areas of opportunity for anybody trying to make a living out of music are so obvious they are generally not seen. That's probably because they're too large to be taken into focus without first taking a big step back.

Taking that step, though, is not simple as it requires a serious realignment of thinking and a strong independence of mind. We all know from our daily living that it is extremely easy to be seduced by the familiar – and abandoning it in favour of some fresh thinking can be fantastically difficult.

In the music industry, it is no less of a challenge. Think of it from our point of view: as record buyers, our focus is constantly directed towards the charts and our own country. In the UK the media's – and therefore our – attention is solely on this week's listings and what is happening this side of the White Cliffs of Dover.

How many television and radio chart run-down programmes are there each week? Including the venerable *Top Of The Pops*, there must be dozens. Add to that the tabloid papers and the myriad teen magazines and therein is the bulk of the music media, all of whom are interested only in what is in the Top Twenty – and often only the Top Ten.

So, with that constant barrage of stimuli all saying, 'Look at the chart! Look at the chart!' going beyond this, I'll say it again, takes a serious effort of will. However, when you consciously make the decision and readjust your eyes to see it, the submerged part of the iceberg – the nine-tenths of all music sold that isn't chart material – starts to come into view. And once you know it's there, it opens up a lot of possibilities for artists, executives and entrepreneurs.

That, then, is our first new focus: non-chart music. Now let's add another massive area of potential: those 97% of record buyers who don't live in Britain. They may often speak a different language but that only means they are in a different part of the world, not on a different world. Accessing them is – if you have the right material – no less straightforward than going on holiday. We'll look at that a little more closely in a moment, after we've explored a few of those home-grown possibilities.

Staying in the UK for a moment, it is undeniable that the chart is the quickest road to success. But it is also the most difficult route to traverse. To get a record into the chart means having the right material and being able to back it up with the right sales and distribution infrastructure and a significant marketing budget. And, as we know, none of those things comes cheap. That doesn't mean, though, that the chart is the sole province of the majors, but it does make it frighteningly tough going for everybody else. Because size of budget is a factor in chart success, the majors have an advantage over smaller firms simply because they're bigger and have more money.

Bright, independent people have always looked for ways to sell music without having to go head to head with the majors in the competition for chart space. These free-thinkers are the people who first focused on that part of the iceberg beneath the water and wondered what music might it contain. When they plumbed those depths they found there was a world of infinite possibilities waiting for them and, initially, it was one they had pretty much to themselves. Let's look at how their thinking developed and how they demonstrated that there is a profit to be made outside the charts.

The first real flowering of this non-mainstream philosophy was the indie revolution of the late seventies. The motivations for it, though, were more aesthetic than commercial. Iain McNay, owner of Cherry Red Records and one of the founding fathers of the indie sector, says of what drove him, 'It was when the Emerson, Lake & Palmer box set was released. A lot of us thought that there must be more to music than this.'

In Cherry Red's case, that 'more' was Alien Sex Fiend and a host of other non-chart-bound acts. But the fact that Cherry Red is still trading a quarter of a century later is proof that a very nice living can be had from dealing in bands that are never going to make it on to Saturday morning children's television.

So, while the indie revolution may have been ignited by punk, it was fuelled by every other form of music. Once Cherry Red and its contemporaries had demonstrated that it is possible to be solvent while never even dipping your toe in the mainstream, indie labels started to spring up everywhere: in classical, rock, jazz, folk, heavy metal, Celtic, religious and every single other genre you care to mention. Many have gone by the board, either to the great turntable in the sky or, if successful, into the arms of the majors through takeovers and purchases. But a significant number, like Cherry Red, still plough their lone, independent furrow decades after first breaking that new ground.

There are, then, no rules about what area an indie should operate in. Indeed, a large part of Cherry Red's recent success has been in putting out football records. That is, they pick a club, round up every song by fans, bands and players they can find and put it on an album. The resulting series has done very nicely for Iain and the other soccer fans who work at the company. (Iain has often said – not necessarily entirely in jest – that loving football is a prerequisite for getting a job at the label.)

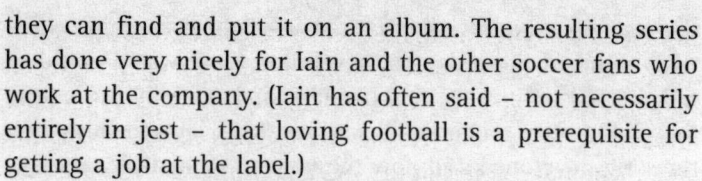

For an indie, the ideal situation is to find a field which has not been previously explored and move full steam into it. Being number one in a field of one minimises the pressures from competition – the majors in particular – and maximises commercial potential.

How is that achieved? Through original, or, if you will, independent thinking. Take, for example, Colin Miles, a man who pioneered – if not actually invented – the concept of reissues. Not only did his original thinking bring significant rewards for him and his company, it added hugely to that submerged part of the music iceberg that lies beneath the tip sticking up into the light of the charts.

The key point is that Colin had the imagination to look beyond the latest list of hits. Once he decided to do so, what he soon found himself looking at was the near-century's worth of accumulated material that the major record companies had in their vaults; and he rapidly realised that the vast bulk of this treasure trove was not even available to the average record buyer. Seeing what was cached away, Colin had a theory that many of those old albums could still command an audience. So he went to the majors and said, 'If you're not using that, do you mind if I release it?' The majors, happy to get some income from dormant titles, agreed to give him a licence to reissue their old records.

All that material Colin wanted to use is called catalogue, so let's take a moment just to refresh our memories about what is catalogue. Major record companies are old – very old in some cases – in the context of a fast-moving market like music. EMI was founded more than a hundred years ago and has a stock of recorded music going back to the first decade of the twentieth century. Now, when those early recordings

BROAD HORIZONS

were originally released, they were the chart hits of their day. They were fresh and new and their singers – operatic tenors like Enrico Caruso – were big, big stars. Not long after, though, such operatic classics were replaced by the ragtime and the popular songs of the 1920s. Within ten years the likes of Caruso became somewhat old hat, passing from the main focus of public consciousness as dance music took over.

The same process continues today. If you're old enough, think about the records you were buying twenty or even ten years ago. Can you imagine somebody ten years younger than you buying them today? Probably not.

In this way a record company rapidly builds up a catalogue of material, or back-catalogue, as it is sometimes called. Catalogue is predicated, then, on an album having a limited lifespan: it goes in the chart, it drops out, it fades from public consciousness. Commercially, it is essential for a record company that this happens because a label could not keep up with the demands of pressing discs – let alone marketing and promoting them – if every album remained popular in perpetuity. Albums have a natural lifespan based on their popularity. Once that popularity begins to wane, so does the amount spent on advertising and promotion to keep them in the public eye.

There are, of course, records that stand apart from that system – though as a percentage of total releases, they are few indeed. These are the albums that, as we saw in Chapter 3, will be in the racks of any mainstream record store anywhere in the Western world, despite the fact that they may be thirty or even forty years old: *Dark Side Of The Moon*, *Bat Out Of Hell*, *Thriller* and anything by the Rolling Stones and the Beatles. All those albums are now so big that they need no further promotion. They simply sell steadily by word of mouth and by reputation.

But, for each all-time classic, the majors have thousands of lesser-selling albums, each a hit to some degree in its time, lying in the vaults. For years and years the major labels let the vast majority of them stay there after the end of their chart run, but Colin Miles reckoned that there was life in those old dogs yet, and the majors were only too happy to oblige. After all, they had nothing to lose. Those old albums were earning no money in the vaults and even a modest profit from Colin's activities was better than no profit at all. So they gave him a licence to reissue.

Now, a licence is an important concept. The copyright laws mean – yes, you've heard it before, but here it is again – that labels own the recordings in the vault like they would own gold bullion. But, unlike bullion, records can be copied. So a record company can say: we agree to you pressing and selling this album in return for you paying us an agreed sum for each copy you sell. This kind of deal is called licensing.

With such permissions in place, Colin established a company called See For Miles and set about putting those old albums to work. His first obstacle, of course, was not persuading consumers to buy them but persuading retailers to buy them, for the simple reason that if a record isn't in the shops, people can't get it. Despite mail order and the advent of the Internet, that remains as close to being true today as it was when Colin was pioneering reissues in the early eighties.

The first step, then, is to persuade a retailer to actually put the albums on his shelves. Colin had a distinct advantage in this over all those other labels who try to break new talent by asking retailers to take albums nobody has heard of by acts with no history behind them. He, of course, was selling albums that already had a history – and though for some of them it might be a small one a long time ago, it was a history nonetheless. Colin's first, and pretty much biggest, obstacle suddenly became that little bit smaller because the record stores were being asked to buy albums they had heard of or could at least look up.

Suddenly, the albums that many of us older buyers had bought on vinyl and destroyed through use, abuse or neglect were available to buy again. And not only those albums, but others that we missed at the time or were too young to appreciate first time around. In this way Colin helped open up the market and to shift some of the music-buying public's focus away from the chart. He tapped into a largely unenthused and unexploited market: those older buyers to whom the chart is often an irrelevance. In commercial terms, he also helped label executives to see that albums they had previously thought to be not worth re-releasing actually had some commercial merit.

And Colin's point was well made, not least among other indies. After his initial success, reissues labels began to mushroom, prompted by his example and, sometimes, by direct experience. One of those men who saw for himself what potential there is in re-releases was Andy Gray. Remember him from Chapter 3? He's the founder, boss and top man at Europe's biggest independent record retailer, Andys Records. (It is merely a rumour that Andy had a team of creative consultants working round the clock for a month before coming up with his company name.)

Back in the late eighties Andy saw that some records in the second-hand section of his shops were fetching £40 or more. High price means demand and, instead of trying to satiate that demand with used goods, Andy and his brother Billy set up Beat Goes On to re-release older albums. For his basic stock, Andy went down the same route as Colin Miles and approached the major record companies asking to license some of the material they had in their vaults. His requests were successful and the labels let Beat Goes On and the other indies in the reissues business have plenty of material. But by now the major labels were getting wise to the idea and decided to get in on the act themselves. Spurred by the success the indies were having with their material, they decided to cut out the middleman and enter the reissues business in their own right.

That's why we now have a huge variety of older albums in the stores, generally at what is called a mid-price point; that is, a lot cheaper than a front-line, newly released, chart-oriented album. Often these catalogue albums are part of a campaign whose main sales pitch is the price: Sony calls the one it runs Nice Price and, basically, it means that if you're a metal fan and you missed Judas Priest first time around, you can now get the band's back-catalogue for a lot less per disc than you would, in relative terms, than when it was new. And though the names vary, every major label now sells exactly the same kind of mid-price, catalogue-album range.

So, what are the advantages of re-releasing an older album? Firstly, there are no A&R costs. We noted earlier that the largest cost faced by a record company is making an act famous in the first place. Well, there's none of that with a re-release. A re-released album is from an act that is already famous to a lesser or greater degree. Plus, there is no need to put the band in the studio, get them to write songs, see them argue with the producer, walk out, come back, sulk and sundry other parts of the creative process.

Rather, an album in the catalogue is done, finished, complete. Even the packaging is ready to go, though, of course, the re-releasing label can update that packaging should it wish to. One label that took this concept to its extreme is Judas Priest's original record company, Gull. Priest did a couple of albums for Gull – *Rocka Rolla* and *Sad Wings Of Destiny* – before moving to Sony (CBS as was) at the end of the seventies and becoming a pretty big global band. Gull have repackaged and re-released these two original albums more times than I can count under a variety of different titles, and much to the distaste of the band, who have argued that fans are being cheated and deceived into buying the same thing over and over again.

(The man behind Gull and the man who signed Priest is David Howells, a genuinely charming gentleman of rock. Later in his career, David ran Stock/Aitken/Waterman's label, PWL. Mike Stock, Matt Aitken and Pete Waterman were the pop writers-producers-everything else behind Kylie Minogue and Jason Donovan's huge success in the eighties as well as Rick Astley and several other teen sensations. Now, when Priest made a concerted effort to break into the American mass radio market in the early nineties, they went to David, who put them together with Stock/Aitken/Waterman. The resulting amalgam of styles found fruition in three songs which were never publicly released.)

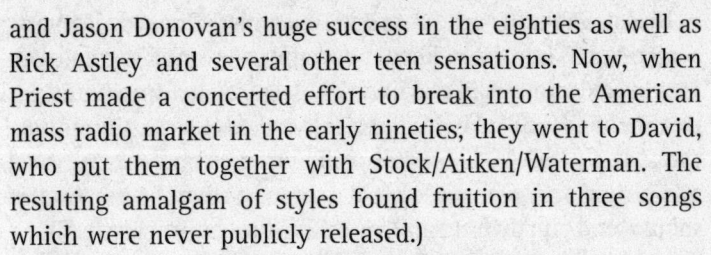

Right, back to the pros and cons of reissues. As we saw, a reissued album is from an act that already has a fanbase, of whatever size. That means there is a ready-made market to be exploited. Any new fans that come to the band on the strength of the reissues are a bonus; and, of course, you are giving new fans maximum encouragement by making the album as cheap as it can be. Any re-released album went through the record company's budgeting process first time round, so profit and loss on it were calculated then. Now it is simply an asset. Of course, exploiting that asset requires some work and cost. Copies need to be pressed and distributed; a sales pitch to retailers needs to be made; advertising (in one form or another and at one level of expense or another) needs to be taken; and, it goes without saying, the appropriate mechanical and artist royalties need to be paid. But, without that initial A&R cost in the mix, overheads are reduced dramatically – hence the attractive pricing of Nice Price and equivalent concepts.

And let's just remind ourselves of the other big advantage of a reissue: an album sitting in the label's vaults is earning nothing at all; if it's in the stores, it has a chance of bringing in a bob or two.

If there's a down side to reissues, it's that it's difficult to get publicity for the albums coming out for the second or even third time. Of course, a label can take a shed full of advertising in all appropriate media, but it's still a problem to get journalists and broadcasters interested. The task, though, is much easier if the band is venerable and durable and is still touring sizeable venues.

Black Sabbath are a prime example. Due to lawyers, accountants and associated nonsense, the band's catalogue was kicked around like a financial football before ending up in the hands of a bold company called Castle Communications. Castle had played a major role in the reissues revolution and I always felt it seemed rather fitting that it should end up owning the rights to the early, classic Black Sabbath albums. Why fitting? Well, just because Castle are active and aggressive in their marketing and, as an ageing headbanger, I was simply delighted to see the Sabs' classic catalogue get the kind of boost the company could give it.

Castle did reasonably well out of this catalogue; they are classic albums, after all, and sales ticked over nicely. But then, without warning, the company suddenly hit pay dirt. When Ozzy Osbourne rejoined the band, the Sabs instantly went from middle-aged rockers to legends once more. They began playing some of the biggest halls in the country and the world and interest in them reached its highest point for twenty years. For Castle, the resurgence in the band's fortunes meant that the Black Sabbath catalogue grew from steady selling to the subject of headline news in every publication with an interest in rock. As Castle counted the profits, every record company with a catalogue hoped and prayed for such good fortune to happen to the older albums in its vaults.

Now let's go back to where we started this chapter. Let's move from Black Sabbath to the Smurfs. That made you smile? It shouldn't. In this chapter we are dealing with all those forms of music that aren't pop-based, chart-oriented material. The Smurfs are just such a thing. I raise the Smurfs particularly because people get sniffy about the street cred (or lack thereof) of these children's favourites. Well, the Smurfs have sold ten million albums and the man who owns the rights has the financial power to buy the half of Wiltshire that Sting doesn't own already. I met him once at a party to celebrate the Smurfs' success; he smiles a lot.

The core point I'm making, just as we noted at the top of this chapter, is that if you look beyond the charts there is a huge music-buying potential to tap into. Take all the niche markets – jazz, folk, country, grindcore, children's, you name it – and they all clock up very decent sales. Each one of those areas represents scope for an entrepreneur who wants to specialise in that field and for those people who don't want to contend with the majors.

Some of these areas have huge, in-built advantages for the people wanting to work in them. Take, for example, so-called lapsed buyers – people over twenty-five who have got out of the habit of buying music. They're an attractive market because over-twenty-fives tend to have more money than under-twenty-fives, often a lot more. Find out what they like – from reissued nineties chart songs and the Black Sabbath albums they grew up with to military bands and Caruso – and you will do well.

Be warned, though. The record industry has been trying to tap this market for years with varying degrees of success. But, even with the combined efforts of the whole record and retail sectors, results have been somewhat patchy. So what has the industry done to attract non-young, non-mainstream customers. Well ...

For their part, the retail chains have created environments that are less threatening to older buyers. Many of the big stores have their classical and jazz departments separated from the louder, trendier areas and some even have their own entrance so that an older buyer doesn't need to be exposed to anything that might stop them venturing over the threshold.

Record companies have done their bit, too, by releasing the music older people might want to hear – and that, as we noted, runs the gamut from hits less than ten years old to brass bands and Celtic pipers.

Labels and store groups have also worked together on specific promotions for stated artists and have come together in what are known as generic campaigns – these things being promotions that don't ask you to buy any particular piece of music but just tell you generally that music is wonderful. In the States these promotions were done under the heading 'Give the Gift of Music'; in the UK the slogan was 'Life Sounds Better to Music'.

It has to be said that neither campaign was a runaway success. When a post-mortem was held on both of them, the feeling was that people don't identify with music as a concept, but just as albums from their favourite artists. If you don't mention their favourite artists, they tend not to flock into record stores. Nonetheless, the fact that labels and retailers tried is hugely commendable, and perhaps the most positive thing to come out of these initiatives.

Ironically, fate has on occasion taken a hand in these matters and has proved far more effective at bringing lapsed buyers into the shops than the industry's own campaigns. And when fate calls, it always does so with a specific piece of music – thus proving the point that a particular sound is far more attractive to people than a notion of music.

A prime example of the kind of good fortune I mean came in 1992 when ITV decided to use Luciano Pavarotti signing 'Nessun Dorma' as the theme tune to its World Cup coverage. Now, generally, opera on telly is less popular than pro-celebrity sheep wrestling (I'm still flogging this concept if anybody is interested) but suddenly millions of people were exposed to it just because they wanted to watch the football and, more importantly from the industry's point of view, millions of people were singing along to it. Now there's a first.

As a direct result of this tune and its singer being heard by us masses, sales of 'Nessun Dorma' went through the roof and Pavarotti's catalogue became the hottest it's ever been. By extension, the whole classical sector got a boost because, as retailers know well, when somebody goes into a store for a specific record, they rarely come out with only the one they went in for; it is far more common to pick up one or two others while they're in there (admit it, we've all done it). The classical market, which, year in, year out, accounts for 10% of all records sold, finished 1992 on around 12% of all sales, its biggest slice of the market for decades. Suddenly, because of one operatic aria being used as a TV football theme tune, record stores served a lot of people that they hadn't seen for a long, long while; those lapsed buyers suddenly found the habit again.

We can see, then, that it is possible – by good fortune and/or clever business skills – to sell a lot of non-pop, non-chart music in the UK. It is also possible to sell such things to a massively bigger market: that 97% of the world's population who don't live in this Sceptr'd Isle.

Now, I am not talking here about having a big hit in the UK and then translating that to foreign countries in the manner of the Miracle Trees from the previous chapter. Rather, what I'm alluding to is taking abroad the same kind of skills that are used to find non-mainstream markets at home. By that, I mean that if you're so unpopular in the UK that you couldn't even get arrested, it ain't the end of the world. Let me explain.

A prime example of what I mean is Smokey. They had their big hit, 'Living Next Door To Alice', in the seventies, then went into something of a decline – except in Denmark. The Danes continued to love the band long after Britain had passed them over. So, what is the band to do? Should they take the hard option and try to resurrect their career at home or take the line of least resistance and be stars in Denmark? Wisely in my view, Smokey went down the latter route and the band found they could make a good living working and touring there. I mean, Denmark is a very nice place to live and the krone is a more than acceptable currency, wherever you choose to bank it.

Even Smokey's small UK resurgence at the end of the nineties with the jokey re-release of 'Living Next Door To Alice' in tandem with comedian Roy Chubby Brown didn't distract them from keeping the Danish market alive. By looking for opportunities overseas rather than moping around bemoaning a lack of success in the home market, they had a lengthy career instead of being dismissed forever as one-hit wonders.

In similar vein, other acts tried hard to exploit what they saw as fertile ground in Eastern Europe after the Iron Curtain fell. Several who felt their careers could do with a boost rushed to those former communist states, the first of any significance to go being Kim Wilde to Poland and Uriah Heep to Russia.

But whether these people should be seen as pioneers or a bit previous is a subject for debate. Those Eastern European states were suffering from the world's worst political and economic hangover back then, and I don't know how either of those acts was paid, but in 1989 and 1990 the zloty (the Polish currency) and the rouble didn't get you a long way when you tried to hand them over at the bureau de change in Bexhill-on-Sea. I trust Kim and the boys in Heep were paid in something more bankable.

But, if Poland, Hungary and what is now the Czech Republic weren't hugely attractive then, they certainly are now. They have made huge strides towards normal politics and economics and the zloty is now what is called a hard currency – that is, it has some real value compared with other currencies. And the beauty of those markets is that they are receptive to older stuff. Though it's more than a decade since the Berlin Wall fell, there's still a good deal of inertia in Eastern Europe. Meaning that, if, like Uriah Heep, you made your reputation as rockers in the seventies, there are still people – a significant number of people – there who regard that as cutting-edge music.

In Eastern Europe's most advanced countries – the three mentioned above – the infrastructure now exists to be able to sell, market and distribute albums reasonably efficiently and certainly effectively enough to be able to make a profit. It's given a whole new lease of life to some records that had pretty much come to the end of their days in Western Europe.

In more mature markets, too, opportunities present themselves. John Sykes had a modest career as a rock guitarist in the UK, but when it began to peter out he took his adult-rock style to Japan and had another couple of hits. Voilà, another career extended through creative use of the global market.

There is always scope, both inside and outside the UK. As we will see in more detail in Chapter 20, music is the only truly global business.

Chapter 8

ONLINE

NOTHING IS HAPPENING.

No, really. Nothing at all.

OK, if you insist, there have been things in the news, the rows over file-sharing services like Napster being the biggest of them. But what is happening in terms of business being done in the online arena? In this virtual world, virtually bugger all.

Beyond question, the biggest current project is the global yak-fest about what the future holds and how online business can be maximised and blah-di-blah and, of course, there's still lots of legal and political fallout over Napster-style services but otherwise sod all. As I write this, less than 0.01% of all music sold worldwide is done so as signals travelling down wires from a website. That's less albums than I've got in my attic.

Even in the third millennium, people still like to buy bits of plastic in shops next to BHS and just round the corner from the pub – despite the fact that the music industry has spent nearly £3 billion globally trying to persuade us otherwise. And just what is it that they are seeking to persuade us to buy into? Well, two things, one of which has been a damn sight more successful than the other.

Let's start with the successful one, the simplest way to sell music online: mail order. That is, a company owns a stock of records and videos and sends them out in the post to whoever buys them by credit card through that company's website. All the main high-street record retailers do this, as do some other dedicated online trading companies and some of the smaller, specialist labels.

It ain't rocket science. It just requires a website and a subscription to one of the companies that handles online credit card payments. From a standing start, the whole thing can be set up in a couple of weeks – and the trickiest thing isn't the Net technology, it's filling in all the forms the credit card payment company sends you to make sure you're not dealing in drugs, children, gerbils or anything else you shouldn't be putting in the post. That, really, is all that needs to be said about mail order. Unless we want to get into the security aspects of buying stuff by credit card online – which I don't, because it's fantastically tedious – there's no more to say. So let's move on to ...

The other way of selling music online – by direct download – is an area far more complex, far more problematical and far, far less successful than mail order. But, before we jump in, let's start by looking at a little of the background.

Way back in the beginning, in 1994, before the Net became the, er, essential tool it is in all our lives today (particularly if you want porn at any time of the day or night and the newsagent's is closed), people had all sorts of notions about what it was going to do for us.

Music publishers in particular had grand ideas that it would be the death of record companies. Indeed, some very senior music-publishing people suggested to me loudly and with passion that history would show record companies as merely a small chapter in the story of music and that labels would be a passing phenomenon that didn't live much beyond the opening of the third millennium. Meanwhile, of course, publishers would go marching on into an ever more glorious future. Hmm ... I'll have a pint of whatever they were drinking; sounds like good stuff.

But, in truth, those publishers making this case were often very serious and sober. The scenario they predicted was that during the nineties everybody would have tired of browsing through record stores and would simply be downloading digital material at home. They saw huge catalogues of music being available at the touch of a button and all the user had to do was pay a subscription charge and download what he or she wanted on to their home system.

Though they were often hazy on which technologies would be used to do this, some publishers even believed there would be no downloading. They felt that a viable system would be for people to subscribe to their entertainment service, then simply access the tune they wanted and have it played from a central location directly into their home – a system which would, they felt, have grown out of digital radio. All the 'records' would stay in one place and us punters would simply pay to hear them.

While we recognise some of these ideas today, this online music thing has not yet become a world-dominating concept. Why? Well, I suspect for these reasons. Firstly, like just about everybody else, I like music that is not necessarily the world's most popular – and even if you are a pure pop fan, there is still something in your desires that isn't in the mainstream. So, however much the people behind the fledgling subscription services of the nineties assured me to the contrary, I couldn't feel confident that they were going to have 'Nude Disintegrating Parachutist Woman' and 'In The Grip Of A Tyrefitter's Hand' (no, I'm not making this up; these Budgie tunes are standards in my house) on the database. And if you ain't got these, er, classic tracks, you can count me out. I am not abandoning my record collection and paying a monthly subscription if I can no longer hear the stuff I want to hear.

The second reason is even more basic and even more valid.

Our species may have technology that does things which would astound a magician, but our bodies are still those of hunter-gatherers. This gives us a desire to want to touch things; we don't feel we own something until we can handle it, feel its shape and its weight. I believe we all get pleasure from seeing our CDs lined up on the shelf and that we like to see a wall covered in discs; it makes us feel proud and happy. And, if you want to take the hunter-gatherer thing one step further, just think how pleasurable it is to finally find, at the back of some obscure record shop, an album that you've spent years looking for. I'd say that pleasure is a lot greater than any joy you might get from being able to just press a button and have the contents of that album delivered to your living room in an instant.

And if you want a final piece of evidence to support this theory, look at vinyl. Before the club scene gave twelve-inch vinyl a new lease of life, the format should have been dead and buried under the relentless tide of CD. But it refused to die. Why? Because people like a square foot of artwork and sleeve notes and what have you, and they enjoy a big, heavy, substantial thing to have around their home, a trophy to show for the money they spent on it.

(As a small digression, several people have suggested to me that the desire humans have to look through each other's record collections is the same desire dogs have to sniff each other's arses.)

So, music subscription services failed to make the nineties the label-free land the publishers desired. Now, in the new millennium, are we any closer to that digital heaven they dream of? Are we bollocks.

In the publishers' ideal world, everybody would by now be plugged into a broadband Internet connection and would be downloading music direct from the publisher for an agreed fee. In their view, there would be no record companies involved; people would simply buy the music direct from the publisher. But, of course, somebody would have to record the tunes for downloading. Presumably, this would be done under the publishers' auspices – which would, thereby, turn the publisher into a record company. Bizarre. It's one of those things you shouldn't think about too much in case it makes your head hurt, like that stuff Arnold Schwarzenegger says about time in *Terminator 2*.

Anyway, this is what publishers wanted and what many of them thought would be happening by now. It ain't.

Instead, what is happening is that the major record companies have launched various sites advertising their own wares. You go to the site – which may represent more than one label – and you can download Bon Jovi, Kylie, Sir Elton John, Westlife and so on, in exchange for an appropriate fee. The record companies like the system, of course, because it means they no longer have to go through the pesky and expensive business of pressing discs and physically transporting them to wherever they will be sold. However, consumers have realised that they are downloading exactly the same music they can buy in a store and have decided they much prefer a good, solid bit of plastic to some electrons, even if they do entirely the same job.

But, for an area that hasn't generated much business, the Net has certainly raised its share of legal issues. I go into them a lot more in the next chapter, but suffice it to say here that, thankfully, the various agreements providing a legal framework for online trading have all recognised that both performers and songwriters have an inalienable right to be paid for the music they produce. This is very encouraging because it is vital for the future of the business that those important precepts continue to be acknowledged, whatever forum they are being applied to and whatever technology emerges.

Oh, and the fact that the rights of the songwriter and performer continue to be recognised in this digital era was why, of course, Napster and the other file-sharing sites got into trouble (before Napster got its sheen of respectability in late 2000 when BMG bought into it).

If you're not familiar with it, Napster was at the outset a US-based service whereby, for a monthly subscription, you could download tracks people had sent to the Napster site. In those earlier days of its operation, anybody could upload and the vast majority of the music available there was from major artists. The site was very popular and lots of people logged on and walked off with lots of free music. Thus, music was changing hands without the people who wrote it or recorded it getting a single penny from it. Napster argued that it was helping to promote the various artists featured on its site and that somebody downloading a track from the site was then highly likely to go out and buy the album it came from. But the US courts took the view that Napster was taking other people's property – their music – and, in effect, selling it without handing over any of the cash to them.

I hope the people behind Napster have now worked out what a bad idea this was. To illustrate what I mean, let's look at this from a different angle, this time with the guys at Napster as the people whose property is being taken away. If I sold the things they owned – their houses, say – without telling them, and scarpered with the money, leaving them to find a hairy-arsed Yorkshireman in their bed when they came home after work, they'd be pretty upset (depending on how they feel about hairy-arsed Yorkshiremen, of course). It's not too hard, then, to work out why the people who toil mightily to create music and the record companies who bring it to us were upset when their property was given away.

And it dosn't take a huge leap to understand why they continue to complain about all the other sites offering music for free that have grown up in Napster's wake.

The larger point remains, though, that, despite a lack of music commerce over the Internet (legitimate, at least), this medium will always play a part in the music industry as a means of publicising various artists. I imagine that the personal sites of the big stars get thousands of hits a day and such a site allows an artist to make an announcement without it having to be passed through the lens of the media first. The star can speak directly to his or her fans and tell them about the new album or some detail of his or her personal life that needs airing and/or correcting. Emerging acts will also take advantage of the Net in this way, too, though on a smaller scale.

In exactly the same way, so will record companies and retailers who use the Internet to advertise their products and stars; to them as well it is a way of speaking directly to fans and consumers. And young acts, of course, will always use the Net as a way of being accessible to anybody who cares to drop by.

But, with labels now in a three-billion-quid hole trying to launch online trading with nowt to show for it, is there a future in this business?

Chapter 9

THE LAW

THE MUSIC INDUSTRY HAS had relatively good relations with the law over the years. Of course, there have been very famous instances of individual musicians getting into trouble for such things as motoring offences, taking drugs and punching photographers (is there really a law against that?), but, generally, the business has had more cause to thank the law than to curse it.

In fact, without the law, there would be no music industry. As we saw in Chapter 4, all that protects musical copyrights is the law and the legal authorities who enforce it. If you have a goldmine, you can protect it by employing a big lad with a stick; but only the full process of the law and the diligence of the police and protection of the courts can stop the bad guys preventing the good guys from making a living from music.

So let's look at the main pieces of legislation which affect the music industry. We'll start with UK laws first, then move on to European directives and international conventions and domestic laws in other countries.

In this country the most important and significant piece of legislation for the music industry, by a long, long way, is the Copyright Act, or, if you want to get technical about it, the

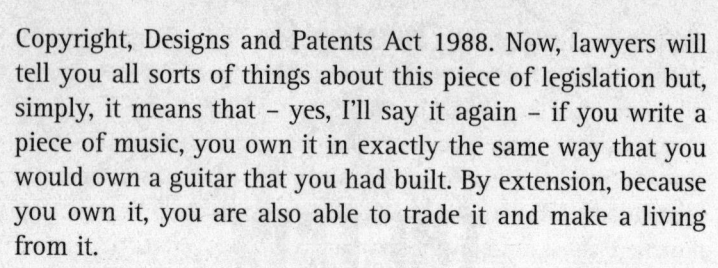

Copyright, Designs and Patents Act 1988. Now, lawyers will tell you all sorts of things about this piece of legislation but, simply, it means that – yes, I'll say it again – if you write a piece of music, you own it in exactly the same way that you would own a guitar that you had built. By extension, because you own it, you are also able to trade it and make a living from it.

Let's do that again because it's important. Though the Copyright Act is huge and complex, this is all anybody needs to know about what it says: if you wrote a piece of music, you own it. Job done.

To be fair, there are some other good things in the Copyright Act, but what I've just said is by far the most important of them. Nonetheless, while we're here, let's look at one of those bonuses – the fact that this law established a useful forum for airing grievances about copyright matters, the Copyright Tribunal. This is a court of law where copyright disputes are debated and, while it still involves lawyers and all the other expensive paraphernalia of the legal process, it is at least specialised in the area of intellectual property, which makes for a speedier and (compared with the High Court, where general disputes are settled) a more welcoming legal experience.

Since being set up in the late eighties, the Copyright Tribunal's work has mainly consisted of settling arguments between two sides over what the level of a royalty should be. Soon after the tribunal was established the record companies and music publishers settled down there for a marathon debate as to what proportion of PPD the mechanical royalty – which is, as we know, the key payment for all involved in the music industry – should be set at. It took them a significant amount of time and made a lot of lawyers a lot richer before they reached a conclusion.

However, since then, new technology has thrown up a whole new set of problems, such as, when is a mechanical not a mechanical? You can imagine the fun the lawyers have had with that one.

The idea, though, is one of huge significance, particularly in the light of emerging technologies, so let's step for a moment into the international arena and look at it a little more closely. As we noted earlier, the concept of mechanicals comes from the days when all music was mechanically reproduced. That is, you inserted a metal drum or a string of punched cards into a player-piano and the machine played the tune according to the instructions carried on the drum or the cards. Everything was carried out mechanically – which, at the dawn of the age of electricity, was all there was.

So, until the digital era which arrived with the advent of CDs at the end of the eighties, the concept of mechanicals was nice and simple. If music was reproduced in a form where a mechanism could make the same song again and again and again until it wore out, that was a mechanical reproduction and mechanical royalties were due.

Now, though, digital transfers and solid-state electronics mean that music can be reproduced ad infinitum without any moving parts in the process. (And if there are pedants out there who want to claim that electrons move down a wire when a current flows, go back to your physics books. Each electron travels only its own width when a current passes across it; one electron doesn't enter the system in Surrey and come out in Sydney when you send an email.)

Back in the real world (well, the world of lawyers, if that qualifies), there has been huge debate over whether the process of sending music down wires is a mechanical reproduction attracting a mechanical royalty. Now, I don't mean by this the music that people buy from paysites; I mean a wacky concept involving things called ephemeral copies. OK, sit back and settle down – this is going to take a moment.

When music travels across the Internet, it goes from one place to another via things called nodes. These are the centres the big Internet companies use to hold information while it passes from one place to another. It's sort of like changing trains. If you're going from Brighton to Norwich by train, you have to travel to London, wait there for a while, then travel out again. Electronic signals move in exactly the same way. They go from the sender to a central node, then out again. The only difference to changing trains in London is that when they arrive at that central node, they are copied. (I've no idea why, and life is too short to care.)

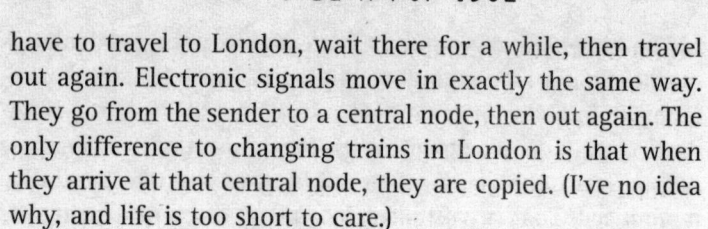

Because they are copied, the music industry has argued that these are reproductions for which a royalty should be paid – in response to which the Internet industry said, in essence 'Are they bollocks.' The lawyers, of course, made a packet out of presenting both these conflicting positions.

The main forum for debating this issue was, appropriately, the conference at which the framework of all copyright law for the online era was laid out: the World Intellectual Property (WIPO) conference in Geneva in 1997. Now, before that WIPO conference, there was no copyright law anywhere in the world relevant to intellectual property. Nothing. Bugger all. Nowt. The purpose of the conference, then, was to set out, once and for all, the rules for doing business over the Internet and who got what from whom by way of payment for it.

This issue of what is a mechanical in the context of the Internet was a central point and it brought the two sides into head to head confrontation. And just who were these people? Well, in the blue corner were those who represented the telecommunications companies and Internet Service Providers (ISPs). Opposing them in the red corner were the copyright community, the creative people.

It was an ugly battle as both these sets of mass debaters regarded the other with a distaste that bordered on disgust. The creative side hated the Internet side because the telecoms companies always described the people who make music and art as 'content providers'. Nic Garnett, head of the International Federation of the Phonographic Industry (IFPI) at the time of the WIPO conference, says this is akin to calling Beethoven a concert-hall filler. The description, he reckoned, treated music as a mere commodity and gave no consideration

THE LAW

to the creativity behind it or the pleasure it generates or the importance it has in many people's lives.

The Internet side hated the creative side because it rejected the argument that the ISPs and telecommunications companies were presenting a whole new avenue for creative people to access markets that had not previously existed.

So, in the pleasant, if boring, city of Geneva, they argued the toss. And how they argued. But eventually they came up with an agreement, in the form of two treaties (and I'm not going into the details of how and why, because the only thing that matters is what it means in practical terms). The deal was that:

1. No royalties would be paid for the ephemeral copies, but those ephemeral copies would be strictly controlled and kept within the ISP's systems.
2. Copyright holders and copyright owners – they are different people, but we'll go into that in a moment – have the right to prevent or allow the use of their works on the Internet.
3. If works are technologically protected, it is illegal to try to circumvent that protection technology.

In essence, the WIPO treaties reinforced the basic principle that music is property. That is, they set out the idea that we have revisited several times now: if somebody makes music, they own it and, as with all other property, are entitled to protect it.

While the acceptance of this idea of music as property seems very small and simple and not much to come out of a month-long legal yak-fest, it is actually a very significant development. Without it, the Internet companies and any entrepreneur offering an Internet-based service would have been able to give away or sell other people's music with complete impunity. That would have had terrible consequences: any record released could have been available for free on the Net within minutes of hitting the streets. Such free access to music would have meant that the composers and performers who created it would receive no income, being instantly turned from motivated professionals into keen amateurs. And, by extension, why would a record company go to the time, effort and expense of recording, making, marketing and distributing an album if it knew for certain that nobody would buy it because anybody could just download it from the Internet?

The WIPO treaties were something of a triumph for creative people, even though they fell far short of what the music industry would have liked. And the reason I say it was a small triumph is, as we have noted but we'll do it just one more time, the treaties did, at their most basic and most important level, enshrine forever the massively important principle of extending the copyright protection of the physical world to the, er, un-physical world of the Internet. Hooray.

So what happened to these things after they had been signed? Well, bear in mind that a treaty is only an agreement in outline, so the WIPO documents then needed to go to the various national legislatures around the world to be put into domestic law.

In the US, after the usual consultation, arguing and political process, they emerged as the Digital Millennium Act. In Europe they came out as the Copyright Directive, which, as I write this, is awaiting adoption by the government into UK law. That is, the European Union does not make law. The EU is a club to which the UK belongs and, as equal partners, the members discuss what rules the club should have. Once those rules have been adopted as a Directive, the members of the EU (the fifteen national governments) go home and make law that brings those rules into legal force. All UK law comes from Westminster. No UK law comes from Brussels; that is merely the forum where our government discusses what shape future laws might have. Thus, everything discussed in Brussels has to go through the UK legislative process just like everything else. And right now, the Copyright Directive is going through that (or maybe it went through that ten years ago if you've just bought this second-hand from the Oxfam shop).

Where, then, does this leave the professional British songwriter and muso? Well, he or she is protected in terms of physical records because of the provisions of the current Copyright Act. The songwriter and muso is also protected when his or her works are performed merely as vibrations in the air, again because of the existing copyright law.

Musos are also protected by a thing called the Copyright and Related Rights Regulations. This modest piece of legislation says that performers must get a fair share of performance income from records played to an audience. Before this was enacted at the end of the nineties, only record companies were entitled to broadcast royalties and any money they gave to artists was out of generosity and a desire to maintain good relations. Because of it, labels and artists had to come to a more formal arrangement than their previous gentlemen's handshake understanding in which labels got the lion's share of income; and, without much fuss, they agreed on a fifty-fifty split of all the royalties accruing from public performance of records. But there is a big hole in the protection these regulations provide, and it is an issue that has been a big source of irritation to the music industry. If a pub or shop or any other public establishment plays a record for its customers' enjoyment, it must pay a royalty. If, however, the pub or whatever plays music on the radio or television to its customers, no royalty is due. This is certainly an irony, and one that annoys no end those who ought to receive the royalties.

Moving on, though, to newer legislation and the newest media, once the Copyright Directive becomes law, copyright holders and owners will also have the right to say yes or no to their works being used on the Internet. Now, having a legally enforceable right to say no means that an acceptable sum of money has to be offered and agreed before those works can be used. This is just the same as a man selling his house: unless I offer him a sum of money that is acceptable to him, he has the right to say he is not going to sell it to me.

Songwriters and performers are, then, protected in the physical world and, very soon, will also be protected online. The laws are in place (or very quickly will be) to make sure that they can earn a living from their music, no matter how it is performed and through what medium.

I think we're ready now to have a look at how all that works in reality and to go back to that idea of the copyright holder and copyright owner and their differing roles within the legal framework. See, I promised you this was coming, now here it is. Blimey, has a book ever been so full of fulfilled promises?

Eyes down, then, and we'll get started. But I warn you that, though these are simple concepts, they can take a bit of assimilating, so make yourself comfortable for a while.

The copyright owner is always the person (or persons) who produced the work. The copyright owner can be a composer who wrote a song or a performer who recorded it. So, if our songwriting friend Beethoven from Chapter 4 writes a song, he owns it. If the Miracle Trees record it, they own that recording (though not the song itself, remember).

However, both these sets of people, each copyright owners, designate copyright holders to act on their behalf. For a songwriter like Beethoven, the copyright holder is his publishing company. For a recording ensemble (or band, if you want to get technical about it) like the Miracle Trees, the copyright holder is the record company.

Now, this just means that one person owns the rights, another one administers them. Don't be confused by this because it's just a standard business practice. It's not hugely dissimilar to your relationship with your bank: you own the money but the bank holds it on your behalf.

So, the copyright owner owns the work and the copyright holder holds it on his or her behalf. That is, one organisation – the publisher or the label – is acting as agent on behalf of the person who created the work. It is exactly the same as the publisher of this book, the copyright holder, working on my behalf as the copyright owner.

The key point is that a songwriter does not have the time or inclination to market his songs to the people who might like to use them – advertising agencies, film companies, solo artists or bands etc – so he gives his copyrights to a publisher to hold and to market for him. Similarly, a solo artist or band give their rights to a record company to hold and to market for them because most of them are not in the business of pressing, marketing and distributing bits of plastic.

So, a copyright holder acts on behalf of somebody else. The copyright holder does, though, have the legal power to say yes or no on the copyright owner's behalf. (All right, this is not always true, as the power the copyright holder wields depends entirely on the terms of its contract with the copyright owner. However, in the vast majority of cases the copyright holder is able to make decisions on the owner's behalf and to act on them without reference back – though there will be plenty of earache later if the copyright holder has done something the copyright owner doesn't like.)

All this means, then, that the yes or no for the use of a work – either in the real world or on the Internet – can be given by the owner or the holder. You can understand that it is important that these two sets of people have a good relationship and see eye to eye. Remember how vital we saw a good A&R relationship was in Chapter 5; that kind of trust and cohesion must extend to all else that the label or publisher does on the copyright owner's behalf if everybody is to remain happy.

This is particularly significant because once a deal has been done by the copyright holder (the label or publisher), the copyright owner – the person who made the music – is going to have a fantastically difficult time getting out of it if he or she doesn't like it. Generally, though, creative people and those who represent them tend to be on the same side financially and on good terms as humans. Serious conflicts are rare – but extremely bloody when they do happen.

That, then, is the difference between a copyright owner and a copyright holder. Though they are separate entities in law, they both enjoy protection under the law and have the same legal responsibilities. Let's look at one of these, an area of the law that has been of interest and concern and the source of massive controversy for creative people: obscenity.

We saw in Chapter 2 the effects of the Obscene Displays Act. Now let's move on to its big brother, the Obscene Publications Act. This piece of legislation is famous – or infamous, depending on how you see it – because it is the law that precipitated the most famous trials of creative people's work: the publishers of DH Lawrence's *Lady Chatterley's Lover* were prosecuted under this act, as were the people behind *OZ* magazine's 'Schoolkids Issue'. Lots of porn has also been found illegal under this law, though without the same public profile as the Lady Chatterley trial.

(Sorry, I can't mention Lawrence without alluding to this remarkable fact. He was from Eastwood, a Nottinghamshire pit village a few miles from where I grew up. Now, despite being a tiny little community – really no more than a big village – Eastwood has produced a major author, DH Lawrence, the founder of the Salvation Army, William Booth, and two England centre forwards, Jeff Astle and Tony Woodcock. Not bad for a dodgy place with one decent pub. And look at all these free facts you get in among this music industry stuff. Lordy, this book is worth the money.)

Right, where were we? Ah yes, the Obscene Publications Act. Now, there are those people who would have you believe that the government is always looking for ways to clamp down on the challenging thinking of radical groups. There are even those who would have you believe that the government is always seeking to find new ways to oppress us and that the obscenity laws are the means of doing that.

But, in my experience of governments, they're too busy

trying to get the trains to run on time and stopping the hospitals bursting at the seams and keeping the country safe from the perceived threat of the marauding legions of Johnny Foreigner to worry too much about the artistic community.

Still, the law is there to protect society and the line has to be drawn somewhere. However, where lies that division between phwoar and forbidden is a subject of great debate and, as the years go by, great change. For instance, when I was a young man, hardcore pornography was unheard of. Back then, in the sixties and seventies, just as sex was starting to become a bigger issue in my life than the Beano, pictures of consenting adults having sex were illegal. These days, when it is possible to find images instantly on the Net of any combination of sexes or species shagging, the obscenity laws are applied a lot differently – which is a damn good thing considering what most of us have stashed away somewhere on the computer.

Just as the coppers stopped seizing any magazine with an erection in it back in the eighties, the obscenity laws pretty much gave up on music at the same time. The last case to come before the courts was a single called 'Sheep Farming In The Falklands' by Crass. I don't think they ever made it on to *Top Of The Pops*, though. Now, 'Sheep Farming In The Falklands' was about ovine sex, or sheep shagging to the less discerning of us, in those South Atlantic islands (where, it has to be said, those long winter nights must get pretty lonely).

The case was kicked around for a week or so until the judge, who confessed that his cousin was a sheep farmer in the Falklands, said he could find nothing wrong with the record and everybody should go away and find better things to do with their time. This was the last time any record came before the courts and, even though a prosecution was brought, it is important to note that there was no conviction. In fact, no record ever released in the UK has ever been banned or been deemed to be obscene.

That's right. Take your pick from 'Sheep Farming In The

Falklands', 'God Save The Queen', 'Die You Bastard' (that cute little singalong Motörhead ditty) or all those records advocating the violent overthrow of the state, the violent overthrow of established religious practices or the violent overthrow of one's lady friend. None of these or any other record has ever been found by the courts to be obscene.

Now, there have been all these suggestions that record x, y or z (most famously, I suppose, the Sex Pistols' 'God Save The Queen') has been banned by the BBC or WH Smith or somebody else. This is not so – and in any case they do not have legal authority. Rather, the BBC simply chose not to play 'God Save The Queen' and WH Smith chose not to stock it.

It's exactly the same as when I choose to frequent a boozer. I go to my local and not to any one of the other nearby pubs. I am not banning those other pubs from my life; I simply choose not to go there.

No record, then, has ever fallen foul of the law of obscenity. Ever. And I am pretty damn sure none ever will.

If action is ever to be taken against a record – particularly in the light of the legal changes in the wake of September 11 – it will be for inciting racial hatred. To date, though, all the Oi movement records from the late seventies and many others subsequently that have advocated a neo-Nazi ideology have been left alone.

I suspect that this will remain the case unless somebody goes out of their way to release something utterly offensive. But even then, the law is likely to ignore it. Utterly offensive records have tiny, tiny fanbases and even smaller sales. Taking the producers of such a record to court would only bring that offensive song to public attention. I think the legal authorities are much more likely to let it come and go without leaving a stain on the public consciousness.

Oh, and if the law does get heavy with some pillock singing a eulogy to racial intolerance and nail him to the wall – in the legal sense, of course – I shall still sleep soundly in my bed.

Chapter 10

THE INDUSTRY ORGANISATIONS

THE MUSIC INDUSTRY IS full of organisations with bizarre acronyms – something which, I imagine, is also true of every other industry. But, just as we noted at the start of the book, there is absolutely no reason why anybody should feel any part of the business is impenetrable. Though the acronyms may seem opaque if you don't know what they stand for, the function of the organisations hiding behind them is straightforward.

Let me say again, before we get really stuck in, that nothing these organisations do is beyond human comprehension. That statement must be true because all the people who work there are human: they talk, think and behave like humans and respond to human interaction. With that in mind, now let's have a look at the most significant industry organisations.

The big one is the BPI – the British Phonographic Industry, often erroneously described in the media as the British Phonographic Institute. This is the main trade association for record companies and it is responsible for arguing their case to politicians and the media and, more practically, for organising the Brit Awards, overseeing the official UK charts and hammering the music pirates. As a trade association, the

BPI is a bit like a trade union. That is, labels join and, by sitting on the organisation's council, by arguing their case to the membership and by voting, they decide its political direction. Through the subscriptions they pay, they also fund staff to do the work that this political direction requires.

That staff issue is a very important one, for this reason: though the labels individually provide the cash to pay the staff, these people are independent from any individual record company because they are employed by the BPI as a whole; that makes them honest, neutral brokers. This is the only way the BPI, or any trade association, can operate: there must be people at the centre whom everyone trusts to be unbiased and even-handed.

But what do these people do exactly? Well, the BPI has, in essence, four departments: numbers, legal, events and anti-piracy.

Numbers sounds boring but is hugely important. More properly, it is known as business information and it is so significant because the industry needs to know precisely what state the sector as a whole is in. Record companies, retailers, music publishers and all others with a financial stake in music need to understand what is happening in the market – and the BPI numbers department is there to tell them.

The department is able to do this only because it is in that unbiased, disinterested position we noted. Record companies would rather eat glass than give one another their sales information, but they are prepared to give their figures to the neutral BPI for the good of the business as a whole.

Because the BPI's members account for virtually all records sold in the UK, their total sales figures add up, pretty much, to the total market. Thus, by analysing the labels' data and comparing this year's figures to last year's, the BPI can give a picture of what is happening in the total marketplace – that is, whether overall sales are up or down, whether particular genres are growing or waning in popularity, what regions of the country are doing best and worst in terms of sales, and so

THE INDUSTRY ORGANISATIONS

on. It is massively valuable information for the whole industry, and, without it, nobody would be able to make any kind of business plan.

Moving on to the legal department, the lawyers are involved in all things that the BPI does. So what do BPI lawyers do? Well, they oversee the legal aspects of all BPI operations, keeping everything above board and making sure contracts and agreements are in order.

The most obvious part of their work is in the field of anti-piracy, helping to bring charges against some fairly unpleasant villains. Indeed, the reason why the BPI was set up in the first place in the early seventies was to fight piracy.

Piracy is the unlicensed reproduction of records. It varies from well-meaning fans selling bootleg recordings of live shows by their favourite band to big, almost industrial criminal gangs turning out discs meant to look like the real thing. (More on this in Chapter 20.) These discs, called counterfeits, are made using relatively sophisticated reproduction equipment, both in terms of pressing and printing. At a casual glance they look like the real thing – the new Westlife album or George Michael disc or what have you. However, what distinguishes them is a) the price; if a new, mainstream pop album is being sold on the street for half the price it is being sold in HMV for, there's something wrong somewhere; and b) where it is being sold; if a man has a market stall or a bench set up on the pavement, it is probable that he is not conforming to the same standards of business and legal ethics that a multiple high-street retail chain is.

So, there is an alarming amount of unlicensed discs out there. The BPI's legal department has the task of ensuring the people making them end up before the courts.

The people on the ground who implement that policy are the anti-piracy department. This collection of former coppers and ex-trading standards people does the hard graft of chasing up leads and following cars across the country (yes, it really is like a poor man's James Bond) to find out where the discs are being made and by whom. The anti-piracy department monitors villains, gathers evidence and tries to persuade the police to take action – for instance, raiding the relevant premises – once the evidence mounts up into a case.

Now let's move on to the events department. This is the one responsible for the Brits and a hundred other smaller-scale events during the year, such as seminars, workshops, showcases and presentations. Events is the public face of the BPI. The things this department does give people their few insights into the workings of the BPI and the record industry. It is important, then, that those events look good and present the right impression of the business – one that is dynamic, active, upright and honourable.

That is significant in terms of not just public consumption but also political attitudes. See Chapter 15 for more on the awards shows, but I think it is easy to appreciate that what people see of an industry in a public forum is hugely important. In fact, for most people – and for everybody who hasn't bought this book – the only glimpses they get into the music industry are through the windows of the Brits. It is vital, then, that the business looks good when showing its face to the public because a business that doesn't look good will soon see its standing – then, soon after, its sales – going down.

Now, just like the record companies it represents, the BPI has another department, one above and beyond the day-to-day matters: the Big Boss. In the BPI's case, he's called the director general. While he has lots of work to do in overseeing all the things that happen within the BPI, much of his time is spent externally in keeping the politicians onside. Like all business, the record industry is affected and changed by new laws and there is always something in the pipeline that is going to impact on the way its commerce is conducted. Sometimes the proposed changes are minor but sometimes they can turn everything upside down. The director general makes sure the politicians understand the record industry's

THE INDUSTRY ORGANISATIONS

position and/or concern over those laws. (See Chapter 13 for more on this.)

And though the BPI performs a whole range of valuable functions in the big, wide world, just by being the BPI it fulfils another massively important task for its members in that it provides an impartial forum in which all the heads of the UK's record companies can talk. Why is this so valuable? Well, day to day, these guys compete with one another with a ferocity that would make fierce things shudder, so getting them to be calm, considered and rational when in the same room takes a neutral venue and a conducive atmosphere.

So, the managing directors, chairmen and presidents who make up the decision makers of the British record industry regularly sit down at the BPI to discuss the policies the organisation needs to implement on charts or the Brits or the government or the state of the market or whatever it might be. In so doing, they come together on that neutral ground and in that conducive atmosphere needed to make them able to talk to one another more informally. It's like football managers gathering for a drink at the national stadium rather than on the touchline when their teams are playing each other. The neutral environment is far more likely to bring out a positive, constructive, creative discussion than one in which a head-to-head battle is taking place: boxers are not known for their far-sighted discussions while they are in the ring together. In this way the BPI fosters not just practical and beneficial discussion, it also helps engender human relationships between the various company heads – and that must be a good thing.

The BPI is, of course, the British Phonographic Industry. It has equivalents all over the world representing the record companies in whatever country they happen to be in: BPW in Germany, SNEP in France, NVPI in the Netherlands, and so on. They are grouped together globally under the banner of IFPI – the International Federation of the Phonographic Industry. This organisation does exactly what the BPI does, but on a global scale. It operates everywhere in the world except the US, where the record industry goes it alone under the Recording Industry Association of America (RIAA).

Just like the BPI, the IFPI compiles numbers, only this time on a worldwide basis. This is absolutely vital once more because, as one of only a handful of truly planet-wide businesses, it is essential that the music industry knows if the Japanese market is in recession, the German market is expanding and whether CDs are finally overtaking cassettes in South Africa. Just like in the UK, it is only with this information that business plans can be made. Without it, a lot of time, resources and effort would be wasted as the industry would be operating blind.

Again, just like the BPI, the IFPI fights piracy – once more on a global basis; and it is hugely important that it does so because pirates also tend to work on a global basis. Considering that the BPI's remit ends at Dover, I think we can see it is vital that somebody can go beyond the White Cliffs and fight this problem on a multi-national footing. Much of the pirated material that comes into the UK does so from overseas, and the BPI can counter it only after it gets here, whereas the IFPI can try to stop it at source.

And, in a final parallel with the BPI, the IFPI also runs international events; one of its big ones is the Platinum Europe Awards – see Chapter 15 for more on this – but there are many other, less glamorous activities, such as seminars, briefings for politicians, press conferences and so on.

The IFPI and the BPI are, then, entirely on the same side. They believe in and fight for precisely the same things. On top of that, their offices are only a couple of minutes' walk apart in central London and the respective staffs often socialise and get on well together. But, having worked for one organisation and been a consultant to the other, I can tell you there are days when they are utterly at loggerheads and would have difficulty agreeing which way is up. That's both a mystery and a shame because there's lots of good guys in both places.

THE INDUSTRY ORGANISATIONS

Right, back in the good old UK, there is one other significant association on the record industry side: the Association of Independent Music (AIM). AIM was set up by the bigger indie players, prime movers among them being Pinnacle Distribution top man Steve Mason and the Beggars Banquet label gaffer Martin Mills, who felt that the BPI could not represent the needs of huge corporations like those that Warner Music and Universal Music belong to, as well as the interests of the indies, particularly the smaller members of that sector.

So, Mason and Mills and others went about setting up their own organisation to do precisely the same things as the BPI – but with an indie slant. Now nicely established with a significant full-time staff, AIM is involved in the same kind of political, statistical and charts things that the BPI does – but all from an indie perspective, of course, and, in AIM's view, better representing the indies' views and sensitivities.

AIM and the BPI now work in a somewhat gritty equilibrium in that they present a (fairly) united front when confronted with threats from the outside world, but spend much of the rest of the time kicking lumps out of each other behind closed doors. Ah, such is the ever lasting and barely concealed antipathy between indies and majors. A shame, once more. It makes me very sad that people whose agendas coincide so well – the BPI, IFPI and AIM – should expend any effort at all scoring points off one another when the real threats to their livelihoods lie out there in the big, bad world rather than on their doorstep within the music industry. But, when the going gets tough, these three can pull together, so I remain hopeful about their combined effectiveness on behalf of the record industry.

Moving on from the labels side of the business, let's look at what the retailers have to represent them. For a long while they had nothing; they had no equivalent to the BPI, nobody to speak for the retail sector as one, unified whole. That made them feel rather out in the cold. Until ...

In 1986 Russ Solomon, owner of Tower Records in the US, was president of the American retailers' association, NARM – the National Association of Record Merchandisers. He told his European chief, Steve Smith, that the Brits should have an equivalent. Steve, dynamic man that he is, set about putting things in place and in 1987 the British Association of Record Dealers (BARD) was born, with Steve as the chairman.

For a while BARD floundered around, a bit shocked by its own, new-found power and not really sure what to do with it. It did a fine job in collating retailers' grievances – particularly those of the indies, who, individually, have no voice at all – and in presenting those grievances to the record companies, but it lacked an issue to really unite it and give it focus.

It found one, though, in the great chart upheavals of the late eighties and early nineties. It was in the middle of that business revolution that BARD suddenly found its feet and realised that it had a hugely valuable commodity – information. Why was information so important? Well, the UK charts – and all other valid listings across the world – are based on retail information. That is, the stores say, 'This week HMV in Preston sold three thousand copies of the Miracle Trees' new album. Virgin in Carlisle sold two thousand ...' and so on and so forth until the total sales for every album available can be totalled up and compared. The one that sold most is obviously number one, but more on that process in Chapter 12.

Historically, the retailers simply handed over this sales information. There were reasons for this which we'll also look at more closely in Chapter 12. But once BARD realised that without the information it was giving away there would be no chart (and without the chart there would be no *Top Of The Pops* and no chart-based broadcasting of any kind, either on television or radio), it found its unifying issue.

Galvanised and excited, BARD said to the Chart Information Network (CIN), the people who actually put the chart together in those days, that if they wanted BARD

THE INDUSTRY ORGANISATIONS

members' valuable sales information, they were going to have to pay handsomely for it. After much complaining and wrangling and gnashing of wallets, a deal was struck and money changed hands – and still does on an annual basis. (An update: the CIN has now evolved into a cunningly titled operation known as the Official UK Charts Company.)

BARD has given the retail sector a face and a voice and a profile. Because of the deal this organisation did over the sales information, the importance to the whole industry of the retail sector is now apparent and obvious. In addition, the retailers are now on an even footing with the record companies in that both sectors have a representative trade association. The two bodies, the BPI and the BARD, now meet as equals once a month to discuss industry issues and matters of mutual concern and it is a compliment to the BARD that it has brought the stores to the same table and the same-size chair as their trading partners the labels. Having sat in on their meetings several times, I can report that relations are generally cordial, though the occasional spat is not unknown. But, in the meetings I have seen, I am happy to say that both parties seemed to clearly appreciate that each needs – yes, needs – the other if the whole industry is to prosper.

Moving on to the music publishers, the biggest and, in effect, only organisation is the Music Publishers Association (MPA). This monolith oversees the Mechanical Copyright Protection Society (MCPS), the Performing Right Society (PRS) and all the political lobbying and public relations activities that the publishers undertake.

But the MPA is not the most prominent of organisations, mainly because, as we have noted earlier, the publishing sector is not the most prominent sector within the industry. In addition, the MPA also tends to take a back seat to its subsidiary bodies, the MCPS and the PRS, because they're the ones that actually do the work and get their hands dirty and, if anybody's going to get into the news, it'll be one of these two rather than the MPA's secretariat.

The other publishers' body, and one closely allied with the MPA, is British Music Rights, which is largely a political organisation, spending much of its time lobbying politicians, in both London and Brussels, for better copyright protection.

That's records, retail and rights and their respective organisations. There is, though, as you would expect, a plethora of other bodies spanning the whole range of activities and sectors within the music industry. These include, among many others, the Concert Promoters Association, the International Managers Forum, the Association of Professional Recording Studios and the International Association of Entertainment Lawyers.

Slightly below all these in the pecking order is the Musicians' Union (MU). In my seventeen years at the core of the international music industry, these people never registered on my radar. Nobody could ever point to anything they had achieved or done. No contemporary musician ever said they had done anything on his or her behalf and the organisation has had a long policy of not speaking to the press, so even if they were doing anything, I couldn't find out what it was.

There are fine individuals in the MU structure, people I admire and have drunk with. But obvious achievements of the organisation can be summed up in the phrase 'bugger all'.

OK, that small tirade out of the way, let's go back a little and look at who belongs to the big organisations, who works for them and how to access their services. Starting with the BPI, the most active and dynamic of all these groups, who comprises the membership? Very simply, every worthwhile record company in the country. Though many indie labels are also members of AIM, they generally retain their BPI membership. As a result, the BPI represents around two hundred UK record companies, which, between them, account for virtually all of the British record market.

Joining the BPI is not too tricky – you just have to be a legitimate record label and be prepared to hand over your membership fee, around 0.03% of your turnover (or a couple

THE INDUSTRY ORGANISATIONS

of hundred quid, whichever is higher). And what do you get for your membership? Access to excellent market information, a vote at the Brits, plus guidance and advice and the protection of being part of the big boys' gang. The BPI is also a representative force for British labels at international trade shows like Midem and Popkomm (see Chapter 16), and in this way membership of the organisation gives companies an instant presence in the global marketplace.

There's also another advantage in being a member of the BPI: participation. Many times while I was director of communications for the organisation, people would complain to me that it was doing this, that or the other thing that they didn't like. Well, if you're a member, you can change that policy, because you get a vote and a voice and the chance to lobby. If you're not a member, you remain outside the decision-making process and your only avenue is to give a very bored director of communications earache when he's trying to drink his pint in peace.

There are similar advantages to being in the MPA: publishers belonging to the organisation are part of the club and they get to participate – to one degree or another – in the decision-making process. Just like labels in the BPI, they have the protection of a big organisation behind them and, once more just like the BPI, size is not a bar on membership. So long as you are a working publisher, you can join. And, personally, the smaller my company was, the more eager I'd be to be in there with the big boys.

In addition to which, remember, the MPA oversees the Mechanical Copyright Protection Society and the Performing Right Society (please feel free to refresh your memory by turning to Chapter 4) and these two organisations bring in all the publishers' income. So there is a strong incentive for a publisher to be a part, albeit a small one, of the management process.

So who works at the BPI and the other major organisations? As we noted at the start of the chapter, ordinary people and lawyers. There are no barriers to employment there save having something the BPI can use to its advantage, be it a law degree, a flair for statistical analysis or simply a willingness to answer the phone and make the tea. All of which is remarkably similar to trade organisations working in every other area of industry.

In essence and practice, the work of the BPI and of the other music industry bodies is no different to the work of, say, the National Farmers' Union or the National House Builders' Council. All those organisations, within the music industry and without, respond to their members' needs and represent their memberships' views and arguments to the outside world. Very often, as we noted, that outside world means politicians. All the music industry organisations spend significant energy in making sure MPs, MEPs and civil servants understand the issues involved. As we have seen, it can be quite tricky to understand abstruse concepts like intellectual property and it is important that politicos and their advisers know what it is. Having made sure they do understand the basic concepts, the various industry bodies must then bring round the politicians and civil servants to their way of thinking. So, if new copyright law is on the drawing board, the BPI and MPA in particular will seek to ensure that it is at least as good as the old law and, if they're lucky, a helluva lot better. More on this in Chapter 13.

However, they often face a lot of opposition in such efforts from powerful commercial forces who want reduced protection for copyright owners, so the music industry's representatives have to fight extremely hard just to make the business's voice heard.

The only good thing about all those outside threats is that they do tend to unite the industry into a single front. For example, new copyright law that lowers the level of protection enjoyed will get the BPI, MPA and the rest singing from the same hymn sheet. At other times, though, they are like fighting dogs in the same pit. The BPI and MPA in particular can be particularly vicious with each other – not surprising, really, as they are fighting for the same bone all the time.

Take, for example, the issue of mechanical royalties. Remember that record companies do not own the music on the record – they own just the recording – so they have to pay for the music they use. And who do they pay? The publishers in the MPA, of course! So, the level at which payments are set can divide the BPI and MPA mightily. Indeed, the two sides in this area are almost mutually exclusive: the more the record companies in the BPI have to pay, the less happy they are; and the less the publishers in the MPA receive, the louder their complaints. Finding that middle ground where everybody is content is a process that has left blood on the carpet, the walls and the ceiling.

Generally, though, all relations are deeply cordial. No, in truth, they are. Despite the spats, rows and arguments and a background of long-held mistrust, these organisations tend to get on well. All the senior people in these bodies are polite and charming and courteous and diplomatic to each other at all times and the staffs often share a pint and a chat. But if one of those senior execs was on fire and the only other people in the room were the senior execs from the other organisations, it would be interesting to see who would and would not choose to piss on the flames.

This, though, is a side issue. More important is that these organisations exist, can be joined by anyone active in their respective field and provide a great deal of protection, security and guidance for the membership.

Chapter 11

THE PEOPLE

THERE ARE GOOD GUYS and bad guys in the music industry and, as we noted at the beginning of the book, the proportions are about the same as anywhere else.

Taking the bad guys first, it has to be admitted that there have been some very bad ones. The exploitative scum that is Jonathan King springs to mind, along with one other executive who was convicted in the late eighties for sexual assaults on women and who I am prevented from naming for legal reasons (though he could still have a smack if he ever wants to come round to my house; I remember who you are). Then we have Gary Glitter and his convictions for possessing child pornography. But, apart from these three, I am at a loss to think of anybody who is an out-and-out villain or even has a serious conviction (that is, something beyond a minor motoring offence). Not a bad ratio, then: three guys in an industry of twenty-eight thousand people.

Collectively, however, the business is not a saint. While the individuals in the industry are no better and certainly no worse than twenty-eight thousand people in any other sector, the music industry perpetrates one terrible darkness: gossip. Rumours begin apparently without reason, circulate without restraint and create a reputation for somebody that he or she has done nothing to deserve. I could name many, many people who have been hugely damaged by such things, but let me give you the example of one average (yet curiously attractive) bloke – me!

I am a man in slightly better than average health. I have a clean criminal record: I've never been charged with anything, never been arrested, never even been so much as cautioned or warned about my behaviour – save for one glorious incident of riding my motorbike at a deeply satisfying but highly illegal speed on the M1. And I am a man who has been entirely faithful to his partner.

Yet all of these things have all been said about me:

1. I have had a brain tumour.
2. I was connected with a sex ring run out of the House of Lords (not bad for a lad from a council estate in Nottingham, but do I really want to see any of those people naked?).
3. I was arrested and charged over possession of child pornography (and you can imagine how much that suggestion hurt when I heard it).
4. I had an extramarital affair with my old mate Colleen Hue.

I hope you can see from this what astounding things can be generated by one average man leading a normal life. I dread to think what can be said about people who really do get famous.

It has also been chilling to see how rumours are invented and nurtured by the people who should least be doing it – the people who benefited from the support, assistance and love of the person they are gossiping about. People regarded as friends can abandon any notion of truth, loyalty or equity in a fraction of a moment and begin promulgating the most damaging lies.

And I'm not talking here about those people who have spread untruths about me. I am talking about my own

THE PEOPLE

disturbing propensity to join this trade in offal and to pass on salacious innuendoes and unfounded tittle-tattle about others. Call it the dark side of the force or something, but it is the music industry's dirtiest and nastiest habit. I deeply regret my part in this noisome exchange.

I also regret that the four statements above about me are entirely untrue. Of course, while I am profoundly delighted that 1, 2 and 3 are utter fiction with no connection to the reality of my life, it disappoints me that ten years of pursuing Colleen didn't get me so much as a snog. Tell me there's still hope, Col ...?

But, in my view, this tendency to gossip viciously is the music industry's only major vice. Like other businesses, though, we can lay claim to lots of minor ones: tardiness is one that sends me up the wall (I could have built a house in all the time I have spent waiting in record company receptions) and close behind that in irritation value is insincerity. 'How are you?' means absolutely bugger all to most of the people who use it (try telling them how you actually are and see what response you get) and 'We must get together sometime' often means even less.

Then again, I'm sure that this is a common complaint and that many people reading this book who currently work in sectors other than the music industry would recognise these foibles in their own fields.

Moving on to happier matters, it is important to say that there are many attributes of which the music industry can be proud – belief and commitment being the main ones. When people feel strongly about a band they will back that belief to the limits of their ability and, often, beyond the limits of their finances. I greatly admire such acts of faith and, of course, it is through them that the world is richer by a lot of music that would not otherwise have seen the light of day had the conviction of the people financing it been less.

In fact, this level of conviction and commitment is seen right across the music industry. Major record companies will spend millions on acts that they believe in, bands that never make a dent in the chart, simply because of their belief in them. And, if the act fails first time round, the label's passion is such that they will spend many more thousands on a relaunch; prime examples are the way CBS (as was) got behind the Roaring Boys and MCA backed Energy Orchard. Never heard of either of those bands? Not surprising; few people did. But I watched astonished as those companies put everything they had – money, expertise and love – into trying to break those acts into the mainstream. It broke my heart when everybody's efforts failed to be rewarded, and it made me hugely admire the men and women who fought so hard for so long to try to make it happen simply because of the level of their belief. And this is not just a prerogative of the majors. On a different scale but with exactly the same principle, indie companies and smaller entrepreneurs will mortgage their houses and everything else they own to try to break a band, often without any success whatever and even going broke in the process.

This, then, is what unites the people in the industry: a love of and a belief in music. I have often been truly amazed by the commonality of feeling across the business. Indeed, when there's a new outbreak of the kind of bickering between indies and majors that we looked at in the previous chapter, I find it utterly ironic that what unites these two sets of people is far, far greater than what divides them.

Let's look at this a little more closely and give the lie to a few uniformed criticisms. The commonest disparagement of the major record companies and their senior executives is that they are fat cats interested only in money and not connected to the music. I find such an assertion rather offensive, and, in reality, instead of being the general rule, as some people would tell us, I have found it true in only one case I can think of among the hundreds of senior execs I have known. In fact, I tend to hear this accusation only from people who have never met a senior exec, let alone been there when an exec had his shirt off and was jumping up and down at a gig – and, yes, I promise you this happens.

I think it is easy to appreciate that an exec who has worked his way up the ladder of the music industry is going to like music; indeed, without a love of music to inspire him, I suspect he will never have the determination and drive required to make it to the top. But even those execs who have come to the industry from outside, from, say, a legal background, come because of their love of music. There's a lot more money available to a lawyer in the City or in private practice than there is in most music industry jobs and every lawyer I have known in the business was there simply because music was a lot more exciting than insurance or corporate finance or other stuff that's simply too dull for me to type.

There are, of course, some lawyers in the music industry who live their lives as though they were working for Royal Legal Financial Bastard Insurance plc, but, in my experience, they are few and far between. And nobody loves them.

Conversely, the lawyers who make it to the top of the corporate tree represent the absolute antithesis of that attitude. People like Sony's European president Paul Russell, former Phonogram and MCA UK chief David Simone, the late, great PolyGram (now Universal) European boss Maurice Oberstein and dozens of others across the world all came to music from a background in the law and all demonstrated not only a love for music but a real feel for it. Known universally as Obie, Oberstein was finding and breaking hits well into his sixties. Even as a pensioner, he was more in touch with what was happening in the world of popular music, and particularly new trends in pop, than most teenagers. Obie also invented more than a few of those new trends in pop – and did so at an age when most folks are muttering about the good old days.

And much as I have had a go at lawyers in this book, let me say that I have been to gigs with lawyers, taken my shirt off and jumped up and down in the front five rows with lawyers, talked about music all night with lawyers, travelled to far-off places just to see a band with lawyers. Simply, they love their music. And to suggest somebody is not passionate about music because they wear a suit and tie all day is high bigotry – not to mention rather arrogant.

Just like the lawyers, there are financial people who love their music, and human resources people who love music and people who do pensions who love music and people who run CD-pressing machines who love music. In short, I have met nobody at a major label who wasn't an avid fan of one form of music or another. That favourite snipe that the majors are just corporate bastards is simply something for which I have never seen evidence.

OK, so now we're in the realms of senior execs, let's look at another flavour of human that makes up that top echelon. In among the lawyers in that highest bracket is an entirely different type of top dog – the one with an A&R background.

A prime example of one of these people is Rob Dickins, long-time boss at Warner in the UK. Rob is never happier than when getting his hands dirty making records. He produced a string of songs and can claim two major milestones: a number one with Cher's 'Believe' and actually being mentioned in a song lyric, in Enya's 'Orinoco Flow'. (Come on, tell me you remember that from Chapter 5. It wasn't that long ago.)

But even guys like Rob, who are provenly creative and who are in the music business for all the right reasons, are not immune from negative perceptions from the outside world. They get a lot of earache for simply being successful and having plenty of cash. Well, I say they've earned it. Top guys at a major record company are like managers at a big football club. It's a high-risk, high-return business with no safety net for those who fail – and job security is about as common as dragon tears.

The pressure on the head of a major label to keep coming up with the goods year after year after year is enormous. If they get well rewarded financially for being good at that, I am entirely relaxed about it. It's not taxpayers' money they are getting and their pay is not coming out of my pocket. If their employers choose to pay them well for a job well done, good luck to them. Anybody else who is top of their tree in industry expects a decent return, so why should record executives be any different?

Before this gets out of hand, though, and I start making these people look like saints (which they ain't, though Rob Dickins is married to one of the women who used to be in Pan's People, which would certainly be my idea of heaven), let's delve a little deeper into the reality of who they really are.

Execs with a background in A&R tend to have started in, yes, you guessed it, the A&R department. There have been many notable cases of somebody beginning as a young boy listening to tapes and working his way up the ladder to be managing director or chairman or whatever the Big Boss at a label calls himself. I think we can see how launching a career in the A&R basement gives such an exec valuable insights. It means, for example, that he has a massive amount of knowledge of both music and musicians at his disposal. In addition, by the time he reaches the dizzy heights of chairmanship, he should also have some maturity and a breadth of experience of what other departments do and why. It is a formidable combination and execs from an A&R background are often extremely effective. On the other hand, they can be complete pillocks, their main failing being their desire to pursue their creative urges, no matter what the cost. And, on occasion, the cost has been very, very great, almost crippling some big-name operations. As a general rule, it is often wise not to let A&R people near a chequebook. But, of course, no generalisation is an absolute mirror of the truth.

After the lawyers and the A&R people, there's one other broad category of senior executive: those with a marketing background. Marketing people tend to have a better grasp of financial matters than A&R guys. Now, this does not mean that marketing people are without creativity; the best of them have imaginative thinking coming out of their ears and other orifices. But there also tends to be a streak of practicality running through them compared with execs who have a background in marketing.

Perhaps a man who exemplifies this is Paul Conroy. Paul really established his career while marketing manager at Stiff Records and such was his creativity that Stiff became an icon of both the punk and indie movements. Back in those days, though, Paul was but a boy and his imagination had not yet been tempered. So his boss at Stiff, Dave Robinson, often praised his innovative thinking but knew he had to back his ideas with hard cash. 'Never tell Paul how much it costs,' Dave often said when asked about how to get the best out of his marketing chief.

Paul did great things at Stiff, and later, when he allied his creativity to financial discipline, he did even greater things as marketing director of WEA UK, then as gaffer at Virgin UK. His long tenure in the senior echelons of the business – he parted company with Virgin only in 2002 after twenty-five years in the industry – is testimony to how effective a man can be when he has marketing creativity and financial discipline.

Now let's look at another one of my favourite marketing men, Tony Powell. Tony, who currently runs Pinnacle Distribution after years as marketing director at Phonogram and then as boss at MCA UK, climbed the ladder from the very bottom rung. He started out as a sales rep, a man on the road selling to retailers, and gradually moved up from there.

The experience Tony gained in that ascent was invaluable. Through taking the long road to the big chair, he knew how companies worked from top to bottom and how their clients and partners reacted to them, and that gave him a priceless sensitivity to retailers' needs and desires because for years he had to look shopkeepers in the eye and listen to their complaints and concerns. A number of senior industry execs find that they go in stores less and less as they climb the ladder, and they can be accused of being out of touch with how the ordinary indie retailer feels. This was never an accusation levelled at Tony.

I hope you can see that, having looked now at lawyers, A&R people and marketing men, there is no one single background that is ultimately better or worse than others for climbing to the top of the tree. Each of these backgrounds brings with it certain positive attributes and certain shortcomings. No top exec I have ever met was fully prepared for the job when he took it; each one of those people (and, I have to emphasise, bar two exceptions they were exclusively men) had to learn some aspect or another of the post. But that, I suspect, is true of anybody, anywhere who has ever been promoted.

If, then, you are bright, determined and courageous (and lucky enough to get a break in the first place), there is no barrier to anyone with a brain and a backbone earning a reasonable living at a major record company. Why a brain and a backbone? This is capitalism, remember, and those without brains enough to be bright go bust or fail to move on in their career. Backbone is needed because this is the music industry and it is glamorous, exciting and wonderful – and if you don't want it and fight for it as much as those people competing with you for a position in it, you will, and deserve to, lose out to them.

In truth, the doors of the major record companies are wide open. The music industry is a meritocracy – I have never seen any form of racism and the level of sexism is on a par with or lower than in every other industry I have experienced – so that if you are the brightest or the best, you are already qualified for a job. The only challenge people face is becoming the brightest or the best – but that's life.

OK, that was a very brief overview of the majors and the kind of people who work for them. I regret that space meant I didn't have room to go into a number of other interesting areas – like the musicians who cross the fence from performing to being an exec. Top Sony A&R man Muff Winwood is a prime example of that, along with a number of other current A&R

people who have been in Dexy's Midnight Runners, the Undertones and, believe it, Bros in their time – oh, and not to mention the very upright legal brain at the PRS who once had a record deal with his band Faster Pussycat Kill Kill. Our look at the majors also missed out the people who finally break into record companies after half a lifetime spent doing something else entirely or who get a job at a label after years behind the counter at Dead Dog Records & Tapes in Stowmarket. Bless them all.

But, if we're now agreed on the fact that there are no barriers to employment and that there is a huge variety of backgrounds, talents and personalities within the majors, let's move on to the indies and see some of the characters there.

Are they a breed apart from major-label execs? Well, there has certainly been only restricted amounts of crossover between the two sectors over the years – and the only guy I can think of who was boss of a major then went to be boss of an indie is Tony Powell. Bearing in mind that the indies were born out of frustration with the majors' ways and were raised on a diet of determination to be different, it is not surprising that there is a different standpoint, ethic and mindset among the populations of these two disparate but neighbouring countries.

Let me illustrate what I mean by saying a little about my favourite indie sector character, Iain McNay. Iain was one of the original people to say: 'There must be music beyond what the major labels are putting out,' and his label, Cherry Red, is now one of the very oldest indies in Europe. (Come on, of course you remember them from Chapter 7.)

There is no part of Iain that feels connected with the corporate world and he wouldn't last ten minutes in it. That's not a criticism of him (after twenty years of knowing this exceptional man, I have no criticisms of him); it is simply a recognition that there is no corporate hole that would fit this indie peg.

Iain likes to do things that have not been tried before, to

think radically and freely and to have the scope to follow his conclusions and to allow his staff to do the same. In my opinion, he is fairly typical of the indie sector in that the people who populate it tend to be well, more, er, indie is the only way to describe it.

And what does it mean to be indie? Well, often the attitude is predicated on that antipathy to corporate companies we noted above and in Chapter 10 but, beyond that, it depends on the indie. Independent labels cover the whole spectrum of music, and generally the only thing that unites them is the indie ethic of trying to be and do something different and to have the freedom to go their own way. We would not expect the head of an indie classical company to have a lot to say to a man running a grindcore metal label – beyond stating, perhaps, their respective views of the indie ethic.

But, make no mistake, that ethic which unites them is extremely powerful. It has prevented a lot of talented indie people making a move into the majors and anything that can persuade people to resist such temptation is potent indeed.

There are, however, classic examples of people who learned their trade in the indie sector before taking up reins of power in the corporate world, Paul Conroy being prime among them.

Then there are those people who started up an indie label because nobody else would have them. The utter joy of the indie sector is that it takes only hundreds rather than thousands of pounds to join in – and, with the advance of technology, even that modest entrance fee is diminishing all the time. Because of the ease of access, lots of people have started indie labels either as the only way they could get into the business, or the line of least resistance, or as the only way of doing it their way. But whatever their reasons and motivations, they've contributed a lot of music to the world and had a lot of fun doing it (though most of them have had to face the pain of going bust somewhere along the line).

So what motivates all these people in the music industry, be they the gaffer at Sony's European headquarters or the junior

A&R assistant (temporary) at Scrotum & Jubblies Records Ltd? Well, as we noted at the top of the chapter, a love of music is the single common denominator. It reaches right across the business and is a fire in the heart of everyone from top to bottom, lawyer to ligger, Toronto to Tokyo. Sure, there are people who think going into the music industry will make them rich and/or famous, but even those people are motivated first and most by their love of music.

Let me give you an example of that passion and what it can do to people. I once shared a plane ride and a taxi with Andy Gray, who, as we know by now, is head of retail chain Andys Records, and Jon Webster, long-time marketing man and head of Virgin Records UK. These two passed the time on the journey not just by chatting about music but by chatting about catalogue numbers. That is, each carried round in his head not only the title and track listing of a huge number of albums but that album's catalogue number as well. Now, if that isn't the epitome of passion for a subject, I'm not sure what is.

As we know, indie people such as Andy and Jon have this kind of passion by the bucketload – which is why indie people are prepared to put their houses, relationships and, occasionally, lives in jeopardy to pursue their desires. But, just to emphasise the point I was making earlier that the majors, too, are hotbeds of passion rather than feather beds for fat cats, let me say this: I have seen very senior executives from very big companies in highly, almost violently animated discussions over which guitarist is most expressive, who can and cannot sing, which drummer thought timing was something to do with an Olympic event, and the like.

Indeed, watching senior execs from major record companies dancing, singing and shouting with the rest of us at a gig gives the lie to any notion to the argument that they somehow feel differently about music than the rest of us do.

Just to give a little further evidence of the passion these guys have:

- I once walked into the office of Hein van der Ree,

managing director of Phonogram, to find him belting out a tune on an electric guitar at truly alarming volume.
- I shared tears at the most moving parts of the Live Aid show with a managing director I won't name for fear of embarrassing him and undermining his reputation as a hard bastard (you know who you are).
- I've swapped stories on best-ever Budgie gigs and greatest-ever versions of 'Breadfan' with John Love, at the time managing director of PPL.
- I have never bumped into an A&R director, manager or scout in any circumstances – in the street, in the pub or at a gig – when they didn't put a disc or tape in my hand and say, 'You've got to listen to this; it's brilliant.'

OK, I think you get the point about execs and their motivations, but what about the people who actually make the music – the musicians?

Well, in this category of people there is a larger manifestation of the desire to be rich and famous. But then I think that is a prerequisite for making it to the top. If you go into music not caring whether loads of people hear and like your stuff or not, you will simply be trampled in the rush to success by all the people who ache to have their material heard and loved by the widest possible audience.

Also, I believe it takes a particular mindset and a robust ego to not just be prepared to stand in front of and seek to entertain a hundred thousand people at a festival but to actually want to do so. Personally, I'd rather be caught shoplifting lingerie (again).

And, of course, musicians, in common with – and perhaps surpassing – everybody else in the music industry, love music. Every muso I've met spent their whole teenage years listening to and playing music and their young adult life striving to the limits of their ability to make a living from it. They are, in many ways, driven and consumed by their passion for the subject.

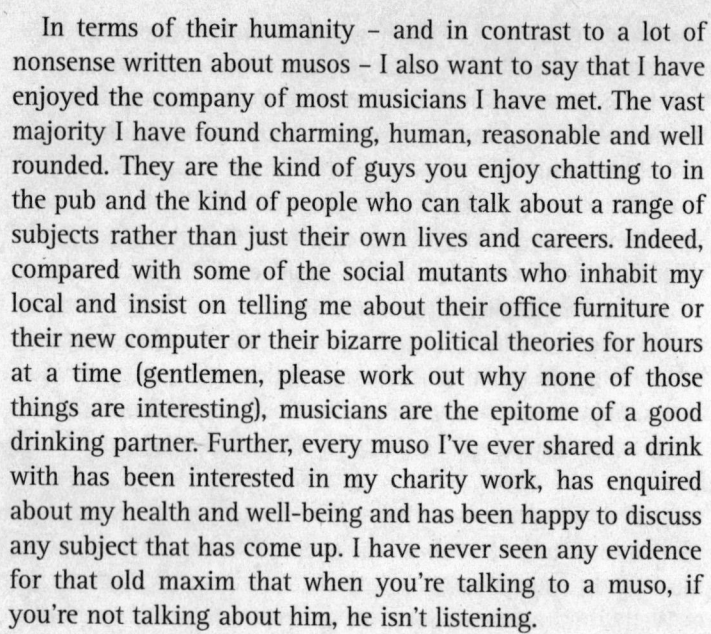

In terms of their humanity – and in contrast to a lot of nonsense written about musos – I also want to say that I have enjoyed the company of most musicians I have met. The vast majority I have found charming, human, reasonable and well rounded. They are the kind of guys you enjoy chatting to in the pub and the kind of people who can talk about a range of subjects rather than just their own lives and careers. Indeed, compared with some of the social mutants who inhabit my local and insist on telling me about their office furniture or their new computer or their bizarre political theories for hours at a time (gentlemen, please work out why none of those things are interesting), musicians are the epitome of a good drinking partner. Further, every muso I've ever shared a drink with has been interested in my charity work, has enquired about my health and well-being and has been happy to discuss any subject that has come up. I have never seen any evidence for that old maxim that when you're talking to a muso, if you're not talking about him, he isn't listening.

I have, though, been somewhat disappointed by the change in some people as they have risen up the ladder. I've known young bands who were totally charming and polite at the outset of their career but then pretend they don't know who you are when you bump into them after they've become famous. And I've seen a handful of performers turn their back entirely on the people who made them famous and pretend that those people never existed. But such disloyalty brings its own rewards. When life turns ugly for the muso (as it inevitably will at some point or another in their career) there are far fewer people prepared to hold out a helping hand if that hand has already been bitten by the mouth it fed.

Happily, though, for every lamentable case, I have seen dozens of examples of loyalty, trust and friendships that have lasted and grown throughout a career. Indeed, in seventeen years at the core of the music industry, I saw many more examples of the positive aspects of human nature than the negative ones.

THE PEOPLE

And we shouldn't leave this chapter on people without relating a story that says a lot of good things about the business's human face. It also reinforces the point I was making about the industry being open to anybody with a brain and a backbone – and not just that, but, if their brain and backbone are big enough, music can be a platform on which they can really prosper. It's a tale of two retailers, Richard Handover and Brian McLaughlin.

South African Richard was an unknown quantity when he took over the running of Our Price, then the UK's biggest record retail chain, in the late eighties. Richard took great pride in the fact that his only academic qualification was one O level – in geography. Now, as I write this, he is Group Chief Executive of WHSmith.

Brian McLaughlin is a man I hold in equal affection and admiration, for the reason that Brian rose from being a shop assistant in HMV to running the HMV Group in Europe, an organisation comprising not just HMV stores but Waterstone's book stores and lots of other impressive stuff.

Two nice guys armed with no more than who they are. What other industry would have given them the opportunity to demonstrate their abilities and rise so far – and allow them to stay nice guys in the process?

Chapter 12

⭐

THE CHARTS

THE CHARTS ARE THE greatest marketing tool ever invented. Steady. Sit down. Let's say that again. The charts are the greatest marketing tool ever invented.

No other marketing concept has ever promoted so much of a commodity for so long. No other marketing concept has ever spawned so many imitators, all adding to the marketing power of the original idea. No other marketing concept has ever attracted so much media attention.

And no other marketing concept has ever had so much criticism.

For all these reasons, the charts are unique.

They first appeared back in the 1950s in the US, but that was a different age and a different world. Charts as we know them today – sophisticated, national and compiled electronically – are really a British invention from the end of the eighties. It was then that modern technology was first employed in their compilation and then that the system really began to have some veracity and true value.

So, leaving history to the history books, we'll look at how the charts of the modern era have grown to what they are today and how the UK provided a model for the rest of the world. Now, if you're sitting comfortably, I'll begin ...

Up until the mid-eighties charts in this country were compiled using diaries. That is, selected stores around the UK filled in diaries of what they sold. They logged each sale of each album and single in a book – the chart diary – and the diaries were returned to the market research company, which then added up the totals. It was a long, laborious process, which was why the chart sales period ran from Monday to Saturday and the chart didn't come out until Tuesday. So, only then did we get to find out what had been popular the previous week.

In addition to such tardiness, there was also another massive disadvantage in this arrangement: it was open to corruption and hyping. We'll look at those two things in a little while. For the moment we'll stick with the mere practicalities of this system, which were, obviously, horrendous. In our digital, electronic age it is amazing that as recently as twenty years ago people were using pen and paper and the totals had to be added up using good old arithmetic, but that is exactly how it worked. Given these obstacles, the most amazing thing to me is that a chart was produced at all in time for Tuesday's radio chart shows.

Only in the mid-eighties, at the instigation of the chart compilation company Gallup, did the first signs of modernisation appear. Oh, I hear you ask, and what's a chart compilation company? Well, the UK charts have always been a joint venture between the record companies' association the British Phonograph Industry, the BBC and the industry publication Music Week, along with, latterly, the British Association of Record Dealers. But this amalgam of organisations, a grouping which commissions, promotes and oversees the strategic direction of the charts, doesn't actually get its hands dirty in collecting figures and putting the listings together. So the people who do those jobs out there on the ground and who actually find out how many records have

THE CHARTS

been sold are always a market research company, or the chart compilation company as they are known. Until the end of the eighties that company was Gallup. Yes, that's the same Gallup that asks people whether they are voting for Colonel Sir Bufton Tufton or Dave Spart at election time.

Gallup is a big, sophisticated company and, because of its forward, innovative thinking, it took the first step towards bringing the chart into the modern era by introducing the so-called chart machine, which was basically an electronic version of the diary. In effect, the process of operating this machine was just the same as filling in a diary.

The machine sat by the till and when somebody bought a record, the shop assistant entered the catalogue number into the device's keypad. The machine – essentially a very unsophisticated PC – logged the number and stored it and, at various times during the week, sent the accumulated sales data down the phone lines to Gallup. Then Gallup added up the totals, but now with the aid of some rudimentary electronic systems to speed up the process. The chart, though, was still compiled using data from Monday to Saturday but was not published until Tuesday. Because of this, in many ways, just like in the days of chart diaries, it continued to be out of date even before it was released. But, back in the mid-eighties, there was only one chart in this country and its backers had no reason or incentive to speed up the operation.

Nonetheless, in that era, the charts compiled using this method were pretty much the best in the world. Why? Mainly because of the depth of the sample. When market research companies like Gallup are conducting political and consumer polls, they reckon their sample is very, very good if they can question one in two thousand of the target audience. Gallup was very fond of pointing out that its chart sample was better than one in three. This means that in the days when there were around five thousand record stores in the UK, nearly two thousand of them were on the so-called chart panel that sent data to Gallup through the chart machines. The system was as good as anybody could make it at the time.

But then came the real breakthrough – electronic point of sale (EPOS) equipment. Don't think this is something exotic and esoteric. It isn't – even though EPOS sounds like a hypno-trance band. But, common enough though EPOS is to us now, it caused a revolution when it was introduced. EPOS, then, is merely the posh name for the bar-code reader attached to the till at the checkout of everything from your local supermarket to the high-street record store.

But, unlike a tick in a chart diary or even entering a catalogue number into a chart machine, the bar-code reader and its associated technology collect lots of data in one go: the item being bought (precisely, not just a record but which record – album or single, artist and label); the time of day; the location of the store; which batch of deliveries the record came from; and, if a card is being used to buy it, just who is buying it and, if they are a regular customer, just how this purchase fits in with the music they have been buying for the past few years.

This is fantastically detailed information and hugely valuable, which is why the British Association of Record Dealers started selling it rather than just giving it away (see, I told you so, way back in Chapter 10). So, all the retailers who belong to this organisation now use EPOS to collect their sales data, figures which they then send to the chart compilation company. Of course, the retailers hang on to a lot of stuff – they don't want their competitors getting hold of the details of their customer base – but all the actual sales information (what was bought, when and where from) goes to the chart compilation company. And because EPOS is in every store you care to name and because virtually all those stores are BARD members, it means that all four thousand or so record shops in the country now supply data for the chart. This is an amazing improvement even on that excellent beginning of a two-thousand-store sample we had in

Gallup's day. In this way the current chart compilation company can monitor every record sold everywhere in the country every day.

Despite the things that the retailers keep to themselves, like credit card details, I think it's easy to see that the quality of information the company receives goes way, way beyond what is needed to tot up the list of who sold most in any given period. This means that the chart compilation company can do a lot more than just tell the labels who's number one. Precisely because it can keep track of every album and single sold everywhere, it produces hugely valuable market research information for the industry.

It can tell you when is the most popular time of day for buying which kind of music, what are the regional variations in musical taste and whether people prefer HMV for rock, Virgin for dance and an indie for indie (or any other combination of those elements). This helps labels enormously to target their marketing campaigns.

So, just adding up the totals for who sold what in a week to find out which was the most popular single and album must be a straightforward matter, then, isn't it?

Well, the numbers are straightforward, of course. If the new Rolling Stones album sold fifty thousand in HMV in a week, fifty thousand in Virgin, twenty-five thousand in Woolworths and twenty-five thousand across all the indies, that's just adding up – and the computer will even do that for you in a tiny fraction of a second. If those one hundred and fifty thousand copies were the most sold by any album in the week, the Stones go to number one. Yes, the figures are simple.

But – and it's a big but – the purchase by a customer over the counter is only the last link in a long chain; and some of those links are not necessarily made of gold.

Just like a vote being put in a ballot box, there's no point in keeping a close eye on the denouement of the system if you ignore everything that preceded it. Thus, in both democracy and the chart there are, all through the process, rules and checks to ensure that everything is above board and, in the case of the chart, also that it is a fair and accurate reflection of the real popularity of a record.

Now, let's go back a couple of steps to see why those checks are needed.

The chart is a bit like Formula 1 racing: there are things you can do within the rules and things that are definitely illegal; and, within the rules, the competing parties will always strain and push at the boundaries to gain an advantage.

Let's look first at what's definitely illegal, and for this we need one further step into history. Back in the days of chart diaries, in the early eighties, it took only a tick in a book to say that store X had sold a copy of album Y. Though it would have been possible to check this against the shop's sales ledger, there was neither time nor resources to check every shop every week. Consequently, a lot of mischief took place; hyping, as it was called.

Young, impressionable sales staff would regularly take a few quid or other inducements from record company sales reps to add a few extra ticks to the sales of the label's big new release that week and, if the guy behind the counter was a fan of a band, he might even add in a few ticks of his own accord, simply out of an innocent but misguided desire to do the band some good.

And less reputable stores even cut out the middleman and let the sales rep get his own hands on the chart diary. There was the legendary occasion when a record company needed, in the days before mobile phones, to contact one of its reps in a hurry. The company rang a shop that they knew he would be at and asked if he was there. The reply came, 'Oh yes, he's in the backroom filling in the chart diary.' That sales rep rose to be a very senior figure in the music industry and later related this story with great pride.

But tales like this show things were getting out of hand and, almost inevitably, the boil of malpractice had to burst. It did so spectacularly when a television exposé of these dodgy practices put all the music industry's dirty laundry into the spotlight.

When it all came out, everybody was embarrassed. The record companies were embarrassed that their shenanigans were now public knowledge; the BBC was embarrassed that the chart it broadcast every week was now held up to ridicule and everybody connected with the music business was embarrassed when friends, family and mates in the pub started taking the piss. All the senior people at labels, retailers and the BBC felt the need for urgent action and they acted decisively. New brooms were brought in and, with the help of all sides of the music industry, they swept clean. A lot of senior and not-so-senior people lost their jobs as a result. Few came back.

The chart compilation company at the time was, as you might imagine, one of the first casualties of this coup; they were replaced by Gallup. This did a number of things. Firstly, it was a fresh, untainted operation now at the helm and, as we noted, the new company was forward-thinking enough to electrify the process of collating sales information.

Soon after Gallup took over, it tried to stamp on hyping by replacing the chart diaries with the data capture chart machines – not bar-code readers, remember, just a little blue terminal into which the catalogue number of a record was input via a keyboard every time a copy of that record was sold.

But the chart machines provided a great deal more information than the chart diaries. For instance, they noted the time that the sale was made and this helped Gallup hugely in its quest to spot inconsistencies in the data. For instance, if a shop appeared to have done 80% of its week's trading between the hours of two and four on a Sunday morning, there was probably something wrong.

More subtly, Gallup's systems could also identify less obvious anomalies. If, when data was being analysed, there was a big blip in sales in a normally quiet period, Gallup could get on the phone and ask for an explanation. I recall one incident where a quiet little indie shop had a big rise in sales about the same time every Friday afternoon, and all in one transaction. It smelt of something nefarious. Gallup called up to find out what was happening and it turned out to be the local mobile DJ calling in during his lunch hour from his day job to buy his weekly supply of chart discs.

Gallup was concerned by such things because any unusual sales patterns smacked of hyping and this practice, as we noted, is the most illegal of all the illegal practices under the chart rules.

Hyping, in the days of chart diaries, consisted of adding phantom sales to the book. But then, in the days of Gallup's electronic chart machine, it evolved into something called buying-in. This consisted of somebody going round a significant number of shops on the chart panel and buying enough copies of a given single to boost it into the lower reaches of the chart. It sounds simple and it felt simple when there were only two thousand shops on the panel.

A chart-return shop (as those delivering data to Gallup were known) was always apparent because of its little blue box by the till. It didn't, then, take a massive amount of research for a team to tour the country establishing which stores had those magic boxes.

Having done their homework, such teams would then sell their services to unscrupulous artist managers and, on occasion, record companies, to hype a record into the chart. Desperate executives could be seduced into purchasing these services because of the power and influence you gained just by scraping into the bottom reaches of the chart. Let me explain: the Top Fifty singles chart was printed by *Music Week* and distributed to retailers every Tuesday morning. If your single is number forty-nine, you're seen by every record shopkeeper in the country and probably pinned to the wall of the store as well, where customers can see you. But if you're number fifty-one, you're invisible. You ain't in the chart; you ain't in print.

So there is a strong incentive to move a single from fifty-one to forty-nine. However, those trying to achieve that by buying-in failed to count on three things: their own profound stupidity; Gallup's sophistication; and the value to a retailer of having that box on the counter. We'll come to why in a moment.

First, let's look at an example of stupidity. One member of a buying-in team back in 1985 was touring the south coast. He started in Southampton and was working his way gradually east, calling in at every chart-return shop along the way and buying a boxful of copies of, let's say, Girl Snot's new single.

Now, this man looked suspicious. What legitimate customer wants twenty copies of a single in the first place? When have you ever bought more than one copy of a record at a time? Perhaps you bought two, one for yourself and one as a gift, but I'd put money that nobody reading this book has ever bought twenty copies in one go. So a man buying twenty copies of something is immediately suspicious. Now let's assume that the purchaser is a nice, safe, middle-class, middle-aged gent and Girl Snot are the loudest, nastiest, most aggressive and anti-establishment band ever to walk the earth, and there's another reason why the sale is dodgy.

You can imagine that, when this happened for real early in Gallup's tenure, the retailers were aware there was something out of the ordinary. So concerned were they that as soon as this guy had made his first purchase, the first retailer in Southampton called Gallup to report something suspicious. A little while later a call came into Gallup from a chart retailer in Portsmouth, just east along the coast from Southampton. Then came a call from Chichester, then one from Worthing ... The guy was leaving a trail like a snail.

By the time the man got to Brighton, a representative from Gallup was already in the store waiting to talk to him and ask him why his car boot was full of Girl Snot singles. I would have loved to have seen his expression.

Moving on to the second of the reasons why hyping of the buying-in variety invariably failed, we see just how bright Gallup are. This company has been carrying out market research pretty much forever and, even without technology, it can spot patterns. Studying patterns of behaviour is its stock in trade. So, after only a few weeks of sales data from a store, Gallup could see what the patterns for that store were – busy times, slack times, times when rock was popular, times when more pop stuff was sold, etc etc. If there was any unexplained deviation from those patterns, Gallup would ignore that store's data for that week.

When Gallup's contract finally ended – for political reasons other than anything else – it was its chart department's proudest boast that no record had ever been hyped successfully during its tenure of running the chart.

And just to bring us back up to date for a moment, let me say that these days illegally influencing the chart is even more impossible. With pretty much every shop in the country returning data and with massively more sophisticated computer systems now, it is easier to fix the football pools than the charts. That's no exaggeration: there are only a thousand professional footballers on the pitch across the country at any one time and there are four thousand record shops. And the footballers spend much of their time away from the cameras; record stores are monitored all day every day.

OK, now let's go back to the third reason for the failure of hyping, even in the eighties – the value of that little blue box. It's a revealing story. Once again I'm going to begin by mentioning the fact that the primary aim of the music industry is to make bands famous. Only just second to that as a motivation is making a new record a success. Even the biggest names and stars have to work hard to break their new release.

So, back in the days when only two thousand stores were on the chart panel that returned sales data to Gallup, there were only two thousand shops that mattered when you were trying to break a record into the charts. Gallup was simply not taking sales information from anywhere else. This meant that record companies obsessively targeted those shops that were supplying data. Understand: a label could sell a million copies of a single through one outlet but, if that shop was not on the chart panel, nobody would ever know those records had been sold and their contribution to chart standing would be completely lost. It's like a football team aiming to be League champions through winning all their friendly matches.

Conversely, every record sold through a chart-return shop scored points for the label and helped propel the record up the chart. So, just like a football team, the labels concentrated hard on the important, points-scoring places and put a lot less effort into the others.

Thus, once the labels had located the chart-return shops – which took about ten minutes on a Monday morning – they regularly gave these stores singles free or at a very modest cost. There were two reason for this:

1. If the retailer doesn't have to pay for the singles, he or she is much more likely to take them into the store.
2. If they're free or very cheap, the retailer can then sell them below the usual price. If a single is in a store at a reduced price, a customer is more likely to buy it than if it is a premium-price product.

Record companies would strain to the limits of their ability to get their records into and then sold by chart-return stores. This gave those shops a great deal of power, and power is a thing that indie stores, by their nature, lack; those indies with a chart machine enjoyed the experience very much, in both human and commercial terms. I mean, how far wrong can you go when every major label is offering you free stock every day?

So, the competition to get and then keep one of Gallup's magic boxes was intense. That's why all stores were always on the lookout for suspicious behaviour. The threat of being taken off the chart panel always hung over them if they were seen to be turning a blind eye to dodgy practices – and being off the panel could mean the difference between being in business and not. Thus, Gallup had two thousand pairs of eyes and ears on the ground looking out for the villains.

OK, that's enough on hyping. Now, happily turning our back on the villains, let's look at the legitimate side of the rules – a place where the intensity of competition drives people to extreme efforts and extreme measures. But let me emphasise that, because hyping is a thing of the past, though the battle for a place in the chart remains utterly merciless, it is now conducted entirely on the right side of the rules. I said earlier in the chapter that this battle is like Formula 1 racing. It is, in that there are things definitely outside the laws – hyping – but, within the rules on what is acceptable, there are teams of bright people working out just what they can get away with and how to do it better and slicker than the other guys. Labels will do almost anything to get an advantage in the race to the charts. Let me show you what I mean.

Chart rules state that record companies are not allowed to give away gifts of any value with a single. Were it not for that, labels would hand out a free fiver with every disc just to get it in the chart. So, because the rules say there must be no gifts of any value, the issue of what is or is not a gift of value has been hotly debated and the rules have been tested time and again as labels seek that winning edge. Some years ago Phonogram (now Mercury) gave away concert tickets with a single, arguing that a promotional ticket has no value. That one didn't go down too well with the guardians of the charts' integrity, as you can imagine.

Another device now outlawed was the old double-packing technique, where labels would use the success of one single to boost the new one. This is how it worked. Say the Miracle Trees have a hit with 'Man, Don't Be A Dog', which has a catalogue number of DOG1. 'Man, Don't Be A Dog' goes to

THE CHARTS

number three, then starts to drop down the chart. Now, a falling single is neither use nor ornament because the TV and radio shows are interested only in songs that are climbing. But it takes a couple of weeks for a single to drop out of the chart completely and the labels exploited this.

So, the Miracle Trees' new single, the follow-up to 'Man, Don't Be A Dog' is 'Cat for Cat's Sake', with a catalogue number of CAT1. The label releases 'Cat For Cat's Sake' as a double package with 'Man, Don't Be A Dog' during the couple of weeks that 'Man, Don't Be A Dog' is dropping down the chart. That is, they are shrink-wrapped together and you can buy them only as a unit. But the catalogue number on this unit is CAT1. So, every time somebody buys 'Man, Don't Be A Dog' – and this is still a chart single, remember – they get a free 'Cat For Cat's Sake' with it and the catalogue number CAT1 is entered into the machine, thereby chalking up a sale for 'Cat For Cat's Sake'.

This may sound abominably complicated but I mention it to show the efforts labels put in to get their material in the charts. In Formula 1, every year the racing bosses set the rules for specifications and every year the teams make their cars go faster within those rules, so the rules are changed again ... It's the same story in the record business.

At this point we should have a look at just who makes the rules for the UK charts. Well, the charts are a joint venture between the BPI, the BBC, the BARD and trade paper *Music Week's* chart arm, the Official UK Charts Company. The rules are made by a committee which features all these people, though the BPI's voice is the loudest. Indeed, the BPI has its own internal committee just to deal with these matters and, should any label be found to be breaking the rules, that's where it has to go to plead its case and hear its punishment. Where, then, does all this leave the chart today? Well, in essence, healthier than it has ever been.

Throughout this chapter what I have meant by the word 'chart' is the official charts – that is, those that say 'The

Official UK Charts Company' somewhere on them. This enterprise is backed by all the big players, has the monopoly on the most authoritative information – the EPOS sales figures from all the retailers in the country – and if its systems can be bettered, I'd like to see it.

There are, though, plenty of other charts in the country. For instance, the Pepsi chart used by independent radio and television. Though not as definitive as the official chart, this has already had a major impact in that its instigation persuaded the official players to get their finger out and bring forward the publication of the official chart from Tuesday to Sunday. This happened when the independent broadcasters' Pepsi chart was first launched. It billed itself as the fastest chart on air and, because it went out a couple of days before the official chart, it certainly was. You can imagine, though, how that claim of being the fastest stung the big boys, and their response was to streamline and speed up their own operation.

This makes the official chart as it now stands hotter, more accurate, more contemporary and far more interesting than it has ever been. Its up-to-dateness is astounding: purchases made up to teatime on Saturday are included in a chart released at teatime the following day. Because of this, the chart remains the greatest marketing tool ever invented, as I said earlier. Why so? Because it promotes current new product through so many and disparate media – in the stores, on TV and radio, in every music magazine and much of the national media. Once you're in the chart you are big everywhere, which is why there is so much competition to get into the chart in the first place. And the exposure comes not just from the Official UK Charts Company chart but all those other charts – the Pepsi chart, mainly – that are compiled with varying degrees of skill and veracity by the media around the country.

In fact, the BPI has often discussed getting out of the charts business altogether. Some of its members have argued that there are so many people putting charts together that the BPI need not go to the time and expense of being involved with creating one of its own. Other voices, though, have prevailed, and these say there needs to be one credible listing and that the BPI needs to have some control over it.

While the BPI has partners in the charts, it has always been an irony that it is both gamekeeper and poacher here. Its members make up the rules for the chart, police the implementation of those rules and also, as they compete in their day-to-day businesses, test those rules to destruction.

Still, chart scandals are a lot less these days than they used to be, largely because hyping and buying-in are virtually impossible under the new systems and because, frankly, the industry has moved on from that type of nonsense.

Chapter 13

GOVERNMENTS AND POLITICS

WHY ON EARTH DO politicians give the music business such a hard time? When I was director of communications for the BPI in the middle of two government inquiries, I used to ask that question regularly. The only answer I ever got was: because that's the way it always has been.

Seems it's a fairly popular way, too. No politician has ever lost votes by saying CDs, and music in general, are too expensive. Indeed, when politicians say music is unfairly overpriced, there is no public outcry along the lines of: 'But what about the mechanical royalty and tax element you seem to have ignored, and how about investment in the future creativity of the business? Where's that going to come from if the record companies have no money to invest?'

But why do politicians hate rock 'n' roll so much? Well, like most hatred, it stems from ignorance. The Establishment – a term I use to encompass the likes of financial institutions, the bulk of politicians and some of the most serious movers and shakers in our society – does not understand the business of music. That is not a statement I have made up. It is a provable truth. Let me give you some of that proof.

Richard Branson floated his Virgin Group – then consisting mainly of music stores and record companies – on the stock exchange, meaning that his organisation was now at the mercy of financial institutions such as the merchant banks, insurance companies, pensions funds and what have you. Not long afterwards he withdrew the company back into the private sector. Why? Because, he said at the time, the City of London and all its financial bodies did not understand his business well enough to allow him to trade effectively.

And His Richardness Sir Branson of Balloon is only the largest of a number of music industry entrepreneurs to say the same thing. Indeed, the first music group to be floated in the UK came to the market only in the second half of the eighties. Some other companies in other sectors have had their shares traded for more than a century, so the markets had only a very late introduction to the ways of the music industry – and they made absolutely no effort to catch up on what they had missed.

How do I know this? Because they never asked any senior figure within the music industry how the business operates, thinks and trades. Certainly, the City and its institutions know about the law and copyright issues, but they did nothing whatsoever to find out about trading dynamics, personalities, interactions or just how things work in the real world. That strikes me as either negligence or arrogance (or both) on a grand scale. And, back in those days, there was no splendid little book like this to help them out.

Now, I've discussed the City to this extent not only to illustrate the level of ignorance of the good old pop 'n' roll business within the Square Mile itself, but also because the City and government are closely linked. The interchange of personnel between the two connects them, as do their sharing of intimate information and the belief that they are the ones running the country.

How, then, do governments react to the music industry?

Well, in large measure, about as well as the City – though that has changed in recent years, and there's more on this later.

Historically, it was a sad tale of ignorance, bigotry and bewilderment.

My old boss at the BPI, John Deacon, spent much of his time just telling new civil servants and ministers what the music industry was. He was not giving in-depth briefings to informed folks about the things needed for the continuing creativity of the British business, but merely telling them what record companies are, what publishers do, what's an indie and stuff like that. What he had to outline were things that were significantly less sophisticated and intellectually challenging than the stuff you have read earlier in this book.

Why? Because the government department that looks after music – National Heritage under the Tories in the eighties and nineties, Culture as I write this under Labour – has never been one of the most important departments. Ministers and civil servants often see it as a stepping stone on their way up or as a quiet backwater when they are put out to grass after being demoted from a more senior position: witness Virginia Bottomley, who was appointed head of National Heritage after being sacked as Health Secretary.

Let's look more closely at the Ginny Bottomley situation. After the humiliation of being dismissed from her high-profile post at the Department of Health and, certainly in the public perception, relegated to a backwater, do we think that her heart and soul and every ounce of her energies were committed to the concept of enhancing the nation's cultural life and creative industries? If they were, she is a better human being than I am. If it had been me in that position, I would have wandered round in a sulk for a month – and I'd have been angry for even longer than that at the thought of the public humiliation of it all.

So, even if she was fantastically well motivated, Ginny had had her head in the health service for the preceding few years and therefore came to National Heritage knowing next to bugger all about the music business. Good old John Deacon – the most patient man I ever met – then had to set about his education task once more and Ginny, in the middle of the huge number of distractions a minister and an MP has to face (including imminent election defeat), then had to concentrate her mind on the task of listening intently to all the things John was saying. Not easy.

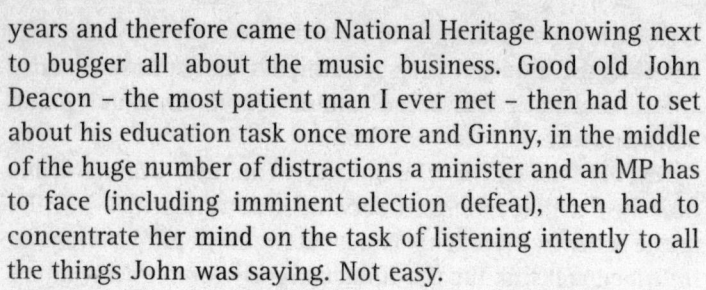

Even with the best of intentions, governments don't always understand the challenges the music industry faces and the conditions it needs to prosper. And governments don't always have the best of intentions.

I suppose at some point we have to discuss the old CD prices inquiry thing, and this seems like as good a time as any. But let's do some of the background first. As we've seen, government attitudes to the music industry have not always been helpful, and politicians – particularly those of the last Conservative administration – are not known for their closeness to music industry issues.

(While I was at the BPI, we had a Tory trade minister visit us. He toured the building and, just as he was about to enter my office, a flustered BPI colleague came in and told me to remove the pictures of the heavy-metal bands I had on my wall. Shocked, I refused, and when the minister came in I made a point of telling him that Iron Maiden – a band signed to EMI – were making more money for the UK's balance of payments than some of the EMI Group's more mainstream activities, things like light bulbs and television rentals. His face was an absolute mask of incomprehension. Not that he didn't understand the words; but public-school-educated, army-trained and Conservative-committed as he was, there was no room in his brain for the fact that hairy, sweaty, tattooed heavy-metal musos could be good for the country. He hated the idea and had a face like thunder when he left my office. Oh, and lest you think this is an anti-Tory rant, it ain't just that. Read on ...)

GOVERNMENTS AND POLITICS

Back in the early nineties, government was distant from rock 'n' roll and held the industry in pretty low regard. I think the image of the business in politicians' minds stemmed largely from two things:

1. How the industry is portrayed in the media, with only the glam things and/or the naughty antics of its stars generally making the headlines.
2. The fact that the music industry has never received a penny of taxpayers' money in subsidies and, unlike the film industry, wasn't constantly going to government with the begging bowl pleading poverty in the face of competition from all those naughty foreigners who keep making more popular films than us.

Though this second point sounds like it ought to have the opposite effect, it actually alienated politicians. It was precisely because the business was capable of standing on its own two feet that the people at Westminster in 1991 and 1992 started getting the idea that it was more opulent and overfed than it should be. Seizing on this political – and, by extension, public – mood, a number of journalists at the *Independent on Sunday* and *Which?* magazine then added fuel to the flames with their constant claims that the music industry was full of fat cats who were taking the cream by keeping CD prices artificially high. Though the BPI tried to counter this with the truth about finances in the industry, public opinion became a powder keg.

The spark that finally ignited that volatile mixture could not have come in more incongruous circumstances. There we were, one glorious Wednesday morning, near Sloane Square, relaxed and content in the sunshine in this extremely posh part of London, when, without warning, the explosion hit. And it happened like this ...

Sir Malcolm Field, managing director of WH Smith, was at the press conference to announce the company's results. Though I can't remember the exact conversation, I can recall a journalist pushing him on why WH Smith's results for the period were so desperate. Sir Malcolm, an utterly charming man and lovely human being, but not a person who I ever saw think effectively on his feet, started casting around for reasons. The one he came up with was: 'Because record companies make CDs too expensive.'

Cripes (or words to that effect), I thought, now there's trouble.

A-ha! That's the truth, then! thought the politicians.

Already genuinely motivated by their own uninformed gut feeling that the record companies were running a villainous cartel, the politicos heard Sir Malcolm Field's words like a clarion call. And, fired by their beliefs and also, of course, by the knowledge that their public standing would, in this climate, be enhanced by launching an investigation into those naughty record companies, they started to conceive their plans.

Within what felt like moments, the National Heritage Select Committee – a cross-party body of MPs chaired by the dapper if somewhat physically alarming Labour MP Gerald Kaufman – announced that it was mounting an investigation into CD prices. Then, a few moments after that, the Office of Fair Trading (as was) said it was to hold an inquiry into 'the supply of recorded music in the UK', which everyone read as an inquiry into CD prices.

The BPI was obliged to respond to both these things simultaneously. Making a gargantuan effort, it marshalled its arguments and awaited a forum in which it could present them. As the organisation's director of communications at the time, I, like my colleagues, was acutely aware that it was not going to be an easy ride and that if we got a fair hearing we could count ourselves very lucky.

For me, the tone was set when I was doing a radio interview about these issues. My opponent from the Consumers' Association – a guy I was utterly sick of after arguing the toss with him fourteen times in the same day –

made his argument on air about how record companies were making enormous and unreasonable profits from CDs. At the end of this speech, the presenter said, 'Yes, that's right. What you've said there is right.' This presenter, I thought, an influential man, has not done any research, has not even listened to what I've got to say, yet has decided already that the other guy is right. And that was the tone not just for that interview, but for the rest of the campaign. In every public forum the BPI and the record companies got earache.

Mr Kaufman's National Heritage Select Committee maintained the theme. While the BPI was waiting for its day before the committee, a whole string of its opponents appeared before the group – and on television – to make their claim that the labels were in league with one another and with the devil.

It was a sight the BPI did not enjoy, for the sole reason that it all seemed a little too cosy. While the organisation understood clearly that its opponents were entitled to put their case, the feeling was that Mr Kaufman was making life far too easy for them. To the labels, it appeared that every statement arguing for cheaper CDs was welcomed as profound wisdom and guided serenely into the committee's records by a host of parliamentary angels.

Whether that was an accurate perception, only history will tell us.

What is not a matter of conjecture, though, is what happened on the day the labels were asked to give their evidence. Let me set the scene ...

When the committee sat to hear the record industry's arguments, appearing before it were BPI leading lights Maurice Oberstein, Roger Ames and David Clipsham, all heads of major labels. But, from the outset, the questioning of these guys was hostile and aggressive. Whereas statements from their opponents had gone largely unchallenged, these men got the hardest time I have seen. Instead of pressing them to get at the truth, Mr Kaufman simply harangued them and told them they were wrong. Not much of a way to extract the facts, in my view. In contrast, as a newsman over the past twenty-five years, I have found that the best way to get facts from people is to listen quietly and sympathetically and ask insightful questions here and there. Mr Kaufman just delivered a public bollocking to people he had judged long before he had heard anything they had to say.

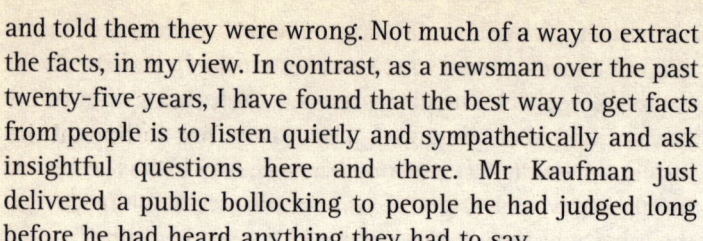

It's a good job he didn't know anything about these guys. Trinidadian Ames is the most placid and relaxed man I have ever met, but he had an expression that day that said: 'I'm going to rip Kaufman's head off.' It's always the guys with the longest fuses who end up going most ballistic when they go, and that day Ames's fuse was nearly at the end of its decades-long slow burn. But he didn't explode, and maintained an outward calm throughout the proceedings. Shame. A bare-handed beheading in a House of Commons committee room would have made great telly.

The hearing came and went and the committee, as expected, later issued a report saying that the labels were all evil scum (or something similar). Commons committee reports, though, don't count for a lot in the real world and the BPI wasn't unduly concerned about it – particularly as the real fight was just beginning. While the National Heritage Select Committee had been conducting its public humiliation, the Office of Fair Trading was calmly, quietly and, more importantly, privately considering the facts of this CD prices business. Having done so, it decided that the best place for all the complex issues to be discussed and analysed was the Monopolies and Mergers Commission (MMC) and it referred the matter to its big brother.

When this was announced, it was my duty to say in public that the BPI welcomed the inquiry. I say to you now that this was entirely true. After what was felt to be a kangaroo court under Mr Kaufman, the BPI reckoned the calm, measured analysis of the MMC was the way in which the true facts could finally be made known.

So it was. When the MMC started work, it wanted to know only the facts – no politics, no spin, no show, just the facts. But it wanted to know all the facts, which meant the record industry had to respond with a massive effort to find all the answers. The MMC's teams of investigators grilled execs by interview, by questionnaire and by directly looking at the processes involved in selling music – and they did it every working day (and some others) for six months. Now, this is my kind of inquiry: calm, quiet, methodical, thorough. It strikes me as a much better way of getting at the truth than Mr Kaufman's method of sitting in a committee room and shouting at a man who wants to kill you for your impudence.

So, having looked at all the facts and having delved in detail into the business of music and how it really works, what did the Monopolies and Mergers Commission conclude? Did it decide that the record companies were working in collusion to keep CD prices artificially high, or did it conclude that the labels were engaged in cut-throat competition and that CDs were at a reasonable price the market will bear? The latter, of course.

Why 'of course'? Because any bimbo who knows anything about the way the business really works knows that two record company heads in a pub couldn't agree whose round it is, so the chances of them getting together to fix prices was, is and always will be truly absurd.

(I once witnessed the most adolescent, testosterone-fuelled argument between a major-label president and his opposite number from another company, a chairman. Like stags locking horns to prove dominance, they spent quite some time debating whether president or chairman was the higher, more prestigious title. Now, if two men can't agree on which of them has the grander moniker, they are unlikely to agree on a strategy for keeping prices as high as possible.)

On the other side of the coin, it was certainly true that labels were charging a premium price for a premium product. But, as a man whose income has never been above the national average, I look at it this way. A CD is around £16. That's not enough for a night in the pub and a curry on the way home. Even if it was, a night in the pub and a curry are gone in hours. The disc I am listening to as I type this has been giving me pleasure for the past ten years and, provided I keep it in reasonable condition, will give me equal pleasure for another fifty. That's not bad for a product that cost £16. What else could you spend your money on that will still be giving you fun when today's teenagers have become the cantankerous middle-aged?

How did this fallacy about CD prices arise? Simply put – I say it again – it arose from ignorance. The argument that CDs were too expensive used to run like this: a CD costs less than a pound to make but costs £16 in the shops, so the record companies are making £15 from each disc.

Well, let's have a look at this with a little more sophistication. Firstly, the price in the stores has absolutely nothing to do with the record companies. Retailers set retail prices. Certainly, the wholesale price from the label has an impact on this, but the actual price we consumers pay is determined by Mr HMV and Mr Virgin and Mr Woolworth and their colleagues in the retail business (who, it should be noted, all compete fiercely to be the shop to offer the lowest price; these gentlemen watch one another like hawks and expend every effort they can to be the cheapest in town).

So, at a time when CDs were around £16 in store, those discs were leaving record companies at a list price of around £8 – and, often, as a result of bulk-order discounts, at an actual price much, much lower than that. Even so, it is easy to say that a disc costing £1 to press selling for £8 still leaves a substantial profit for the label. And, yes, it would, if that were the case. But pressing a disc is only one cost of many. The single biggest of those costs, of course, is the A&R and marketing budget that goes into it. Every album is backed by a marketing campaign of one size or another, and a big TV promotion costs millions. This money must be recouped and then some, otherwise the label goes out of business. In addition, the costs of finding, nurturing, developing and launching new acts is, as we are aware, enormous.

In the music industry this process is, of course, known as A&R. In other industries it is called R&D, research and development, and in business in general it is seen as essential investment to keep an industry viable into a future fraught with unknown pitfalls and beset by fickle consumers and massive competition.

Now, if A&R costs in music equate to R&D in other sectors, the record industry – as a proportion of income – spends more on R&D than the pharmaceutical industry does. A&R, then, is a huge cost – and one that is unavoidable. If record companies stop spending on A&R, where is our next generation of talent going to come from? Labels must seek it out and develop it, then record it and market it if we consumers are ever to hear it.

In addition to having to pay for A&R – and all the tedious things that record companies have to face, like rent, council tax, staff costs, power and water bills – labels, it must be remembered, don't own the music on the records they release. They merely own the recording. That means that they have to pay each time they use the music – and that comes in the form of the mechanical royalties we looked at in detail in Chapter 4. So, by the time a label has paid its A&R and marketing costs, its mechanical royalties and staff wages, there is not a lot left over from the £8 wholesale price of a CD – and often there is nothing left over; remember nine out of ten albums released makes a loss.

And there is one final element in a CD price that nobody, except the government, wants: tax. It is an irony that magazines are deemed to be a cultural good and therefore attract no Value Added Tax (VAT) but records are not a cultural good so get VAT at 17.5%. This means that 17.5% –

or nearly one fifth – of the retail price of every CD goes straight into the government's coffers. And what does the government give back to the music industry in financial terms? Absolutely, totally, utterly bugger all. As we noted earlier in this chapter, the music industry gets not one pound, euro or Matabele cocoa bean from the government in any form of subsidy.

And finally, just as the ultimate irony, may I ask you to consider this. Because magazines are deemed to be a cultural good, no VAT is paid on all those shiny tomes on the top shelf of your local newsagent, yet CDs of Beethoven's symphonies are not a cultural good and VAT is payable at 17.5%. *Big Ones International* is cultural, Beethoven is not. Discuss.

But what's the music industry's relationship with the UK government like now? Better – for two reasons.

The shallowest of these is Tony Blair's personal connections with the pop 'n' roll business. A friend of his during his formative years as a politician was John Preston, long-time head of BMG UK and a former chairman of the BPI. Because they were friends and political allies and John Preston's wife worked in Tony Blair's office, our present prime minister was closely aware of record industry attitudes and concerns.

In addition to this, he is a lot more rock-'n'-roll than previous prime ministers. Having been in a student band and being of a generation that grew up with the Beatles and the Stones, he is a lot more connected to contemporary music than all of his predecessors. And if it turns out that John Major is a closet headbanger with an extensive collection of Judas Priest records that he used as background music for shagging Edwina Currie, I am prepared to stand corrected.

However, seeing the look of transported delight on Tony's face when the BPI presented him with one of Eric Clapton's old guitars convinced me that, in his heart, he is truly one of us. I can imagine his predecessors in that high office

GOVERNMENTS AND POLITICS

being politely grateful for such a gift, but Tony nearly wet himself. Good on yer, son. So you should. Not many people get such an honour.

There is, though, a much larger reason why all governments since 1994 have taken the music industry much more seriously: money.

It all goes back to a brilliant idea from a music publisher called Andrew Potter. Andrew decided the government could be impressed if the true financial worth of the music industry to the country could be identified and he set about collating every penny the music business earns from exports. He put into his calculations sales of British albums abroad, income from Lord Lloyd Webber's musicals in New York, sales of UK-made musical instruments around the world and the kitchen sink.

Eventually, Andrew came up with a figure of £2 billion, showing music to be the third biggest invisible exporter after tourism and insurance – and therefore bigger than shipbuilding and steel put together and utterly eclipsing a lot of industries that the government held in much higher esteem.

Faced with such concrete facts, the government performed a U-turn. Conservative ministers, as they were at the time, went from being utterly opposed to the long-haired, tattooed, drug-taking yobs (as they saw it) in the music industry to being impressed by what these people achieved.

The evidence of that political about-face is clear. Before 1994 nobody from the world of contemporary music had been knighted – well, not for their music contributions anyway, though Bob Geldof did get an honorary knighthood for his charity work with Live Aid (and, please note that, as an Irish citizen, he is not Sir Bob). Now, though, we have gongs just for being a muso. Witness Sir Cliff Richard, Sir Elton John, Sir Paul McCartney, Sir George Martin, Sir Mick Jagger and, I hope, a few others who have been added to that list since I wrote this.

Because of the efforts of the BPI and the brilliant

inspiration of Andrew Potter, the music industry is now getting some of the respect it always deserved. Took about a hundred years too long, though.

And just as a little postscript, Andrew Potter has said to me a couple of times that I helped him significantly in the early stages of that report. Andrew, I have to confess: when you called, I thought it was a mad idea and I was just trying to get you off the phone. It's taken me this long to see the true genius of what you did. Nice one, sir.

Chapter 14

MAJORS AND INDIES

THE SIMPLE WAY OF separating majors from indies is to define them by size: one is a lot bigger than the other. But hidden in that statement are divisions which go far deeper than the eye can see and penetrate every level of thinking, policy and action.

Let's look at those different ways of thinking for a moment, and, to give the most graphic illustration, we'll take two retailers as our example.

The ultimate indie retailer in my view is Andy Gray. But how does Andy run Europe's biggest indie retail chain? What is the management structure? Well, being an indie, that structure is very nice and very, very simple. Three people make all the management policy decisions for Andys Records: Andy, his brother Billy and the finance man. That's it. Three people and no scope for political factions to develop (particularly as two of those people share the same mum and dad) and very little room for damaging political conflicts.

At the other end of the spectrum, let's take HMV UK. HMV UK is part of an enormous group of companies. Not only is that group big, but it is a public company. This means it has shareholders – and that means that not even the boss is master in his own house.

Andy and Billy Gray can decide today to sell the chain and move to Thailand and they can start the process of putting the shops on the market before the sun goes down. Or they can decide to sell half their stores and have it done before the end of the month. Or they can decide to get out of the music industry altogether and become Britain's largest porn retailer within a few weeks.

In contrast, the boss of HMV can do only what shareholders will accept and has to justify his actions to his own boss, the chairman of the parent company, on a regular basis. If the chairman of the parent company decides to sell HMV or close half the stores, there is only so much the boss of HMV can do about it. Though the boss of HMV has massive power and control of the tactical and strategic activities of the chain, he still has people to answer to; only Andy and Billy Gray are truly masters in their own house (unless their mum comes round).

Some while ago Andy told me that the secret of being happy and successful in business is never borrowing money. If you owe money to the banks, they have a say in how you run your business. If you owe nothing to anybody anywhere, you may do as you please – a luxury a company with shareholders, each of whom has both a voice and a stake in the business, never has.

This concept of indie and major goes further still: there is no part of what a company does that is not affected by whether it is an indie or a major. Let's stay with retailers for a while to see more about how that works.

First of all, let's establish who is who. To illustrate what I'm saying, let me create an archetypal indie shop: Independent Discs and Tapes in Brighton. It is a two-person operation, owned by husband-and-wife partners Tony and Denise Williams. The store is on the edge of the city's main shopping area because that's as close as Tony and Denise can afford to get to the action.

Five hundred metres from Independent Discs and Tapes is the local HMV. This large, glossy shop is in the middle of the city's shopping centre and is seen by many thousands of people every day.

Right at their most basic decision, then – that of location – the indie and the major diverge. For both Independent Discs and Tapes and HMV, their decisions are almost made for them.

As we have seen earlier and as is exemplified again here, Tony and Denise, as indie retailers, can't afford the rent on a big, swanky central location. They have already taken out a significant loan just to get the store trading on any basis and their modest outlet on the edge of the main shopping area is as far as their money will stretch.

HMV, in contrast, can go nowhere else but the main shopping mall. Its stores are lavishly appointed, expensively stocked and extensively advertised and it absolutely needs to be in the heart of the shopping centre to ensure it gets the customer traffic to justify all that investment.

OK, having decided where to be, both these stores then have to decide what to stock. HMV's decisions are largely made centrally. That is, one person at head office in London will order all the chart stock for the whole country. That person will also order the main catalogue items – *Dark Side Of The Moon*, *Thriller*, *Sergeant Pepper*, *Bat Out Of Hell* and so on – and much of the more contemporary stock as well. The manager of the Brighton store will certainly have input, though; it will be his or her job to tell head office which bands are big locally, if the city's football club has a single or a video released and generally what conditions and tastes prevail in the city. But the local manager determines what happens at the margin, not the core policy.

Tony and Denise Williams, on the other hand, have a completely free hand. They have a store in which the racks are entirely bare and the decor is white and neutral. They have to make all their own decisions about what to put in the shop. Aware from the start that it is folly to get in the ring with

HMV – they can't compete on price or depth of stock – Tony and Denise decide to fight a different fight. They decide to take only indie label stock. Though indie labels cover every style and genre of music, Tony and Denise believe people will identify enough with the indie concept to want to come to their store. They decide not to stock indie classical, jazz and folk but fill up the store with indie rock, pop and dance. Checking in HMV, they realise only a tiny fraction of what they plan to stock can also be found in the local major chain stores, and they are greatly encouraged by that.

They start to believe they have a winning concept as they are not competing head to head with HMV and Virgin and are instead offering music that cannot be found elsewhere in the city. In contrast with HMV and its chain-wide design, Tony and Denise decorate the inside of the store themselves in colours and concepts intended to reflect their indie consciousness.

As time goes on, both HMV and Independent Discs and Tapes find they are making a reasonable profit – reasonable being hugely different amounts to these different sets of people, of course. And that concept of reasonable is not only different amounts, but is measured by entirely different criteria at these two stores.

Tony and Denise go home each evening and discuss what they've got, what they need to invest in new stock, rent, maintenance and electricity and suchlike, then what they can take out of their income to buy food, pay the mortgage on the house and, if they're very lucky, take a holiday. When they look at their income, they can also decide on whether they can afford some advertising or a little promotional campaign.

The manager of HMV sends his accounts to head office each week. It is there that decisions are made on advertising budgets and promotions, many of which are handled on a national level. The manager is also told how much he can spend on staff and pressure is put on him to keep sales high and costs low. Indeed, the measure of him as an employee, and with it his prospects for advancing up the management chain, is almost entirely how much money his store makes.

Tony and Denise have that pressure to make money, too, but in their case it is because if they don't make money and if they fail to pay the mortgage on their house, they will be out on the streets.

It is easy to see that the manager of HMV and the owners of an independent store think in entirely different ways. Though their desire to make money is the same, one is motivated by pressure from his superiors and his ambition to rise higher in the company and the other two are motivated by keeping a roof over their head and feeding their children. I believe that creates different responses and different thinking, in both commercial and human terms.

Moving on to record companies, here, too, there are massively different ways of thinking, acting and trading, depending on which side of the indie-major divide you sit.

Location, though, is not so much of an issue here. Email, the Internet, phones and the good old-fashioned post mean that, wherever you are, you're connected to the rest of the world. An indie label, though, will find life more difficult if it is based in Preston rather than London, simply because it is away from the major media and the music industry milieu. However, being in London doesn't mean you have to have offices in posh places like Park Lane. All the leading indies do well working out of offices away from the West End and some even thrive from premises in the less salubrious parts of town (which is a euphemism for the kind of places where even the Alsatians go round in pairs).

So, even if an indie has chosen relatively modest offices in a relatively modest part of town, as soon as it puts in basic things like phones and a Net connection, it is entirely equipped to go about the business of A&R and actually signing some acts.

As we have noted, indies operate in all areas and styles of music and often flourish by doing so. In fact, it is a wise move for an indie to try to work in a niche market, as we saw in Chapter 7, but, unlike indie retailers, indie labels are not precluded from taking on the majors. Let's look at a tale of two indies to see what we mean, and we'll stick with a couple of hypothetical old friends to do it.

Tony and Denise Williams sell Independent Discs and Tapes and get divorced, both realising that they could attract a younger, prettier partner with the money they now have at their disposal. Separately, they both decide to use some of the cash from the sale to set up a label.

Tony is a fan of deep turbo nutter bastard folk, a genre which he believes is emerging in popularity but has yet to be discovered by mainstream A&R staff. He decides he is going to operate in this field while the going is good, so he signs two of the hottest deep turbo nutter bastard folk acts he knows and spends money on recording their respective debut albums.

Once these are recorded, pressed and packaged (most likely at an independently owned plant offering its services in these areas), Tony goes about selling the albums to the rest of the deep turbo nutter bastard folk fans. Though the market is small, he has it to himself and so makes a tidy profit on both albums. He then uses that profit to try to break out of this niche and bring deep turbo nutter bastard folk to a wider audience by advertising in the music press and also by hiring a plugging company to work for him. Plugging is, remember, the art of getting media interested in your product. There are companies which specialise in this and, just like the pressers, sell their services to those who need them.

But it is important to bear in mind that Tony's power to bring attention to this new musical form and his ability to advertise and promote it is severely limited by an important factor: money. Tony is, of course, an indie and, like all indies, his resources are relatively modest (if they weren't, we'd call him a major, of course). The only money he has to spend is what he made from selling his record shop, plus anything else he can scrape together, and he ain't going to set the world on fire with that kind of cash. If he is lucky, though, he might just light a spark.

Now, as with everything else in the music industry, there are both advantages and disadvantages in the commercial direction that Tony has chosen for his label – that of breaking new musical ground. His advantage is that he is number one in a field of one. If people want deep turbo nutter bastard folk music records, they have to come to him. The disadvantage is that not many do. If Tony tries to increase his sales by breaking this style of music into the mainstream, it can be a long, expensive task and, at the end of it, the media and, by extension, us punters may still be no more interested than we were at the beginning – that is, not at all.

Let's now take a look at an alternative possible route to success for an indie label by revisiting Denise, Tony's ex-wife and business partner. Denise has decided on a different path for her label. She believes that being in a genre that consumers are already familiar with, mainstream rock-pop, holds the greatest potential and therefore the greatest rewards. She knows that, because most records bought are in this area, she doesn't have to take a particularly big share of this market to become an even wealthier woman.

However, Denise also knows that the majors operate mainly in this market (though a major operates in all markets all the time, of course) but she believes that, because the public are so familiar with this style, there is room for everybody in it. So she spends the next eight months on the road looking for an act to sign. Then, having found a good, pretty, hard-working four-piece band, she records their debut album and begins marketing it.

Because of the competitive field in which she is working, Denise has invested more money in the infrastructure of her label than Tony and has set up an in-house team of pluggers, who are employed by her and work exclusively for her. Once the album by her first band is complete, she sends off her promotions staff to the main radio stations with the finished product. The album is, the radio producers admit, a slick and interesting product. However, it is not as slick and interesting as a similar album by an act signed to Universal which has had a hundred times as much spent on its recording and development.

Denise, though, still manages to sell enough to cover her costs and make a modest surplus by taking the music to the more indie-oriented magazines and radio programmes. These hit a much smaller section of the record-buying public than the prime-time, mainstream outlets, but enough people buy Denise's records to keep her in the comfort to which she has become accustomed.

She also plans to use her profit to sign another mainstream act and to record a second album by the first band. If these next two albums also bring in a reasonable return – and, it has to be said, scoring a profit on your first three releases is a bit like three lottery wins in a row – she will continue releasing and continuing investing and her label and earnings will grow and grow.

OK, so there's two happy indies trying to live happily ever after.

Now let's look at these two scenarios from a major label's point of view. By looking at the other side of coin, I hope to demonstrate just how majors think, behave and operate differently to indies.

Major record companies, like all record companies, are constantly on the lookout for anything new; their A&R departments are driven by a whole raft of burning desires, as we saw in Chapter 5. The major labels relentlessly seek new bands in both existing genres and new genres. They expend huge effort in searching out anything that is likely, in their view, to sell records.

So, if Tony Williams starts putting out records in the deep turbo nutter bastard folk genre, the major labels will be watching like hawks to see what happens. If Tony begins having success, the majors will do one of two things: either they will look for their own deep turbo nutter bastard folk act or they will go to Tony and ask to get involved in his. Such involvement might mean buying all or part of the label – if Tony is willing to sell – or handling one of the infrastructure functions, such as distribution, sales or marketing.

Majors, though, are not averse to using their financial clout to buy an indie company just to get their hands on one act on its roster. But this is not some gross misuse of economic power: nobody is holding a gun to the head of the owner of the indie company and making him sell. He is selling because the amount of money offered to him is attractive. And often the amount being offered is very tempting indeed. Just like it was when Warner Music bought Magnet Records simply because it wanted Chris Rea, who was signed to the label. But while I would not criticise a major for making such a purchase, I do raise a question mark about what happens thereafter. In this case, all the other Magnet artists and staff and offices gradually disappeared once the label and Chris Rea had been acquired. (And a small additional fact for you: the founder and owner of Magnet was Michael Levy, who, as Lord Levy, went on to be a Foreign Office minister in the Labour government. Not bad going for an East End boy who made good in the music industry. Nice one, Michael.)

So, if Tony's deep turbo nutter bastard folk is truly a successful genre, the majors will get into it, one way or another: they will either do it themselves or they will get involved, in whole or in part, with Tony. If, however, deep turbo nutter bastard folk remains tiny, it will not be worth their while and they will let Tony and others of his size have it to themselves.

Now, in Denise's mainstream rock-pop, the majors are already there and, in fact, consider this their own home ground. A new label entering the arena is not going to worry the majors too much. Their bread and butter is finding, developing, marketing and promoting talent in this area and not only do they have plenty of money to spend on it, they are also hugely experienced in their work. EMI is now over a hundred years old and in that time has built up a massive bank of expertise.

So, EMI and the other majors have more money than Denise, more A&R staff on the ground and, yes, more experience and expertise. Meaning that she's on a hiding to nothing, right? Well, not necessarily.

A&R people can't be everywhere all the time and if Denise is bright and looks for her new act in places where the majors aren't represented, she has a chance. She has even more of a chance if the act she signs is musically wonderful. Music is, remember, the heart, the soul, the core, the *raison d'être* of the music business.

Assuming that Denise signs a very hot act, what do the majors do about it? Initially, nothing much. They have stables of hot acts of their own and plenty more where they came from, so day to day Denise isn't going to upset them to any degree. However, if she produces the biggest act the country has seen for years, the majors will want a piece of it and to get it will try to buy the act or, if they need to, the company.

These, then, are some of the main differences in the A&R thinking of indies and majors. Of course, there are many other factors which separate them, and one of the biggest is the international dimension. Let's take a look.

If EMI and Denise's label are competing to sign an act, EMI will say to that band, 'Not only will we spend a lot more money on you in this country and bring all our expertise to bear on your behalf, but we will use the global EMI family of companies to make you a star across the world.'

Denise will say, 'Ah yes, but at EMI you'll be a little fish in a big pond. If you sign to my label, you will be our biggest star and get personal attention.' She will also argue that her network of indie partners around the world who give her label representation in Japan, the US, Australia and everywhere else will also give the act personal attention. This may or may not be true.

Such contrast in approaches to the international arena indicates another huge difference in indies and majors. Whereas majors have everything in-house, indies buy in many services, and this affects the thinking of both of them greatly. In practice, this means majors have their own distribution, their own pressing plants, sales teams, pluggers and so on. For indies, obtaining even something as basic as distribution can often be tricky.

Only a handful of indies have their own distribution operations; the rest all have to buy this service from a third party. Distribution, remember, means the actual act of getting the records to the shops and even in our relatively small country it's still seven hundred miles from the most south-westerly record shop to the most north-easterly. No indie label can handle that without some kind of outside help and most indies in the UK use a company called Pinnacle to manage that tricky business of delivering records to the stores that have ordered them.

Pinnacle's systems are, though, finite and the company can accommodate only so many labels. New labels seeking to have their records distributed by Pinnacle often have to demonstrate a track record or some kind of commercial substance to get through the door.

Majors do not have such difficulties. They own their own systems, so there is no problem with handling any given material. But these large facilities that the majors own bring a different set of problems. Facilities and staff mean costs – often very big costs. A major label faces pressure all the time to meet those costs and still generate a profit. But it has to sell a fearsome amount of records every month just to cover its overheads, so that it has to run hard just to stand still. In addition to that, there is always the big international boss wanting to know what's going on and, behind his shoulder, shareholders. It's pressure that Tony and Denise Williams, with their little two-, three- or four-person operations, simply do not have.

Let's sum up, then. What's the difference between an indie and a major? Well ...

- Majors have the power to influence a wide range of publics. Indies have much less power.
- Majors have a responsibility to be perceived well by that same wide range of publics. Indies generally don't give a stuff about how they are seen by people outside those with whom they trade and work.
- Majors have corporate and financial people to whom they must answer. Indies, by and large, do whatever they like
- Majors are big. Indies ain't.
- Majors can succeed or fail spectacularly. Indies can fail or succeed spectacularly

I throw in this last point because what unites majors and indies is, in my view, far, far greater than what divides them. Let's look at labels again for a moment to see what I mean.

Indies say of majors that they are big, corporate, full of people who neither know nor care about music. Well, as I said in Chapter 11, I've never met anybody from a major label who was not passionate about music, from the guys in the postroom to the man at the top of the international tree. In addition, each of the majors has put more music, of all kinds, into the world than all the indies put together. In any major label's catalogue, there will be plenty of things to suit all tastes. Thanks to the majors, the UK and the world has a rich musical heritage.

Conversely, majors say of indies that they are disorganised and unnecessarily difficult to deal with. Well, it's difficult to be disorganised when there is no money to spare. If you are paying the wages by taking out a second mortgage on your house, you tend to be organised because if you aren't, a lot of money from your own pocket will head straight down the drain. Difficult to deal with? OK, but so is everybody else. Take a hundred people from the indie sector and a hundred people from the major sector and there will be the same proportion in each of saints and sinners.

And that musical heritage the majors created? The indies have added to it and made it richer.

Is one side of this coin superior to the other? Is it the majors or indies who are more morally sound, more commercially dynamic and more lovely as human beings? Well, in my experience of both these areas, it's a dead heat.

I say again that it is a shame there is not more mutual respect between them because they each add something very special to the mix. In fact, let's look more closely at what they do add.

Indies, in my view, bring an innovative way of thinking. To the international music-lovers' party, they bring more music, different kinds of music, non-mainstream music and generally the stuff the majors either can't or don't want to do.

The majors – retailers, labels and publishers – bring power, and that is not necessarily a bad thing. Only through that power can the music industry compete in that big, ugly world out there. Major labels have the advertising and the creative power to make music a viable alternative to all those other things, from films to computer games, looking for people's leisure spending. Major retailers, as we noted earlier, are a presence for music on the high street. Without that presence, for many people music out of sight would be music out of mind.

In short, I believe the indies and majors are like a hedgehog and fleas: without the other, one will die.

Chapter 15

THE AWARDS SHOWS

FOR THIS CHAPTER ON awards shows, I'd like to thank my parents, my friends and all those people who have stuck by me over the years. (And what happened to the rest of you? Did you lose my number?)

There are, of course, awards shows across the world, though they vary massively in value and status – some are utterly pointless, some are revered and respected. And what's the difference between the two? Simplistically, the number of people who watch.

The purpose of awards shows is to showcase acts and to celebrate and laud the abilities of the area of talent on which the event is based. There is, then, a great deal more kudos and commercial advantage in being showcased to a global audience of a billion than to five pensioners and a dog.

I might win the award for the best writer in the room I am now sitting in (actually, I came second last year) but: a) what is it going to do for my career? b) how is it going to publicise this book? and c) how much do I care? All those reactions are, of course, linked. The bigger the award show, the more potential impact it has on my career, the greater its ability to publicise my work and, therefore, the greater my level of emotional engagement in whether I win or lose. You can see, then, that the prestige of an award show is intimately connected with how many people are watching.

Award shows don't, though, generally command instant audiences. More often than not, they take a while to build up into something special. That's not entirely true of honours run by television companies, but it certainly tends to be true of other, more organic events.

Let's take the Brit Awards as an example of what I mean by 'organic'. This is an event that goes back to the early eighties and, in its origins, it was just a cosy night out for industry people. Now, as we know, it is a huge media event watched not just in the UK but in around seventy countries worldwide. It is a fantastic showcase for British talent.

How did it get there? By making itself more marketable and more televisable. And how was that achieved? Well ...

That original cosy night out was not much of a televisual feast. Rather, it was lots of people wearing dinner jackets eating their food, chatting to their mates and then handing over a few awards at the end of it, with the odd band on stage for entertainment. Not exactly rock 'n' roll - even if it was the rock 'n' roll industry.

So, the organisers of the event, the BPI, decided there was more to be had from this event and they began talking to the television companies. The BPI pointed out that its members had all the biggest bands in Britain and some of the biggest in the world, and the TV companies said that they were, well, the TV companies. Together, they tried to work out what they could do for one another.

What they agreed on was a slicker event that was less pure conviviality and more appealing for a wider, record-buying, television-watching audience. Simply, it became focused on the people watching at home rather than on the people in the room. Such a focus makes a lot of sense: there are fifteen hundred people in the room but, if you are very, very lucky, there are fifteen million people watching on TV. Work out which of these two sets of people buys more records.

So how did the organisers achieve this sea change in emphasis? First by sharpening up the presentation and bringing in recognised presenters to host the show. Then they dropped some of the awards that are less interesting for the home viewers – the classical awards, the best producer, the best engineer and suchlike. These are vitally important industry honours (without producers and engineers, there would be no recorded music and a Brit Award used to be one of the few chances these people got to step into the limelight for a moment), but most producers and all engineers are not household names (not even in their own house, some of them), so TV wanted that bit out. It went.

Then dinner went the same way. The awards had, in the early years, been an adjunct to a very nice dinner at a posh hotel, the honours being handed out only after we had all been handsomely fed and watered. However, dinner is not entirely conducive to good TV, so, at the behest of the television people and the ready agreement of the BPI, the show moved from the Great Room at the Grosvenor House Hotel in London's Park Lane to the Royal Albert Hall; that is, it went to a dedicated venue rather than being held in a big dining room with a makeshift venue at one end. Then, in that quest for every greater slickness and sharpness, it went to Alexandra Palace, then Earls Court and finally the Docklands Arena, then back to Earls Court. (You work out which is the best venue, because nobody else can.) Throughout this time, though, the show was each year becoming less and less an event geared for the people there on the night and more and more a spectacular run by and for the TV companies. In ten years it went from being a cosy little evening out that happened to be on television to a slick, sleek piece of entertainment.

It evolved, gradually and over time, taking a while – with more than the odd hiccup en route (and let's not mention the Sam Fox and Mick Fleetwood thing) – to get to its final destination. And that's what I mean by 'organic'.

Apart from their pure entertainment aspect, what other functions do the Brits perform? Well, these encompass politics, promotion and public relations.

The political element cannot be overstated. As we saw in Chapter 13, the relationship between the business of music and politicians is often fraught and it is vitally important that members of parliament and civil servants understand what happens in the music industry and how their decisions affect it.

So, every year at the Brits there are politicians and their administrators – plenty of them. They range from ordinary MPs to Commons Committee chairmen to a deputy prime minister (John Prescott) and a prime minister in waiting (Tony Blair, before he ascended to high office). Now, the advantage the BPI has over other, bigger businesses is that the MPs actually want to come to the Brits. The International Insurance Association (or whatever it's called) has, I suspect, a significant problem in attracting to its annual awards show an excited crowd of people who truly want to be there.

MPs want to come to the Brits. They want to come because they're only human and enjoy a good show the same as the rest of us, they want to come because they want to say they were there, and they want to come so they can bring along wives, teenage offspring, friends and what have you.

In this way the politicians become a captive audience for the BPI and other music industry interests. Dinner is still served at the Brits, but it is at the back of the arena, out of sight of the cameras and long before the show starts. But it remains an integral part of the event. So, though you neither can nor want to talk during the show itself, MPs get well plugged over dinner. The politicians sit with their hosts – generally one of the major record companies, big publishers or industry organisations – and are gently apprised of how the said organisation feels about this, that or the other aspect of government policy. The MP has no option but to listen and, hopefully, by the end of the evening, a good show and a first-hand view of what is at stake if the record industry ever stops being successful – that is, the music and musicians – will have persuaded him or her that this is a business worth fighting for.

Now we come to the promotion aspect, but, just like much else in life, there's plenty of politics in this, too.

Appearing at the Brits is a major boost to any act's career. Just performing on the show helps sales of the band's current single, album and its entire catalogue in the week after, and getting a major gong provides an even bigger boost. An act receiving, say, the award for outstanding contribution can expect big publicity, not just on the show and its television broadcast but in all the other media that cover the event; the resulting surge in sales is often huge. And the act doesn't even have to have a new album or single to feel the benefit – though a bright record company will try to ensure one is available, even a re-release if the band aren't working any more. Rather, everything the band has ever done will benefit, and generally for a fair time.

That promotion does not just apply to the UK, of course. These days the Brits is seen in a fearsome number of countries, most notably in the biggest music market of all, the US. This helps boost the careers of the established acts who appear on the show and, more importantly, launch the career of the newcomers. As I've stressed repeatedly in this book, the whole purpose of the music industry, its focus and its challenge, is making bands famous in the first place. And, as we saw in Chapter 6, just making them famous in the UK is rarely enough. Breaking them worldwide is the aim of every major record company for every one of its new acts. Appearing on the Brits and being seen by a global audience – even if it is only to pick up an award and say, 'Thanks to everyone who voted for me' – at least gets that person's name on to a worldwide platform. If a little music by that new act can be played, too, that's an even bigger bonus.

The Brits is good, global promotion. But where's the politics in all this? Well, the record industry has consistently argued that, left to its own devices and freed from government interference, it can be a global success for the UK. The Brits provides a platform for it to be able to demonstrate that.

Moving on to the public relations aspect of the Brits, for the music industry this is the final icing on the cake. As we know, the poor old rock 'n' roll biz gets so much criticism generally – everybody loves music but seems to love to hate the industry that makes music – and the Brits allows that industry to show its prettiest face, to have a smile and celebrate what it is. And because the show is so slick these days, the coverage in the media afterwards is generally positive and uplifting – the only time of the year when the business can expect such a plethora of supportive stories.

What other awards shows are there? Well, there are many, as we mentioned, and they work in every musical genre and take place in every country. Indeed, while I was at *Billboard* I once worked out that if I went to every awards show everywhere in the world that I was invited to, I could spend a whole year out of the office. Funnily enough, my gaffer didn't want me to do that.

The world's awards shows come in all shapes, sizes, philosophies and histories. Some have grown up over generations, others are a lot less organic. While the Brits, for example, spent more than a decade evolving into the event it has now become, others were born into greatness. All these newer events, of course, are the progeny of music-TV stations. And why do TV stations do it? Well, the broadcasters can pull in big audiences with awards shows; and, of course, they love holding their own events because it means the show is entirely under their control. Thus, we have the MTV Awards, the Comet Awards, run by German-based music-TV station VIVA, and many others.

Away from the public spotlight, there are even more awards shows. In industry terms, these are no less important than the Brits and the rest, but, because they are not open to outsiders, they have a much different tone and direction.

THE AWARDS SHOWS

Prime among such events is the Platinum Europe Awards, an affair whose purpose is purely political. Bear in mind that a show with no television audience can focus entirely on other issues, and for the Platinum Europe Awards that means sending both an internal and an external message about the European record business.

The internal message is intended for industry consumption and is designed to show that Europe is a real market: that is, it is equivalent in kudos to the US. The Platinum Europe Awards, set up by the International Federation of the Phonographic Industry (remember them from Chapter 10?), help to do that by honouring any act whose album sells a million copies in Europe. The idea is that, while acts get naturally excited about selling a million copies in the US, if a fuss is made of them once they achieve the same mark in Europe, they might feel even better about selling records here than they do already. And, of course, the better an act feels about the market, the more likely they are to work here – and the more they tour, smile and do all the PR stuff in Europe, the happier the European labels are.

Indeed, because the US is the world's biggest record market, it is possible for American stars in particular to lose sight of the need to go abroad to tour and do promotion things. The Platinum Europe Awards are there to remind them that there is a world beyond the borders of the good ol' US of A. In addition, these awards also help purely European artists feel better about their achievements. This concept is based on the fact that there are many acts who, though huge in their own country and/or language, are so little known in the US that they'd find it difficult even to get arrested. The Platinum Europe Awards honour them for their achievements and, thereby, put these purely European artists on the same level of kudos, the IFPI hopes, as those people who have sold a million in the US.

OK, now we come to the external politics of the Platinum Europe show. The event is held in Brussels every year, and, funnily enough, within walking distance of the European Commission and Parliament. The show, then, is packed with politicians and their advisers. The purpose is much like that of the Brits – to show the politicos what the industry is, what it can achieve and, most importantly, what stands to be lost if the conditions are not right for it to prosper.

It's easy to understand these motivations. Back in 1998 the European Commission and Parliament was discussing the Copyright Directive, a document of truly massive importance for the music industry right across the fifteen nations of the EU. During the debate the music industry was losing several of the arguments to its opponents, the hugely powerful telecommunications and Internet companies. That's not surprising, because politicos are much more likely to be influenced by companies like telecoms, who create hundreds of thousands of jobs in the EU and pay billions in taxes, than an industry that employs only thousands and produces far, far less in terms of revenue for governments.

So, the music industry was coming second best in terms of what it wanted from the Copyright Directive. Now, this situation could not be remedied overnight, but it was certainly helped significantly by the Platinum Europe Awards that year. The star turn that night was the Corrs, and, for anybody unfortunate enough never to have seen this act, they are a band of three stunning sisters and their far-from-ugly brother, Jim. Not only are they excellent musicians and hugely likeable and intelligent as human beings, but the women are also some of the sexiest in the world.

That night the then Commission president Jacques Santer was giving away the awards. This is a man who is, of course, used to having a fuss made of him. But he is not used to having a fuss made of him by the Corrs. They chatted to him, charmed him and presented a cogent argument for why the Copyright Directive should be skewed a little better in favour of the creators rather than the people who disseminate their works.

For sure, things didn't turn on their head that night, but the Copyright Directive certainly worked out much better than it was before.

Like all the pure industry events, the Platinum Europe Awards take place behind closed doors. This means that the industry can relax a little there rather than being somewhat clenched and tense, as it can be at the Brits, knowing the world is watching. That makes the Platinum Europe Awards much more relaxed, casual and informal – and that despite the fact that Europe's most powerful politicians are present.

There is a very similar atmosphere at the UK industry's most fun domestic celebration, the Silver Clef Awards. This charitable event celebrates both good works and big talents and it is the warmest, happiest, funniest show in the calendar. Again, because it is a behind-closed-doors event, it is wonderfully relaxed. Speakers tend to give speeches that they would never make if the cameras or mainstream media were present, and that makes for the most marvellous spirit of camaraderie. Pete Townshend's monologue a few years ago and his diatribe against Eric Clapton was one of the funniest things I've ever heard. Not only was it massively libellous – though done with huge affection – but it was littered with the kind of language that even Channel 4 would baulk at. For those of us present, though, it was a wonderful celebration of all that is good in the music industry: talent, friendship, humour, honesty and solidarity.

And the Silver Clef Awards each year raise thousands of pounds for the music industry's favourite charity, Nordhoff-Robbins Music Therapy.

This organisation uses music as a means of accessing autistic and brain-damaged children and helping them connect with the world around them. Its achievements are internationally recognised and receive the most heart-warming tributes from the parents of the children it works with.

The final event I'm going to mention in the UK calendar is the Ivor Novello Awards. Unlike the other honours, which are predicated on record sales, the 'Novellos' (or 'Ivors', take your pick) celebrate the songwriters' art – which is what you would expect for awards named after one of the greatest composers of the early twentieth century. (He wrote 'Keep The Home Fires Burning', among plenty of other stuff.)

Once more, the television cameras are not present, but the print media are, so those on stage are sometimes a little more guarded in what they say. It remains, though, a glorious celebration of the people who are the strength of the music industry – the men and women who actually create the music.

Awards shows, then, perform a variety of different functions, often all at the same time. Many come and go without making an impact on the public consciousness, but many others have become part of the entertainment calendar. What would February be without the Brits? Just that much colder and darker and less fun. This may be the biggest compliment there is to the music industry – that things would be worse without it.

Chapter 16

⭐

THE TRADE FAIRS

SO WHAT'S A TRADE FAIR? Well, every industry has events at which it gets together one or more times a year to talk to colleagues, cement contacts with existing trading partners and generally seek out new opportunities. The event where an industry does that is called a trade fair and these things are wonderful opportunities for businesses scattered across the globe to meet in one place. For the music business, it means that a UK label can talk to its German, US, Australian and Japanese partners all in the same afternoon.

And, though this is never stated in the advertising brochure, trade fairs are also a chance to get fantastically drunk and shag anything of the opposite or same sex, depending on your tastes, who is up for the same no-nonsense rut as you are. The music industry's desire for this kind of mixture of commerce and consumption is exactly the same as that of every other business. And, like every other business, the music industry is very good at both these aspects.

In the music industry there are only two trade fairs worth talking about, though there have been hundreds of pretenders to the crown over the years. The only ones, though, to have stood the test of time are Midem and Popkomm. Midem is held in late January or early February in the French coastal resort of Cannes and Popkomm takes place in August in the very attractive city of Cologne in western Germany.

But let's start at the beginning with the grandaddy of all the trade fairs, Midem. This French operation stands for Marché International du Disque et de l'Édition Musicale – records and music publishing, to you and me, and takes place in the very posh Palais des Festivals in Cannes – yes, the same building in which they hold the Cannes Film Festival. Midem consists of four main elements: the trade fair itself; the gigs; the conferences and fringe activities; and the drinking and socialising. Don't underestimate the importance of this last element, but we'll get to that after looking at the others.

The trade fair itself is essentially a market – hence the 'Marché' of the title. Across the whole ground floor of the Palais and spilling on to several other levels are stalls selling wares. Remember that music is a commodity which is bought and sold like any other, and this is a market where rights are traded.

But the stalls, usually called booths or stands, do not look like a street market selling fruit and veg. This is still the music industry and this business does things with some style, plenty of pizzazz and, often, a good deal of money.

For a big company, a stand at Midem is a lot like a mobile, rather glamorous office: it may well be large, superbly or imaginatively decorated (regularly both) and will contain all the accoutrements of doing business – phones, computers, meeting rooms and, more often than not, something like a café and bar. Smaller companies with less money will go in for something a little more modest, but the purpose of all of these stands is the same: to sell as much of the company's products as possible.

To do that, they will display the company's wares – that is, its copyrights – in the most attractive fashion possible. The labels will show artwork, play music to the passers-by and do whatever it takes to attract attention, just like any other trader

THE TRADE FAIRS

– and this concept of doing whatever it takes often involves exposed female flesh and/or people in outlandish costumes. Mind you, I have to tell you that after being accosted by your fourteenth alien on your way to work in the morning, the novelty and attraction of it all can wear a little thin. And your desire to know which company and/or planet the alien is representing is very small indeed before you've had your first cup of tea (and not much bigger after).

Who are these people selling to? In short, anybody who is buying.

Remember, the essence of Midem is that it is an international market. That is, people from one country trade with people from other countries. This is vitally important commerce for indie labels in particular; without it, they could never have a hit outside their own country.

Indies, as we know by now, are small companies, and generally they operate only in the country of their birth. That means that they both like to and need to trade copyrights between them. We've already looked at this concept briefly, but it's important, so we'll do it again, this time in the context in which it actually takes place.

The concept of buying and selling copyrights, or rights as they're more often known, works like this. A London-based indie label – let's call it Nine Windows Ltd – signs the hot new band the Miracle Trees. Nine Windows has distribution for the UK and a relationship with UK retailers but operates nowhere else. It believes the Miracle Trees can be a hit outside the UK, but it needs a trading partner to launch the band in overseas countries. So, Nine Windows takes a stand at Midem and declares as its marketing pitch: 'We own the rights to a hot new band, the Miracle Trees. We are certain you can have a hit with this band in your country. Want to buy the rights?'

Nine Windows will have on its stand pictures of the band, a sampler CD it is giving away and, perhaps, a couple of members or all of the act there to play a few songs and generally make a fuss of potential clients. (And this is the kind of thing I alluded to earlier when I said musos must work.)

Let's assume, then, that the delegates from the Deux Oignons label in France happen along and, having heard the sampler, think the Miracle Trees could sell a lot of records in France. They express their interest to Nine Windows and the two sides sit down to thrash out a deal. The nature of that deal, we'll come to in a moment.

Later in the week of Midem, Nine Windows invites representatives from the German label Drei Kölsch to listen to the band's music. Drei Kölsch's delegates are equally impressed and, just like Deux Oignons, do their deal to handle the Miracle Trees in their home market of Germany.

In this way, and one country at a time, Nine Windows is gaining global distribution for the Miracle Trees. It is like doing a jigsaw of the world, and Nine Windows is completing the picture one piece at a time.

But what kind of deals is the company doing? The most comprehensive is what is known as a licensing deal. That is, Nine Windows says to its partner: we will give you a licence to sell as many copies as you like of the Miracle Trees' album. You may market it as you see fit, you may promote it in any way you like (within the bounds of legality and some parameters of taste) and you may do whatever deals you wish with the retailers. In return, you will pay us an agreed number of pounds, euros or dollars for each unit you sell.

Through such a deal, Nine Windows is leaving all the effort to the label buying the rights. The advantage for Nine Windows in this is that it need not get directly involved in a foreign market. Instead, it has somebody doing the work on its behalf – and that somebody is a company that speaks the language, knows the territory and has pre-existing distribution and infrastructure. The disadvantage for Nine Windows is that it has no control.

And though Nine Windows may try to keep a measure of control by building a number of safeguard clauses into its original contract, it won't tie its partner's hands because it is important and essential that the overseas label has a large degree of autonomy. Why important? Because Nine Windows has to allow the partner the freedom of movement to do the job Nine Windows hopes it will do. If the UK company stipulates: you may not market in this manner or sell to that kind of retailer, it is stopping its partner doing an effective job. In addition, allowing freedom to a trading partner is essential because no company is going to enter into an agreement in which it can't use its own judgement and skills. (Nor is a company likely to want an agreement in which it feels it is not trusted.)

Now, should Nine Windows decide it wants more control and is happy to do some of the work itself, it can enter into what is known as a sales and distribution deal, in which the partner handles these two functions. That is, Nine Windows does the marketing and promotion in the country in question but its partner handles the practical matters of selling the records to the retailers and making sure they get from pressing plant to stores. Nine Windows will pay for such services – either as a flat fee or, much more likely, as a percentage of sales income.

The advantage of a sales and distribution deal over a licensing agreement is, as we noted, that Nine Windows has much more control. The disadvantages, though, are two-fold:

1. Nine Windows is now having to operate away from home, possibly in a culture and business environment with which it is not familiar.
2. The label handling the sales and distribution in that country has much less of a stake in the record's success and, therefore, much less of an incentive to make it succeed.

There are, though, no hard-and-fast rules about which of these kinds of deals is the better. It depends on many, many individual circumstances concerning markets, companies, type of acts, personalities and economics. It is certainly not a case of one size fits all; deals are tailored to meet at least some of the needs of all parties (and there is not an equitable deal in the world that meets all the needs of all parties).

So, if Nine Windows can do a couple of deals for representation around the world, it will reckon it will have had a good Midem.

Now, what about Drei Kölsch in Germany? What constitutes a good Midem for them?

Let's assume Drei Kölsch is a well-established indie. It has been trading for fifteen years and has a solid financial base and a decent back-catalogue. But, because it can't compete with the majors in terms of A&R power, it has been missing out on Germany's hot new acts. How, then, does it find something new, young, fresh and exciting to give it a presence in the youth market and, hopefully, the charts? Well, the company goes to Midem and buys it.

The delegates from Drei Kölsch will spend their time going around the market looking at what is available and what is suitable. Like any potential purchaser in any market of any kind, they will visit all the relevant stalls, look at and listen to the merchandise on sale and make a decision on whether they want to buy. That decision will be based on the material's appropriateness for the task in hand – whether it is capable of selling loads of records in Germany – and, of course, its cost.

Above all, the people from Drei Kölsch are eager to snap up a bargain – that is, something brilliant going at a price that is right. Indies like Drei Kölsch will look hard to find such a thing because success with this kind of find can make the difference between profit and loss and even between staying in business and going bust. If the Drei Kölsch people can locate and license what turns out to be a big hit, it will make a great Midem for them; and if they manage only to find and license a couple of albums with more modest sales, this will make it a very good Midem. But even if all they do is meet up with their collection of existing trading partners and renew friendships and

THE TRADE FAIRS

motivations, that would still make for a good Midem.

However, labels like Drei Kölsch do not have the field to themselves in their search for new talent and new music. Major labels are red in tooth and claw when it comes to competition and they, too, are on the lookout for anything with the potential to be a hit. Nothing irritates a major label like missing out on a record that becomes a chart success for somebody else.

The majors do, though, have several weapons they use at Midem to sniff out a hit. The first is bodies: one major will have more people on the ground at Midem than ten or twelve indies put together. Their second weapon is that old attraction of power. While a number of indies feel great antipathy towards majors and wouldn't give them the time of day, lots of other small labels would love to get into bed with somebody so big and strong. Assuming our friends at Nine Windows feel no philosophical animosity towards the majors, they would be delighted if one of the big boys bought a licence from them. If Sony Germany rather than Drei Kölsch took the licence for the Miracle Trees for the German market, Nine Windows and its band would get a much greater profile in the country because Sony's marketing and promotional power is hugely greater than Drei Kölsch's. So Nine Windows might well be tempted to offer the licence for the Miracle Trees to Sony first. If Sony accepted the deal, poor old Drei Kölsch would never get a sniff of the action.

Staying with Sony for a while, what constitutes a good Midem for them? Well, if Sony UK or Sony France or Sony anywhere else picks up a hot new act, that justifies the whole expedition. More prosaically, though, Midem is a chance for each of the national chairmen to meet up with their colleagues around the world, find out face to face what's happening and, if necessary, sort out any disputes that may have arisen.

In my experience, it is a lot more difficult to misunderstand someone if you are facing them in the same room than if you are communicating by telephone or email. Midem is an opportunity for Sony – and every other – global organisation to get its top players together.

Ironically, this eye-contact-communication aspect of Midem is even more important for the indies than it is for the majors. Sony, as a huge, multinational company, can afford to get its top executives together as often as it likes, but if little indie Nine Windows has a licensing deal with a Japanese label, it won't be able to afford a return air ticket to Tokyo very often. So, as we noted at the top of the chapter, Midem is a chance for Nine Windows to sit down with its partners around the world and talk. And, again, this kind of face-to-face talking provides benefits that no amount of electronic conversations can.

So, that's the market itself. Let's move on to the second aspect of Midem, the gigs.

Every night across Cannes there are shows – dozens of shows. Many of them are showcases for emerging acts, others are full-blown, arena-size gigs by established artists, many more are club-size concerts by young bands and some are small, intimate shows in out-of-the-way places.

The concert programme is run by the organisers of Midem and is designed to be as attractive as possible – which means it needs to contain as many big names as can be booked. This list of headline bands is also augmented by plenty of acts that most folks haven't heard of, these bands' obscurity coming from the fact that they are either still learning their craft or that they come from far-away lands (Belgium).

With all these elements in place, the official programme will, then, consist of all the artists Midem's organisers have managed to attract – big and small – plus the shows arranged in conjunction with its partners. Those partnership shows will be events like 'The Best of British', a showcase for British acts run mainly by the BPI, and similar gigs presenting other nations' prime talent organised by their national record industry organisations. In addition, one record company or another may have decided to have a particular presence that year and laid on one or more showcases of its own artists. Thus, through Midem's own efforts and the promotional activities of its partners, there are plenty of shows to attend each night. Generally, provided you are a registered Midem delegate, you just walk through the door at any of the gigs that takes your fancy. It's a nice situation to be in and most of the time delegates are spoiled for choice. For me, the best part about that choice is being able to sit having my tea and, while taking in one of that town's exceptional pizzas, only then decide which show I want to go to.

Now for another out-of-market experience – the conferences and fringe activities. That phrase, though, covers a multitude of events, from the tedious to the terrific. Let's start with some of the terrific ones.

The Palais des Festivals, where Midem's trade fair element is held, overlooks Cannes' new harbour, a place where some serious marine hardware is moored. On these boats many parties and receptions are held, hosted by anybody from accountancy and legal firms to record companies and individual bands, distributors and music hardware manufacturers. While they are not all wildly exciting, it is, of course, very pleasant to be having a drink and a (small) bite to eat at somebody else's expense while savouring the warm evening air of the south of France.

But, as with all pleasure, there is obviously a price to pay for it – and the price is somebody yakking at you for a while about a subject you may or may not be interested in. But if you are eating the host's food, drinking the host's wine (I wouldn't wash my dog in the beer they serve up), it is only fair to listen for at least a short time to what the host has to say about his or her latest project. The people throwing the receptions know that, by providing good hospitality in an attractive location, they are likely to get people coming along to hear their tale who would not otherwise have done so.

For some people, such fringe activities are all there is. Some folks never bother to go into the Palais at all and don't even register. They spend all their time on a boat or in their hotel and hold all their meetings there. A whole range of people do this – from tiny indies who can't afford to buy a pass to the Palais to massively important and influential executives who feel they can get more done from their hotel suite than from the floor of the fair.

Moving on to the tedious aspects of the fringe activities, nothing comes more monstrously dull than the conference programme. Midem is very proud of its conference programme and it puts in a lot of effort to attract speakers of worth and fame. But the end result is the most boring way I can imagine of spending an afternoon. Now, that is just an opinion. Hundreds of people go to the conferences that form part of Midem and many have said to me that they have come away feeling enlightened about the law or technology or new A&R developments or whatever the subject happened to be. As for me, I have simply heard too many self-important pillocks rambling on about things that nobody cares about to ever set foot in one of those things again. In fact, if Midem ever ask me again to chair one of these things (which is unlikely after this diatribe), my advice to Midem delegates is: don't come; you'll be bored.

Personally, I have learned far more from just being at Midem and chatting to the people I find on the floor of the show than I ever have in the conferences and seminars.

All of which happily brings us on to the best bit of Midem: the drinking and socialising. Now, as I said earlier, don't be fooled – this is a very important part of Midem. However, as you might imagine, it is not the most arduous (though it has produced several hangovers that I didn't think I was going to survive).

But such socialising truly has enormous value. Let me explain. I am a newsman by trade and that meant that, while news editor at *Music Week* and *Billboard*, I had to understand and be informed about a lot of topics. Just wandering through Midem or walking down the street in Cannes, I might see somebody who was central to one of those topics. While it may have been impossible to get this guy on the phone while he was in his office with all its distractions, it is very easy to see him in the flesh and say, 'Got five minutes for a cup of coffee?' In those five minutes I learned a lot.

Then there are those times when I arranged to meet somebody for a coffee (the tea in Cannes is worse than the beer) just because they were a mate and I only got to see them twice a year. In many of those conversations that mate said something that really helped me understand an issue better and/or raised a whole new idea I had never thought of.

And there were also those times when I had been dealing with somebody over the phone for months but never met them; Midem gave us the opportunity to finally put a face to the name. Getting drunk and doing something stupid with some of these people (and, trust me, we did some things that were the height of folly) really cemented our relationship.

As we noted, email and the phone are fine as far as they go, but there is no substitute for simply sitting down with somebody and chatting. The conversation may start with football or the weather, but it always ends with business. In my experience the best ideas emerge when there is no pressure. The phone certainly creates pressure – who could cope with a thirty-second silence in a telephone conversation? – but a chat over lunch, coffee or a pint (yes, I do know one good place for beer in Cannes) generally helps relationships move forward in both commercial and human terms.

That was Midem in a nutshell. But what, I hear you ask, about Popkomm?

Well, what unites these two trade fairs is far greater than what divides them (though neither of the two organisations would admit as much). The basic precepts behind Popkomm are exactly the same as those behind Midem: it aims to bring people together, get them talking and doing business. Its name even evinces what it's about – it combines 'pop' and 'komm' from the German for 'communication'.

The elements are even the same as at Midem: there's the trade fair in a big exhibition hall, gigs around the city of Cologne, peripheral events and entertainments and, of course, a conference programme that is just as tedious as Midem's.

For me, though, the biggest difference between the two events is the intangible one – that of the atmosphere created by their settings. Midem is in Cannes, an ethereal other world of money, glamour and show. Popkomm is in a very pleasant but no-nonsense German city that has industry and bad weather to keep its feet on the ground. Cologne is a city that most of us would recognise and feel at home in; Cannes remains another planet to me despite the fact that I've been going to Midem since the mid-eighties. So, when I'm in Cannes, I tend to think about the starry end of the music industry; in Cologne, my mind is more fixed on the nuts and bolts of the business's day-to-day graft. But maybe that's just me.

There is, though, one real, measurable difference between the two locations – cost.

Now, I have had a charmed and privileged existence in which I have never paid for a hotel room in Cannes. I am told, though, that the prices are utterly stupid. For sure, just eating and drinking in that town is a very major expense and not for the faint-hearted.

Cologne, though, is far more rooted in the real world and prices are much more reasonable. (With twenty-two breweries, the beer is also infinitely better than in Cannes. But, then again, what comes out of Satan's willy is infinitely better than most of the beer in Cannes.)

As for the setting for the show itself, in Cologne the Köln Messe, where Popkomm takes place, is a massive conference and exhibition site about twenty minutes' walk from the city centre. Unlike Cannes, there are no nice cafés just over the road, so once you're in Popkomm you tend to be stuck there for the day. It does concentrate the mind on business a little more, but it reduces the opportunities for a pleasant cup of coffee and a chat away from the hubbub of the trade fair.

And if, despite these minor differences, the purpose and *modus operandi* of Popkomm still sound remarkably similar to Midem's, they really should. Notwithstanding their different styles and tones, these two shows perform exactly the same excellent function. They bring people together from around the world and get them talking. That has to be a good thing: for business, for people, for music.

I salute both of you. Now stop bickering.

Chapter 17

⭐

THE MEDIA

MUSIC IN THE MEDIA is a concept that covers a lot of ground these days. It used to be that coverage of music was confined to specialist magazines, but nowadays there is not a newspaper in the country that doesn't feature music of one kind or another, and the TV news regularly adds to that. In each of those media the stories range from award shows, big gigs and the latest big star to hit town to the antics of some famous young person who's in trouble with the law and/or his mum.

This opens up plenty of opportunities for people trying to make a name for themselves – and it also has a plethora of pitfalls for people who have already achieved it. But let's take it one step at a time and look at the various types of media covering music.

An area that is often ignored in accessing the music industry is the trade press. These magazines deal with the business of the music business and they are a fantastic and hugely under-recognised resource. In the English language – and therefore in the world business – two titles dominate the field: *Music Week* for the UK industry and *Billboard* for the global business. Let's look what they've got to offer.

The job of these two publications is to get stories about the industry first, before anybody in the outside world gets a sniff of them. In fact, if *Music Week* and *Billboard* don't do this, there is simply no reason for the people in the industry to buy those publications. Thankfully, though, they both have a long tradition of being first with the news. The job of these trade publications is to be limpet-close to the industry they serve, so if they don't get stories before anybody else, they truly want their respective arses kicking.

In my fifteen years as news editor at those magazines, I can count on the fingers of one finger the ones we missed and that taught me something very important about the value of these publications: that they can give a competitive edge to their readers that is so great as to be almost unfair.

If I'd had hair, I would have torn it out at the number of times some other publication in the general media claimed an exclusive on a story we had carried two, three or, on one famous occasion, nine months earlier. From this I realised that virtually nobody outside the music industry is reading *Music Week* and *Billboard*. Thus, it becomes obvious that anybody who actually chooses to do so has a huge advantage over the competition. Knowledge is power.

How can new musicians and budding entrepreneurs make use of the trade press? Firstly, of course, by reading it to find out what is happening in the business. Secondly, by using it to make the wider industry aware of who they are.

Remember back in Chapters 2 and 3 we noted how important it is to get the business on your side before even thinking about customers. We saw then that the first step in selling a record is getting it into the stores because if it ain't in the shops, people can't buy it. The industry, then, always has to come before customers.

So, if you have a new label, you need to let distributors, retailers and others know that you have a new label. And, if you are a new artist, you have to make an impact with the industry so that it gets behind you rather than being excited instead by all the other new artists competing with you for attention.

How, then, to get a story in either *Music Week* or *Billboard*? Well, first of all, have a story to tell. Secondly, be aware of who you are telling it to. It was another cause of frustration for me as news editor at both those magazines that I would receive exactly the same press release about a new album as would the teen-market magazines. Work it out: one release cannot be appropriate for both the serious, worthy trade paper and an ooh-super-look-at-his-new-haircut magazine. Think hard, then, about how you are going to present your story and what are the needs and desires of the people you are presenting it to.

Then, when telling your story, do it with both creativity and honesty. Be aware, though, that the creativity element doesn't mean making something up, but rather just looking hard to find something worth talking about. There is no point calling *Music Week* or *Billboard* and saying, 'I've just released a new album.' Their response – either stated or silent – will be: 'So what. So have a thousand other people this week, including U2, Westlife and Pink Floyd.'

Instead, find something they can write about. Find something different about you, your label or your album. Something. Anything. Find a way in which you stand out from the crowd (though, sadly, if you can't identify anything that makes you different, you may not have much of a future in the music industry).

Then, after that creativity in finding your story, comes honesty in telling it. This is essential, because there is absolutely no point in lying to these publications or trying to build up what you are doing into something it ain't. Despite the fact that *Music Week's* and *Billboard's* greatest and baldest talent has moved on to writing books, there are still bright boys and girls at these magazines. They know a very large amount about the industry and about musicians and the likely success of an album. If you try to pull the wool over their eyes, they will spot it in seconds and not treat you seriously. Being open and honest with them is the only way to proceed.

And, to make them most receptive to what you are saying, be conscious of the different things they do. *Music Week* is based in London and covers the UK industry with a small eye to the rest of the world. *Billboard* is global, based in New York, with an office in London to handle non-US stuff. If you're not in the US, you go through the London office when dealing with *Billboard*. But mark well the difference in emphasis for the two magazines; by being conscious of what they are, where they circulate and who reads them, you have the best chance of giving them a story they'll actually use.

OK, let's move on to the national media – the newspapers and mainstream TV and radio news shows. Newspapers have, in the past twenty years, developed a real interest in what happens in music. All the red-top tabloids have dedicated columns dealing with popular music and, should a big star be in town, on tour or in court, they are all over it like a rash.

Now, the tabloids do not always bring their most rigorous standards of truth to their coverage of popular music. Of course, they do so if the issue is legal or serious, but if the story is that star X has been eating only sausages since the age of twelve or star Y was seen on the town with a mystery blonde, they tend to relax somewhat. In fact, the star's record label is often complicit in this. The label's job is to keep the star in the public eye and making up trivial stories – ones that will get in the paper but won't harm the star's reputation whether true or not – is part of the PR department's art. Often, both the paper and the label know a story to be untrue, but they decide to suspend their better judgement and print it anyway. This system tends to work well provided that the star involved knows what's happening and approves. If, however, the star hears for the first time that he's a Buddhist or a Baptist or a pigeon-fancier by reading it in the *Sun*, he is not likely to be best pleased.

But, above and beyond all this trivia, are the stories the tabloids love most – those with a whiff of scandal about them: a marital infidelity, a drugs misdemeanour or even a family tragedy. At that point fame is an utter curse as, just when the star least wants to show his or her face, the tabloids will be hungrier for pix and an interview than a vegetarian in a sausage factory.

It's an irony of the tabloids: either they are not interested in you at all when you want them to be, or they won't leave you alone when all you want in the world is to be left alone. It's a funny old world, guv'nor.

But, should the day actually come when the tabloid press pack do seek to feature you, just remember this: all they are interested in is the story. Nothing you say to them is off the record, everything you do will be recorded and used in evidence against you. Do nothing and say nothing that you are not prepared to see in print later.

Dealing with the broadsheets is another matter – more civilised, more discerning. But they are also far more choosy about what they will print than the tabloids. There is no point making up something to go into the broadsheets, because they will see it coming and simply won't use it. Just as with *Music Week* and *Billboard*, you have to have a good story to tell and you have to tell it well – that is, simply and to the right person.

A key point in that process is to not send these people – or any other journalist – pages and pages of stuff about what you've done or are doing; send them three paragraphs of clear information. The staff on national newspapers are busy and if you don't get them interested in three paragraphs, you don't get them interested at all. And if you can't sum up what you're doing and why it's interesting in three paragraphs, again, sadly, you may not have a story to tell.

(Try this. Imagine yourself on one side of a busy road. Your friend is on the other side and, above the noise of the traffic, shouts, 'What's happening with your new company/

album/project?' The truncated details you would struggle to convey over the sound of the road between you are the essence of the story you have to tell, and these are the things – and the only things – that you should put in any press release.)

When you have your story and you've written your release and start wondering about who on a paper to send it to, do this simple thing: send it to the editor. You will see many names in the paper attached to articles about music, but there is no way of telling whether that person is the editor responsible for music coverage, a freelance correspondent on a one-off job or even whether it's a pseudonym for nobody in particular. Send everything to the editor and his or her staff will open it and direct it to the most appropriate person.

Now let's move on to the music press. By music press I mean all those magazines that have music either as their only subject or as a large part of the lifestyle mix they cover. Between them, these magazines cover every style, sector and sub-genre of records and we all have our favourite, no matter whether our passion is line dancing or headbanging.

The first thing in getting these publications interested in you is knowing what style of music they deal in: don't send grindcore heavy metal to *Smash Hits* and don't send romantic singer-songwriter material to *Kerrang!* because that's just a waste of everybody's time and effort. First, push at an open door – and the most open door is that of the people who write about your style of music and understand what you are talking about.

But don't talk too much. Your music will speak for itself, so it is important not to overwhelm whoever is giving first read to the incoming post at the magazine with too much information. Once more, send everything you need to say in three paragraphs and definitely on one sheet. This is certainly true if you trying to attract interest in the band and even more so if you are sending an album for review. The album will speak for itself; there's nothing you can say on paper that will change how the album sounds. If, though, the album gets the attention you seek and the magazine wants more information from you, they'll get in touch. So, let me say this again because it's important: the music speaks for itself. If, having heard the music, the magazine needs something further from you, they will ring you. All they need is a phone number; give them one in the release – and, because in a busy office, releases and albums often get separated, make sure there are contact details on the disc itself.

Then, as and when an interview is arranged, there are a number of important steps to follow. Firstly, all the members in a band must say the same thing. If it happens that the singer and guitarist end up doing separate interviews with different magazines, when asked what style of music the band is playing, the answer must be the same – exactly the same. I find it a useful tactic to work out well before the interview exactly how the band is going to describe the music they play. A short, tight description of the band's work is useful in so many different ways, not least because if the musicians can't describe what they are doing, how can they expect anybody else to accurately communicate that notion to lay readers?

Secondly, when doing an interview, don't show off. If this is your first interview with a mainstream music magazine, and possibly the magazine that you've been a fan of for ten years, it is very easy to let the excitement of it all overtake you or to feel you have to try hard to be wacky and/or cred.

Well, you don't. If the magazine is interested enough in you to actually come to talk to you, it means you and your music are interesting to them. You've got them already; you don't have to try harder. Besides which, it looks pretty ridiculous when some young person is trying to out-rock 'n' roll the true wild men of the genre. Keith Moon was so rock 'n' roll it killed him. Not much chance of trumping that in a half-hour interview. Just speak the truth simply. Everything else will fall nicely into place.

Another thing to remember when dealing with the music

press is their knowledge. Collectively, the people at the magazine that covers your style of music know a lot more about that style of music than you do. If they ask you for your musical reference points and/or heroes and heroines, make sure you have them right. If you're not sure what you're saying, say nothing.

But don't forget, and I know I'm saying this again, if they're interviewing you they are interested in what you do. You have already won the first half of the battle. Plus, most music magazines don't have an aggressive agenda; it is not their first desire to make you look like a dickhead – unless you really go out of your way to encourage them into that. The best tactic is, then, relax and be yourself.

Now another route to, er, fame. Perhaps the easiest and most gentle way of getting coverage for your new project – and, remember, by that I mean either something artistic or commercial – is local newspapers. Certainly, a story in your local paper is not going to do a huge amount for you in terms of launching your career into superstardom, but it is at least a starting point. A local following or a regional profile is better than no following or profile at all.

A big advantage of local papers is that they are relatively easy to access. Young reporters there get all excited about the idea of writing about something involved in music; it makes a very pleasant change from reporting TV licence dodgers at magistrates' court and chip-pan fires on the local housing estate. Believe me, I made a living out of courts, fires and council committees for years as a boy on local newspapers, and a bit of rock 'n' roll was more than welcome.

So, if you get a young reporter on your side, they will want to keep coming back to you for more stories because you give them a reason for writing about something they are actually interested in. Besides which, they might actually think that your music has something to offer.

And when doing interviews with local newspapers, the same principles apply as with music papers. Don't make things up, don't try to sound more rock 'n' roll than you are. Those who do just sound false (which they are) and/or egotistical (which nobody likes). Once more, speak the truth simply and everything will fall into place.

In terms of interesting your local paper in your story in the first place, here again give them something they can actually write about. But for most local papers, the mere fact that somebody on their patch is doing something musical is a story in itself.

And while getting stories in your local will not, as we noted, thrust you immediately into the media spotlight, a set of cuttings from the *Long Eaton Advertiser* or the *Stamford Mercury* does no harm at all as background material to send out to more influential publications.

Somewhat further up the scale, for most professional musicians the biggest encounters they have with local and regional papers are during a tour. It's then that they sit down and do the dreaded 'phoner'. This means sitting in a room at the record company and talking to every local paper from every city on the tour.

Musicians tend to hate it because of two things:

1. Sometimes the person doing the interview is particularly ignorant of the band and its music.

2. Twenty different local newspapers will tend to ask the same questions twenty times over.

But, as we saw in Chapter 6, the phoner is an essential part of publicising a tour. Assuming that the musician involved can be persuaded to take up this task, he or she can hit a lot of people. If you talk to twenty regional newspapers, that can equate to over three million readers – not bad for a day's work.

And, as in all other circumstances, it is vital when talking to regional newspapers not to invent things. In particular, if you are trying hard to keep the *Derby Evening Telegraph* interested, it might be tempting to say, 'Oh, and I went to school for a couple of years in Derby.' The reporter's next question will then be: 'Interesting. Which school?'

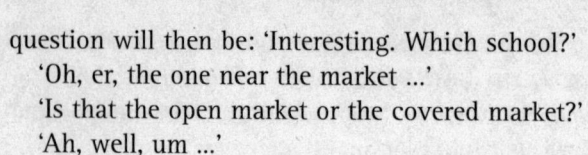

'Oh, er, the one near the market ...'

'Is that the open market or the covered market?'

'Ah, well, um ...'

A reporter on a city paper will know that city inside out and will spot any attempt at deceit a mile away. Simply, don't.

However, there is one thing that reporters love to hear – praise for their city and the local fans. It also gives them a story they can write about. The reporter might say, 'Are you looking forward to your gig at the XX Club in Derby?'

A good response is: 'Yes, last time we played in Derby, the fans were superb, better than anywhere else on the tour.' Or, if this is the band's first time on the road: 'Yes, we've heard the fans in Derby are the best in the country. We know they're going to appreciate our show and our music.'

In this way the fans feel good about themselves and, by implication, about the band, before the show has even started. And, of course, it is important to say that the fans in such-and-such a city are the best in the country, no matter what city that is.

That was something about dealing with the kinds of media musicians are likely to encounter. But what about actually working for that media? How does that happen?

Well, the basic grounding for any journalist is the professional qualification given by the National Council for the Training of Journalists. This, though, requires graft and application and that tends to put off those less blessed with backbone. But, as news editor at *Music Week* and at *Billboard*, I would not consider any applicants who did not have this qualification. That was for two reasons: having this qualification shows you are a competent newsperson; and it also demonstrates you are not a jellyfish who is going to be put off by having to work and study hard for three years to get it.

The same is true of national newspapers and other national media. Local and regional papers do, though, regularly take on trainees and see them through their examination course.

Working on the pure music media is a different matter. These people tend to be writers rather than newspeople, although having that news qualification makes you a better writer, in my view.

To be a writer, you have to demonstrate only that you can write. The first step in that process often entails reviewing shows in your home town and sending them off to the magazine most appropriate.

Now, it is always tempting to try to show off when doing a review, to demonstrate how cutting and cruel and contemptuous you can be. Often, though, that is self-defeating. If a band are playing at the Free Butt in Brighton they are not in the big league, so are not going to be of big-league quality. It is rather a waste of ink to tell people that.

Better, for me – but every publication sees this in their own way – to describe simply what happened there, what the gig was like and so on. This is a much safer option and, in my view, the one with the broadest appeal. Let me explain ... When one of my favourite bands has started its tour in another country before coming to the UK, I am very eager to find out what the show looks like as early as possible. So, when I ring my friend who went to see the band yesterday in New York or Sydney or wherever, I want to know from him what songs were played, how they sounded, what the show looks like and stuff like that. I don't want a detailed critique and I certainly don't want wonderful prose; I just want information.

A fan of a band just needs to know what's happening and what to expect. In addition, somebody who is not necessarily mad about the artist in question is much more likely to read a straightforward, informative report than some esoteric ramble full of puns and allusions that only the cognoscenti will understand. To my taste – and, remember, my taste is one very personal point of view; there are thousands of others – I enjoy reading a description of what happened at a gig. You were there; I wasn't. I'd like to know what it looked and sounded like.

Indeed, *Q*'s success was predicated on this. I reviewed heavy-metal albums for the magazine for five years (and for much of that time under the pseudonym Emily Fraser, which led to the occasional amusing confusion), and the instruction I was given was just to describe. I was told to explain that an album sounds like this, is a development from that and includes the other. *Q*'s huge popularity indicates this is a wise editorial policy.

A digression about Emily Fraser. I adopted this name so nobody would connect my work for *Q* with my work for *Music Week*. My work for *Q* had to be a secret because I could have been sacked from *Music Week* for writing for another publication. So, as a big, ugly bloke from a council estate in Nottingham, I like beer, football and motorbikes. Consequently, Emily Fraser's reviews often had beer, football or biking analogies. When I once drifted into a boxing analogy, I got a letter from a fan saying: Dear Emily, You are wonderful and we have so much in common. Would you like to meet for a drink? I wrote back saying: 'We've got more in common than you think.'

And another thing: I was interviewed for the deputy editor's job on metal mag *Kerrang!* while I was doing this Emily Fraser stuff. One of the leading lights on *Kerrang!*, a very nice guy called Mick Wall, was extremely supportive of my application, speaking well of me to the management and encouraging me to take the post. Simultaneously, and without knowing who Emily Fraser was, he described her as a 'three-eyed lobo job' for her views and lack of knowledge. Mick, you broke my heart ...

So, if you're dealing with the media, speak the truth simply. That is the whole of the law.

Chapter 18

TOURING

WHY ON EARTH WOULD anybody bother to haul themselves, several tons of equipment and a hangover around the country and possibly the world when one television appearance would hit just as many people?

Well, there are many, many answers to that, one of the prime ones being that musos, particularly young musos, love it. People who have performed in front of several thousand adoring fans tell me there is no feeling like it – thus proving that rock 'n' roll is indeed superior to sex and drugs.

A second answer is: because we've always done it that way. From the days of the very first wax cylinders, acts have toured to promote sales of their works. Now, more than a century on, nobody has found a better way of doing it.

So, a third answer to the question is that it is the most provenly effective way of selling discs and is a tool available to all professional acts, most semi-pros and a lot of amateurs.

Let's take this, though, one step at a time, and we'll begin with the best of all reasons for touring (or anything else): pleasure.

Though this statement is far too general to be completely accurate, in large measure it is true to say musos like to tour.

They like it because, uniquely in entertainment or, indeed, life, they can stand in front of anything from a hundred to a hundred thousand people and enslave them. Yes, enslave them. I am pretty sure that, like me, you have stood watching your favourite performer and, for the duration of that gig, have handed over your soul to them. I think we have all been transfixed and enslaved in those moments; we have been willingly and happily transported to a state where only the music mattered. Or at least I hope you have. It is a sublime pleasure and if you don't get it at a gig, you should ask for your money back. Mind you, I'm pretty sure you do recognise the feeling, otherwise you wouldn't have been interested enough in music to buy this book.

So, if we can feel all this pleasure from being transported to favourite-band-land, imagine what it feels like to be able to do that transporting. Think of this: instead of being one of the masses looking adoringly towards the stage, imagine for a moment being the man or woman who commands such adoration. Imagine for a moment how it feels to have the population of a small town hanging on your every move and word and prepared to do anything – yes, anything – you tell them to. I believe them when the musos say there is no feeling like it.

Consider, then, that if you have had some of this rare and potent drug, how hard it is to give up. Ye Olde Brian Clough (the footballer and later football manager, if you don't know him) said that once players stop playing, the authorities should just take them out and shoot them. Such is the pain, he says, of the awful silence when thirty thousand people are no longer chanting your name that it is kinder just to be put out of your misery.

Now, a footballer's career is limited by the age of his legs (and all his other bits, too) but a muso can go on much, much longer. Witness the Rolling Stones, who are now officially older than Stonehenge. None of these gentlemen needs the money from touring any more, but, nonetheless, the only thing that's been on the road longer than they have is the white line down the middle. What makes them do it? Well, if it ain't money, it must be the pleasure of it.

Indeed, ask them and that's what they tell you. As do Status Quo, Elton John, Eric Clapton, AC/DC (a bald schoolboy? Are you sure?) and all those other monsters from another age who aren't short of a bob or two but who would just die without the fix they get from touring.

Now, our second answer to the question of why acts tour was: because it's always been done that way.

Even in this day and age of innovative thinking, digital connections and a new millennium, record companies, artists and their managements still remain deeply attached to the album-tour-album-tour method of marketing.

As we have noted several times in the book, the most traditional way of breaking an act into the public consciousness is to take them on the road and get them to play to as many friendly faces as possible. Then, once that tour is complete and the band have produced their next album, do it all again.

There is a good reason for continuing to rely on this methodology, and that reason gives us our third answer to the question of why tour – simply, nobody has ever come up with a better way of promoting an act and their music. (Have a look again at Chapter 6 if you want more on this.)

So they're the reasons for doing it. Now let's get down to brass tacks and look a little harder at some of the advantages it brings. One of the big ones, of course, is publicity, because a tour gives a big, sharp, clear, long-lasting focus to any publicity campaign.

Think of an extreme example of this, such as, say, a Madonna tour of the UK. Much as she now has a house in London, the fact that she is over here and working is a major event. She will, then, appear on all the chat shows and do interviews with the music and general media simply and solely for the reason that she's out on the road and the media are interested in her tour. Thus, the mere fact of touring becomes news in itself.

And, not only does the tour generate pre-publicity, the stories will just run and run. For instance, the first night will produce more coverage of who was at the gig, what the show looks like, is there anything outrageous happening on or off stage, etc. etc.

The best analogy for all this that I can think of is that of a film première. A tour is like having a première of a new film every night for a month – and, on each night of the tour, a different set of media is activated and interested. That's because, unlike a film première which takes place in central London, a music tour takes place in a different city every night for two months and each of those cities has its own newspapers, magazines and television and radio stations. A film première, big and glitzy and media-attracting though it is, is a one-off. Two days after it has taken place, it's as cold as yesterday's chips. But a big tour coming to town is a hot news event somewhere in the country thirty or forty times over.

If, then, Madonna is touring, it is likely she will do all the interviews with the London-based national media before the concerts start. But then comes the big bonus. If she is playing at the National Exhibition Centre in Birmingham, the papers, radio and the telly in the West Midlands will get excited about the show and will want to feature it with competitions for tickets, interviews with Her Madgeship, reviews after the gig and so on and so forth. The same will be true if she plays Sheffield and Edinburgh and everywhere else she goes.

This regional effect has several benefits. Firstly, it keeps her tour alive as a news item long after her first set of interviews have faded from public memory. (In journalism we always speak of nine-day memory: most events have entirely vanished from the public consciousness within the space of nine days.) Regional media, then, help keep the tour hot and current.

The second big bonus is the breadth of the coverage.

There's a lot of people in and around Birmingham who read, see and hear the media there – many millions more, in fact, than the number of people who will get to see the show. Thus, by being in all the local media just because of her tour, Madonna and her new music are being presented to more people than would fit into the National Exhibition Centre if she played every night for a month. And, as we have noted many times in the course of this worthy tome, publicity equals record sales (unless you're Gary Glitter).

Another advantage of touring is, as we noted, the publicity not just for the person on tour, but also for his or her new music. How many times have you stood at a gig, enjoyed the first three songs from your favourite band then heard those words: 'Now here's a song from the new album ...' Every single time. This is why, of course, the band is there on stage in the first place: to promote the new album.

Sometimes your heart sinks a bit when the singer says, here's a new song, because we all like classics. But songs are not born classics; they have to become so, and often take some little while to become embedded in the public's affections. That first airing on stage during the tour to promote a new album is the traditional square one.

OK, now we've looked at why people tour and what they can expect to get out of it. But who runs the tour? In short, concert promoters – but that term doesn't mean exactly what it used to.

The business of concert promotion basically falls into two eras: before Peter Grant and after Peter Grant.

Before Led Zeppelin manager Peter Grant, concert promoters used to have all the power. They controlled all aspects of a tour, from which venues were used to which band played in them. This is still true to an extent of up-and-coming acts, but for established performers the balance of power has shifted mightily. The late – some say great, others say he was a complete pig – Peter Grant was the man who saw to that.

Peter started out feeling the same way as everybody else in the business in the sixties: that promoters ran tours and a band were fortunate if they could persuade a promoter to put them on the road. But, as Led Zep rose to superstardom, Peter's attitudes started to change. He began to believe that an act with the commercial and marketing power of Led Zep should tour on their own terms and nobody else's.

Thus, the day came in the early seventies when Peter said to a concert promoter, 'We're going on tour. You sort it out.'

I can't overemphasise what impact this had. In this one moment, all concert promoters working with big acts were shifted from the position of senior partner deciding all the moves to being the hired help carrying out the client's wishes. I'd have loved to have seen the look on the promoter's face in that first meeting.

Peter told him, 'We want to play x number of venues in y number of countries. Let me know when you have it set up.' (Not that Peter ever spoke in such polite terms, but that's at least the gist of what he said.)

That left the promoter with the job of attending to all the practicalities and details of that. And what does this entail? Well, it's a mammoth task of logistics and organisation that requires teams of people working round the clock for several months and would take an encyclopedia to explain in detail. So, for our purposes, let's just look at the main areas needing attention and take an overview of the jobs to be done. The agenda goes something like this:

1. Finding and hiring venues

This requires a great deal more skill than is immediately apparent. Firstly, the venues must all be of the appropriate size. For example, Madonna, her stage set and her fans would not fit into the Beachcomber Club in Brighton and, should I ever tour, it is unlikely that the National Exhibition Centre would be appropriate for my one-man show of Armenian baldy jokes (trust me, though, it's a winning act). Secondly, the price of the venues must be appropriate. Above and beyond all else, a promoter must stay in business; that is the prime motivation of any commercial operation in the capitalist world. So the promoter must negotiate the best price he can get from the concert halls. If the price is too high relative to the number of people likely to attend the show, that is a recipe for commercial disaster. Thirdly, the venues must be appropriate technically. That is, the power supply must be adequate, there must be space to accommodate all the effects, scenery, dancers and so on, and the seating (or lack thereof) must be appropriate to the type of people likely to come. Finally, the venues must be available on the right dates. There is no commercial sense in playing Penzance one night, then being in Edinburgh the next, then back to Truro for the third. The venues for two consecutive nights must be as close as possible to each other, to both minimise transport costs and save everybody a lot of time, effort and energy.

2. Organising the crew and transport

Even a medium-size music show won't fit into the back of a Ford Transit any more and the problem of how to get all the tons of guitars, drums, PA and everything else from one place to another is a major logistical task. Not only is it a physical challenge – just how do you get all that stuff from here to there – but it is also a commercial challenge. Logistically, the problem is a relatively simple one to handle if you hire one wagon for every bit of kit, but that, of course, is financial stupidity. So, to keep transport costs to a minimum, the question is how few vehicles can all this stuff be crammed into. Packing a lorry, utilising every cubic centimetre of its capacity, is, then, an art in itself. And along with the transport, of course, come the road crew, the legendary roadies. Now, while these boys can be wild – and I advise against drinking with them unless you have nothing to do for a couple of days after – they are also hugely dependable and phenomenally hard-working. The title of the old Motörhead album No Sleep 'Til Hammersmith pretty much sums it up. When you go on the road as crew, you work and work and work until the last gig is done. Even though the conditions they sometimes have to live and work in are often not conducive to giving of their best, these boys do it anyway. I raise my hat to all of them: lighters, riggers, caterers, guitar roadies, the lot. (Oh, and while we're on the subject, here's the roadies joke: how many roadies does it take to change a light bulb? One, two; one, two.)

3. Looking after the band

This can be the trickiest part of organising a tour. Now, we've all heard those apocryphal stories about Rod Stewart wanting only brown M&Ms in the dressing room afterwards and Elton John insisting on blue tulips backstage, but let me tell you, those tales truly are bollocks. If there are any such stipulations in a contract between promoter and act, the only people who would know about them are the promoter and the performer – and you can be damn sure they ain't telling. However, what actually happens in the real backstage world is far, far more bizarre than anything that may be passed off as a 'true story, honest' by some guy in the pub who claims to have been Rod's driver. Now, I have to say I ain't telling either, but just take my word for it that what is requested by acts and what is given to them is pretty weird on occasion. Acts ask for – and, by and large, get – pretty much anything they want. If that begs the question of whether promoters are ever involved in securing supplies of illegal substances, I can only tell you this. All the promoters I've ever known were decent blokes whose only involvement in recreational drugs was a few pints on a regular basis. Indeed, all the promoters I've ever known were round, decent human beings who, because they tend to be a lot older than the acts they are dealing with, often become something of a father figure and regularly try to help young musos stay on the straight and narrow. But they are also businessmen. And if the top star says he's not going on stage without a line of coke beforehand, what do they do? What would you do? Then, in addition to any incidence of illicit substances (which, I have to point out, are not popular with all musos and are certainly not, in the overwhelming majority of instances, a prerequisite for performing), promoters also have to look after acts in terms of more normal things, such as hotels that are to the act's taste, food that fits in with the macrobiotic/veggie/live chicken diet or whatever else they happen to be on, medical cover and entertainment (either virtual or real) for all the time spent hanging about and/or travelling. On top of that, promoters also have to attend to all the human needs we all have: proximity of loved ones, contact with friends and family etc. etc.

4. Paying the bills

My, this is big. Let's start with something we've already mentioned: the venues. They exist to make money by hiring out their facilities, and every time those facilities are used the venue management presents a bill – often a very big bill. Indeed, the larger the venue and the better the facilities it has, the more its management charges. Hiring the NEC for five nights, Earls Court for two or a big football ground for one doesn't come cheap. And on top of that is something else that doesn't come cheap: the band. Even though the act has hired the promoter to handle the tour, the band will still want to take the lion's share of the profits and that money has to come out of the promoter's incomes from ticket sales. Furthermore, the road crew need to be paid, the transport, catering and accommodation costs need to be paid and – a whopping great sum, this – so does the insurance. The promoter must make sure his ample arse is covered if the singer sprains an ankle and is in pain or, worse, if the guitarist breaks an arm and can't perform. The promoter must also be insured if, God forbid, one of us punters comes to grief. It is rare but not unknown that people die at concerts. The promoter must be certain he is not open to a multi-million-pound lawsuit if that happens on his watch.

5. Looking after the punters

Us folk going to concerts must be safe by law. The promoter must have taken all reasonable steps – and some fairly exacting ones, too – to make sure we all get out in one piece. There are plenty of laws and local regulations the promoter has to comply with in this area, and lots of officials always come to the show venue to make sure the promoter does. And, over and above what the law says, we punters have other needs too – like being able to pee when we need to, have a drink (alcoholic or not) when we fancy and eat when we're hungry. The promoter must ensure all these needs are met. And it doesn't end there. The promoter's responsibilities to us don't begin and end at the door of the venue. The venue must be reachable by a number of different forms of transport and there must be somewhere to park for those who have chosen to drive there. In addition, the leaving of the gig should be civilised enough so that it is not a threat to anybody's well-being – and that can take some achieving when anything up to seventy-five thousand people are all trying to get out of a place at the same time.

That is a long, long way short of being a comprehensive list of the things a promoter needs to do, but I hope it gives some idea of the mammoth range of tasks facing anybody putting on a show for profit. There's one other consideration in this mix, too, and it's something I could have mentioned under paying the bills – but I didn't because it's too complex. Let's, then, take it on its own: the small matter of royalties.

As I've said many times throughout this book, music is somebody's property and each and every time it is used, the user has to pay a bill. The law says the user of music at a gig is the venue and, therefore, the venue has to settle up with the PRS (the songwriters' royalty collection body that we met in Chapters 4 and 10, as I'm sure you recall). Now, if there have been seventy-five thousand people at the show, the amount of money paid to the PRS is very significant. The venue, of course, is not going to take this out of its profits, so the fee it charges for hiring out its facilities incorporates an element recognising the cost of paying the PRS. So, while the venue actually sends off the cheque, the money, in effect, comes out of the promoter's pocket.

For the promoter, this is a bizarre situation of double accounting. Remember that in law and in practice the songwriter and the performer are entirely separate entities – and the promoter has to pay them both, either directly or indirectly. But, though they may be separate entities, they can be the same human being.

Thus, if Sting is onstage singing 'An Englishman In New York', the promoter has to pay Sting for his performance and then, through the venue's performance royalties sent to the PRS, pay Sting as the songwriter for the use of his work. So Sting gets paid twice for doing the one job. No wonder his house is bigger than Derby. (Though just to shatter this image a little it does happen that the songwriting royalties paid to Sting, and other singer-composers, are deducted by the promoter from the performance fee.

Now, all these tasks and responsibilities are present whether the promoter is working on behalf of a big act or is doing the more traditional role of having control of the whole thing.

And, in any circumstances, the promoter's sources of income are the same. Let's look at what they are:

1. Ticket sales
Big. The bulk of what promoters earn comes from people buying tickets – no surprises there. That's the tried and trusted method of making money from staging gigs and has been since the days of Bach and Mozart. In this day and age the notion of ticket sales ranges from us punters buying the cheapest ones we can find to corporate clients buying premium tickets in bulk.

2. Merchandising

This is another big element and one that often goes unnoticed. Merchandising is the overarching term to cover everything sold in the venue that has the band's name on it. Typical examples are T-shirts, caps and clothing. Other examples can include, well, just about anything the merchandiser's imagination can come up with. Merchandisers are companies that specialise in this stuff – the, er, merchandise – and they pay the promoter handsomely to have a stall inside the venue from where they can sell it.

3. Catering

The classic example of this is at a festival, where, unless you've brought your own sandwiches, the only things to eat are those which are available from the vendors on site. This means we are a captive audience, and a hungry captive audience will get through beer, burgers, veggie croquettes, you name it, in alarming quantities. The caterers sell lots of this stuff and make big profits and, just like the merchandisers, pay handsomely for the privilege of feeding the five thousand. In a hall where catering is already installed, the promoter and the owner of the venue will come to some arrangement as to who gets what share of this income. Usually, their agreement is along the lines of a lower price for hiring the place if the venue owner gets to keep all the profits from flogging burgers.

4. Media rights

It's a media world out there and a big gig is a media event. Indeed, a big gig is a media event in a league entirely of its own. Over the years there have been lots of foolish statements made that comedy or fashion or something else is the new rock 'n' roll. Is it bollocks. Only rock 'n' roll is rock 'n' roll – and television, radio and other types of broadcasters love it and will pay well to have exclusive rights to broadcast it. In fact, some of them love it so much they bought the company.

It is no coincidence that one of Europe's biggest concert promoters, Midland Concert Promotions (MCP), was acquired by US media giant SFX. SFX could clearly see the advantages in having both a company that puts on big gigs and one that broadcasts them. Cuts out the middleman. Before that, though, MCP – and all the other big promotions companies – sold the rights to broadcast their shows to the highest bidder. (Oh, and a little story about MCP. For its first twenty-five years the company was based in Walsall, in the West Midlands. However, not many Americans have heard of Walsall and US-based organisations often assimilated the word as Warsaw. So, when MCP were dealing with the managements of big US acts and said where the company was based, confusion often arose – and, regularly, it resulted in Mega Management Inc of New York ringing MCP's number but with the code for Warsaw rather than Walsall. I wonder if the little old Polish lady who answered those calls ever got to see any of the superstars who were trying to play in her front room.)

5. Tour support

As we noted earlier in the chapter, record companies gain hugely from a tour because of all the extra record sales it generates. They very often help get the tour off the ground by putting money into it, a sum known as tour support. This figure will vary hugely, of course, depending on the act involved, the size of the tour and the attitude of the label.

6. Support act buy-on

This is indirect income for the promoter and sometimes he may not see any of it at all, the total sum merely ending up in the pockets of the headline act. But the central fact here is that support acts hand over money to be on the same bill as major artists. Hard and mercenary though it seems – and is – whether you get a gig as a big act's support depends on whether you're up to the job and whether you're prepared to hand over the requisite amounts of cash. In return for the money, the support act gains an audience that it could not garner on its own, so it is often a good investment. But, as we noted, what the headline act does with that money is up to them.

Once more, this list of income sources is absolutely not a comprehensive one, but it's a fair outline of main revenue streams.

There is one other element of the concert business that we should mention before we go: booking agents. Bookers seek out gigs for the acts they represent. Of course, Sting's gigs don't take a lot of finding. The man says he wants to play and promoters come crawling through the Wiltshire corn for the privilege of being allowed to do the job. But acts of a lesser stature than Sting need somebody to argue their case and find opportunities for them to play. That's the role of a booking agent.

It should also be mentioned that the live music business provides work for thousands of other people and allows many folks in all sort of professions a chance to get involved with the exciting business of rock 'n' roll. For instance, the live sector employs sound and light engineers, effects and pyrotechnics people, designers, choreographers, dancers, painters, carpenters, musos even ... It's a long, long list – and these roles provide the most ready access to the music industry.

Chapter 19

THE RIGHTS AND RESPONSIBILITIES OF BEING A STAR

THERE IS A GREAT deal of luck involved in become a star and sustaining a career. It is, though, utterly true that the harder you work, the luckier you get.

This is a particularly relevant concept at the beginning of a musician's career, and that's where we'll start this chapter. We saw in Chapter 10 that there are no short cuts to success and climbing the ladder requires more hard graft than most people are capable of. (Indeed, the level of effort required has taught me never to underestimate a successful muso: they've seen more hardship, more hunger and more discomfort than most of us and, for many musos, the hardship, hunger and discomfort go on for a number of years. You have to be very, very tough to survive a life like that. And if you will bear with me a moment, the nicest story I ever heard to illustrate the level of deprivation inherent in making it to the top concerns Jimmy Lea, the man who, as part of Slade, wrote some of the greatest pop songs this country has seen. The story goes – and I am assured this is true – that, at the time Slade started making some impact, the band had their first meeting with their new manager. It was in a greasy-spoon café and the new manager had double egg and chips. As a struggling muso, Jim had never seen double egg and chips before and stared at this magnificent feast on the table in front of him wide-eyed. Eventually, hunger and envy got the better of him and he reached over and scoffed one of the eggs. Afterwards, he was full of apologies but explained that double egg and chips was a whole new experience to him and he had just been seduced by the opulence of it.)

OK, assuming a muso has gone through that painful process of breaking into the public consciousness and is at least a few rungs up the ladder and, hopefully, on the top, what responsibilities does he or she have? The first and biggest, of course, is to work.

As we have noted throughout the book, working means touring, doing interviews with anyone who will talk to you, turning up at album-signing sessions, going to launch parties and undertaking every other promotional activity the label can think of. Without limitation as to time or effort, it means doing all it takes to gain as high a profile and sell as many records as possible.

One element of that, often overlooked, is keeping the team around you happy. These folk – from label staff to managers – are the people who helped the star up the first, most difficult rungs of the ladder, and these are the people who knock their pan out to keep him or her at the top of the pile. They are also the people who will be there for that star when times are tough, the times when you find out who really is on your side. They deserve all the encouragement they can get, plus, if the star wants to look at it from a more selfish point of view, these people will work a lot harder if they get a bit of recognition now and again – particularly so as many of these essential workers are in unsung positions and are easily ignored.

Bright stars, though, know who these people are, how to motivate them and why it is worth doing so. A perfect example of that came with Kylie Minogue and Jason Donovan in the late eighties. They were the hottest pop property in the country at the time – by a long way – but were signed to an

THE RIGHT AND RESPONSIBILITIES OF BEING A STAR

indie label, PWL. Being an indie, PWL of course did not have its own distribution; that function was handled by an outside company, Pinnacle.

Now, there's a job in distribution companies called 'picking' and it's fantastically boring.

A distributor's warehouse is arranged a bit like a supermarket, with rows and aisles, but instead of bread, tinned peas and frozen pizza, the shelves contain albums, singles and videos. A retailer will send in an order for five copies of album a, four of album b, six of album c and four each of videos x, y and z. The order comes into the warehouse, where the manager gives it like a shopping list to a man or woman – the picker – who is armed with nothing more than an underused brain and a shopping trolley of exactly the same kind as you see at your local supermarket.

The picker then goes up and down the rows and aisles locating albums a, b and c and videos x, y and z and putting the correct numbers of each into the trolley before taking that order to the packers to be dispatched. Now, this is a lot like spending your whole day, every day, in a supermarket buying beans. Picking may be in the rock 'n' roll business but it ain't very rock 'n' roll.

PWL, though, being a very bright company, asked Kylie and Jason to go down to Pinnacle's warehouse in Orpington, on the edge of London, to spend an afternoon picking; Kylie and Jason, being bright stars, agreed to do it. That made a great picture for the local paper and for the music trade press and, above all else, it made the pickers fall in love with these people.

Pickers are notorious for getting orders wrong. Not surprising really; undertaxed brains turn to mush very easily. But in this one act, PWL, with the assistance of its stars, ensured every Kylie and Jason album was picked accurately and dispatched as rapidly as possible. Not only that, the people picking them also got a little warm glow in doing so. It was a brilliant move: everybody benefited and the only cost was Kylie and Jason's time.

This, then, brings us back to the crux of this chapter – that stars have to be prepared to give of their time and effort if they want to remain stars.

When people first become stars, they tend to love all the attention. They love talking about their work, their lives and, if so inclined, their loves. In that first flush of enthusiasm they are generally prepared to do anything the label asks of them. However, the attraction of this disappears quite quickly. Thus, the first few dozen interviews are done with zeal and enthusiasm – but then the ennui begins to set in. It is at this point that the stars the record company likes to work with and the ones it doesn't begin to become apparent.

Labels believe that the harder the artist works, the more the label can achieve on their behalf. Indeed, Paul Russell, president of Sony's music operations in Europe, devoted much of one keynote address to the company to exhorting artists to graft – that is, to do the interviews, to pose for the pix, to smile and make nice with fans and other people who matter a lot.

A prime example of how it should be done is James Last. Though this guy's easy-listening big-band music is not to everyone's taste – and it certainly ain't the cutting edge of music – the fact that his albums have been selling like hot cakes and cold beer for several decades is testimony to the fact that he must be doing something right. The press office at his label, Polydor, loved him because whatever they asked him to do, he'd do it. He would cheerfully – and 'cheerfully' is the operative word here – give of his time to do all the interviews and glad-handing that was required. How much has this approach prolonged his career? I wonder. It certainly can't have done it any harm, now, can it?

Such an attitude makes me also wonder about the Waterboys. For those who don't remember, these guys were a highly rated and much-loved band signed to Chrysalis and they were pretty big in the second half of the eighties. Not too long after the height of their success, though, they split, so we

THE RIGHT AND RESPONSIBILITIES OF BEING A STAR

shall never know how durable they could have been. But I just remember Chrysalis boss Roy Eldridge tearing his hair out because they absolutely would not do interviews. As a former head of press for the label, Roy knew all too well the value of a band talking to any and every media person who happens by, so the level of his frustration is something I can only guess at. I can also only guess at the degree of threats and inducements he offered the band to actually sit down with a journalist now and again. How big the Waterboys could have been if they'd stuck together and done what was asked of them, we shall, sadly, never know.

And here's another example of the things that can befall musos not as diligent as Herr Last. A few years ago I called into the Arista offices for a cup of tea. Some young hopeful on his first album was doing all the tedious phone interviews with all the regional papers. After finishing one he started whining about how he couldn't be bothered to do any more. He was bored, he reckoned.

The head of press begged and pleaded with him to carry on. Failing to move the recalcitrant muso, she then fetched the head of the company, who also begged and pleaded and pointed out what a major effect on the young star's career doing all these interviews would have. That fell on deaf ears, too, and the young man eventually left the building.

Where is he now? Who knows, because his career hit a grinding halt after his first album. Now, a lot of careers come crashing down at this point in their development, but I have often wondered whether he would have got over this hurdle had he done all the interviews he was asked to do.

We have noted time and again in this book that the purpose of the music industry is to make acts famous. Once they are famous, though, a lot of the onus is on the star to stay that way by continuing to work at it. Indeed, it is very, very much in the star's interest to do so. To clarify this a little, let's look again for a moment at the relationship between star and record company.

There is one factor which binds together these two entities closer than a stamp to a letter: money – and, specifically, the money that accrues from selling records. It is always possible that a star and his or her label like each other very much as human beings: they may be good friends who drink, dine and chat together. However, they may also detest each other and want to see the other one strangled with their own dangly bits. But, whatever their personal relationship, they make money together or not at all. That is, every record sold benefits both the artist making it and the label releasing it. The more sold, the more money both make.

Doing the kind of work that labels ask artists to do helps that process enormously by raising the star's profile out in the world of us record buyers. And doing the work also has another major benefit for the muso in that it helps his standing with the people who are being paid to and who are trying to help his career – the label.

A lot of the artist's work is, then, about building up relations with his colleagues and partners. The artist can do this, as we noted, by working hard towards the external audiences and gaining standing among the label staff this way. He can also do it by addressing the company directly. The place where stars do this is at the label's own meetings. The most important of these are those that pull in all the company's staff; that is, not just the people who work in its head office in London, but all the sales staff who spend their lives travelling the highways and byways of Britain flogging the label's wares to unsuspecting retailers.

These are quite big gatherings and the largest annual ones are held in a nice hotel each autumn. There, all the company's products being released in the important last quarter of the year – a period which accounts for about 75% of all music sold during any given twelve months – are presented to the sales force.

Many of the products (I hate that word, but it is one which labels often use to describe their releases) are presented just by playing a disc or a video. But the ones that are best received are the ones that the act concerned turn up to play.

Believe me, even a sales conference – the epitome of the music industry, as it is a forum for all the label has to offer – can become a little tedious after a couple of days, and an act on stage really grabs the attention, particularly if everything else on the menu has come at the attendees just via disc or video.

A star has, I believe, a responsibility to work in this respect: to go to the sales conferences, to play and, just as important, to be at the social gathering – generally a dinner – that completes these events where he ought to make himself available to the label staff. Just as with the Kylie and Jason example we looked at earlier in the chapter, I can't tell you what an impact this has on the people there. It makes the sales force that much more inspired to sell the artist's records and raises morale all round.

In addition, this onus on a star to work in such ways is entirely fair in the sense that it is both a reasonable contribution to the success of his or her career and a just reward to the label for showing faith in the rising muso in the first place.

Musos also have a responsibility to help the industry that has made them rich and famous when the business hits difficult times. The most difficult times, of course, are when governments are in the process of passing laws that affect music. We noted earlier that this is when the trump card can be brought out, and I cited in Chapter 15 the Corrs and their impassioned activities on behalf of securing the best possible version of the Copyright Directive. No other industry can match this. I mean, who is the most famous and sexy person in the telecommunications and Internet sector? Nobody knows and nobody cares.

But the music industry's playing of this trump card would not have been possible had it not been for the Corrs' willingness to get involved by turning up at the appropriate functions and taking the time and trouble to understand the issues.

Out in society at large, I think there are other responsibilities, too. People who have made it big in music are hugely influential to the nation's youth. Thus, it is incumbent on them, I feel, to be aware of that and behave appropriately. Now, what anybody does in the privacy of their own home is up to them, but when in the spotlight, I believe stars have a responsibility to encourage the positive. What does that mean? Who knows, but these are the things I have asked of those acts I work with:

1. Don't smoke and don't make it appear that smoking is sophisticated or attractive.
2. The same goes for drugs.
3. Be conscious of your power and use it for good causes – either a charity you believe in or a political cause or helping the government with some information campaign like encouraging young people to vote.

Of course, for some musos, smoking or drugs or – God forbid – guns and violence are part of the image they seek to present. Each to their own, but I'd rather wear John Prescott's unwashed pants than make a living out of any of that kind of imagery.

And all these things are important because musos have such huge power to influence. I was standing watching Live Aid – you remember, the big charity gig run by Bob Geldof in 1985 – when one old industry hand remarked to me that no other business could do this. I asked him what he meant, and he pointed out that novelists writing on stage would be boring, and actors couldn't maintain this level of intensity and interest over the course of a whole day, so there was nothing that could focus attention and inspire action like good old rock 'n' roll. I realised he was right.

With that realisation, I understood the degree to which musos have power – and that this power can be ignored, used

THE RIGHT AND RESPONSIBILITIES OF BEING A STAR

for good or used for bad. But, so long as musos are switched on enough to realise they have such influence, it is down to their conscience and personality as to how they use it. But not realising is just naïve or deliberately perverse.

OK, that's responsibilities. So what rights do musos have?

Above all, of course, they have the same rights as the rest of us to freedom from fear of violence or intimidation. They also have a right to privacy but, of course, where the boundary between public and private lives is drawn is much open to debate. If my lady is topless on the beach, she can be pretty certain that nobody is going to take pictures of her. However, if she had had a chart single, you can be damn certain that if she gets her tits out, pictures of them will appear all over the press not long after. Is that an invasion of her privacy? Discuss.

I feel very sorry for stars in this respect. If I get so drunk that I can't get home or have a row with my lady in public, nobody notices or cares. If Sting does it, he's in the papers and his personal life is laid out for all to see. It's a high price to pay for fame.

Importantly, though, musos have rights under the law, just like the rest of us. The law is, as we noted in Chapter 9, more the muso's friend than his enemy, for that simple reason that it gives him rights – rights as a human being, as an entrepreneur, as an artist and as an owner of things. Just as it does for the rest of us, it protects his person, his property and his work.

This last issue is an important one as it raises a thing I detest: piracy. Musos have the right to be protected from piracy. So what is piracy?

Well, we looked at this briefly in Chapter 10, but let's go into a little more detail here. Piracy is the name given to the practice of making unlicensed copies of music. Unlicensed means they are reproduced without permission and that means they range from bootlegs – that is, recordings made via an up-the-jumper microphone by somebody at the back of a gig – to counterfeits, discs that are high-quality copies designed to look like the real thing and often almost indistinguishable from it.

Piracy is a menace, for these reasons:

1. It deprives the muso of his or her rightful income. When taken to extremes, it can kill a whole industry. In Africa, the pirates are rampant and, should a legitimate disc be released, illegal copies of it are available within literally hours. Because record buyers prefer the cheaper pirated version to the full-price legit version, sales of the legit versions in many parts of Africa are almost nil – the handful that do get sold being bought by the pirates as their master copy. This means there is no profit for the record company, no resources coming in with which it can invest in talent and, ultimately, no incentive for the label to put out records at all. So, legit labels in many parts of that unfortunate continent have shut up shop and fled. This deprives the local talent of their proper outlets, which means most talented African musos never get any kind of hearing. Those that do – the best and the luckiest – have to go to Paris or London or New York to make their mark, as these are the only places where they can access the legitimate industry and all its infrastructure.

2. Piracy undermines all the financial structures of the business. Pirates take but put nothing back; they do not invest in the talent they exploit. In fact, the reverse is true: by depriving everyone of rightful incomes, they greatly undermine the industry's ability to invest in its future.

3. Pirates are not nice people. They are often also involved in drugs, people trafficking and the kind of pornography that decent people don't want to think about. Money that goes into a pirate's hands is not going to some harmless, well-intentioned hippy. It is going to vile scum who are going to use it to finance far more nefarious operations.

A muso, then, has the right to be protected from this stuff. But whether the authorities get round to doing that depends on their priorities and whether they actually recognise this as a problem. Police and customs officials and folks like that often think piracy is a victimless crime and are very relaxed about doing nothing about it. Well, I've seen the kind of pornography financed by pirates and it makes me want to rip somebody's head off. People involved in music piracy are directly connected to villains who exploit the most vulnerable in our society – be it children used for porn or refugees desperately seeking to flee violence – and the sooner the authorities get a grip on that, the better. And, just as a final rant, because this stuff makes me very angry, if the various people in a position of influence had listened to me when I first tried to expose this stuff, we might be a lot further down the line of controlling it by now.

OK, that's enough of that. Let's turn to a happier topic – another right that musos have: the right to recognition. That is, I believe people in the music industry have the right to be honoured and recognised just like any other artist. We give awards to our painters and actors, so why shouldn't musos have a few honours, too, and be treated with the same esteem and accord as their counterparts from other fields of artistic endeavour? We saw in Chapter 13 that it was money rather than anything else that first brought some official recognition to the business – that is, it took Andrew Potter laying out what the music industry is worth in financial terms to get the government's attention – but now, thankfully, because of the ball Andrew started rolling, we have the knights and CBEs et al. that we should have had years ago. We ain't had a dame in popular music yet, though opera has a few, but there is reason to hope now. And the reasons to hope are: Sir Paul McCartney, Sir Cliff Richard, Sir Elton John, Sir George Martin, Sir Mick Jagger – all recognition of talent and service that is long, long overdue.

It is also appropriate, I think, that Liverpool's airport is now named after John Lennon and I look forward to the day when many more public buildings and places are named after musos, just like they are currently named after actors, painters and some very questionable politicians. Musos are both artists and significant people within our society and they have a right to the same standing as their peers.

Further, I believe that musicians should be recognised not just for their success and achievements, but also for the pleasure they put into people's lives and the good they do the country.

That pleasure element is one that is often overlooked. There are musicians working in every style and genre and that means that each of us – yes, each of us, everyone in this country – has been given pleasure by musos' work. And that pleasure can be intense – over and over again. We all have albums we have played to death and they can often give us as much joy now as they did when we first bought them five, ten or even twenty years ago. People who can do that to us (and what other art form makes you want to jump up and down with joy) should be recognised and honoured.

Musos are also fantastically good for the UK's balance of payments. We saw earlier that music exports are a huge source of money for the UK. I think the public should recognise that the people behind that – tattooed, scruffy, hungover and everything else that they are – should, nonetheless, get a fair amount of kudos for such achievements.

Personally, I raise my hat to all of them.

Chapter 20

⭐

THE GLOBAL BUSINESS

IT'S A BIG WORLD out there, and it would be a mad commercial decision to ignore it.

Fortunately in the UK, we are able to exploit that big world to a significant extent. This country is the world's second most important source of music, after the US, and our reputation for producing the music the world wants to hear opens doors for our newer artists. Indeed, it is now a self-reinforcing system: the country's track record of achievement helps the standing of each new generation of music makers, just as it does French chefs (though why those boys can't do breakfast is a mystery to me), Italian designers and German engineers. In all these cases, history and tradition are such that expectations are raised before anything has even happened.

This international standing is vitally important to the UK industry because the British business spends so much on A&R that it is very difficult to make a profit on any given record just through UK sales alone. The British business must sell its products overseas if it is to remain viable.

How, then, is the business configured on a global basis to ensure worldwide reach for those artists who are capable of attracting such a global audience? Let's start this round-the-world-in-eight-pages odyssey by looking at the main area driving cross-border success, the major record companies.

As we have noted – but, yes, we're going to say it again – the major labels are global. Each of them operates in all developed nations and in a number of developing countries, too. While Africa remains a blind spot for the industry, the business has operations pretty much everywhere else: the Americas, Europe, Japan and Australasia are extremely well covered and there are many other offices across the former communist states of eastern Europe, including Russia. In addition, the industry is strongly represented in the Pacific Rim nations like Korea, Thailand, Taiwan and, increasingly, in China, and in places like India and the Middle East, too.

The global coverage, then, is comprehensive – with the exception of poor, benighted, ignored Africa, but even that might change given a little political will.

Back in the more fortunate continents, record companies always hope that every artist on their books is going to be a global success. They know this is like hoping for a lottery win, but even lottery wins happen for some people.

There are, though, pre-requisites for hitting that global big time. The first and biggest is, obviously, having the music that people want to hear. The second is having the global infrastructure and expertise to deliver it. The third is, sadly, singing in English. Every star who is a star on a planet-wide basis sings in English. (It is possible to have an international hit with non-English lyrics if you are German and sell records in Switzerland and Austria, too, or French and sell in Belgium and parts of Canada. However, for our purposes here, we shall look only at genuinely global success.)

I use the word 'sadly' when I say that people have to sing in English to have an international hit because it seems to me that this indicates a lack of open ears among us Anglo-Saxon nations when it comes to record buying. But there it is. It's a fact of life and business, so we might as well just get on with it.

THE GLOBAL BUSINESS

OK, assuming a record company has an act which is going to cross national boundaries, what does it do to break that act?

We looked at this a little in Chapter 6, in talking about making a star; now let's examine somewhat more closely how this business of transcending borders works.

The key point here is that major record companies are not only globally based, they are also globally organised. That is, they operate on a worldwide basis all the time. No decision is taken in any country – not even the smallest – that doesn't have some impact (however modest) on the way the overall, international company is run. This means that every office around the world is connected in a very real sense to every other. How they are connected is through the parent company.

Warner Music, for instance, is a worldwide company operating out of New York. It has subsidiary companies around the world – Warner Music UK, Warner Music Germany, Warner Music Australia, and so on – but those subsidiaries are all part of the whole that is Warner Music.

Warner Music is run as a global operation, which means that there is one central mechanism for supervising everything happening across the world. How that central mechanism is connected to the various offices around the world is through communication – lots and lots of communication. Emails, phone calls and dear old letters pass between the head office and its subsidiary companies every day. In addition, of course, the subsidiary companies – generally called affiliates, remember – talk to one another just as much.

Those communications, whether they go from head office in New York to the affiliates or are simply between affiliates, contain a lot of business data about money, sales figures, supplies of plastic and suchlike; but, more excitingly, they also contain a lot of information about acts and music. Through this exchange of information each affiliate is able to see what each of its sister companies has – and Warner Music HQ can see the big picture.

Now, as we saw in Chapter 6, a large part of this information about acts is a sales job. Warner Music Germany, for instance, might say to all its colleagues around the world, 'We've got this great new rock-pop act and they are perfect for your country.' Of course, Warner Music Germany is eager to have its acts sold around the world because it will get a percentage of the income from each of those sales. That gives it more money in next year's budget, more brownie points with head office, a very nice boost to morale around the company and, most probably, a nice bonus for the boss and selected senior staff at the end of the year.

This kind of sales job also has advantages for Warner Music Germany's sister companies in that it gives them more acts to pick from than just the ones that their own country is producing. It may well be that when Warner Music Germany says, 'This act is perfect for your country,' there is truth there.

Of course, every Warner Music company around the world listens when Warner Music Germany speaks (or so Warner Music Germany likes to believe), but that worldwide family of companies listens even harder when Warner in the US speaks. From that company has sprung Madonna, REM, AC/DC and a host of big, big names – names whose records have been huge on every continent on earth and have made a fortune for each of the Warner Music companies around the world. Naturally enough, then, the Warner family really wants to know what's coming next out of the US.

The same is true, but to a lesser extent, for the UK company, which, after its American counterpart, is the next best source of international talent.

These companies talk to one another all the time from a distance. They also talk to one another as much as possible face to face. In addition to Midem, Popkomm and other industry events, such as awards shows, where many of them get together, Warner Music will invite senior people four, five or six times a year for discussions, exchange of information and whatever else it is that fifty senior executives do in an exotic location a long way from their wives and families.

Through all these kind of exchanges I have described here, bands cross borders. Via the communication that takes place within a global record operation, record companies in one country are constantly aware of their sister companies' successes and talents in other countries. And that brings us to stage two in this process: after a company in one country takes an interest in an act signed to one of its sister labels, what does it do to actually release the album in its home market?

Well, first thing is the practical one of taking delivery of all the bits of metal and plastic (parts, they're called) that are required to actually press the record. It is very rare that albums are exported as actual records; more often than not, they are shipped abroad in the form of all the parts needed by the local pressing plant to manufacture the album, along with a licence to actually make copies. This makes a lot of sense; far better to make records for Europe in Europe than go to the expense of having a million copies of an album air-freighted from the States.

Now, after those practical matters have been attended to, the local label then goes through all the processes of releasing the record in the way it would for one of its own artists. It presses and packages the record, advertises and promotes it and tries to get the act to do as much work backing it as possible.

The complicating factor in this international trade is that this last element is not always easy. If Madonna has a new album out, she is highly likely to go to promote it – with a tour, TV appearances, promotional activities and suchlike – but she has neither the time nor the inclination to do that everywhere in the world. She will certainly do it in the US and in the UK (in this country, partly because it is the world's third-largest record market and partly because she speaks the language and has a house here) and she may very well go to Japan because it is the world's second-biggest market and

Germany and France because they are numbers four and five.

But will she be bothered to go to tiny countries like Finland or New Zealand, one of which is an alarmingly long distance from any of her homes? Hmm, tricky.

Warner Music Finland and Warner Music New Zealand will beg and plead with her to come. They will tell her that her sales will double or treble if she takes the time and trouble to go to those countries and do a few gigs and one or two TV shows. But does having an ever bigger hit in Finland make any difference to Madonna, who could already buy Sting's half of Wiltshire if she wanted?

Perhaps she could most be persuaded by the thought that she is repaying a debt to a company that helped make her famous in the first place. (See Chapter 19.) But I am not privileged to know the contents of the dear lady's thoughts and how she feels about the contribution to her career of Warner Music Suomi (as Warner Music Finland is known to its friends in the north).

We can see that the global marketplace is full of opportunities. But it also contains some mighty big potential pitfalls. By far the largest of these are cultural: when an act crosses borders, sometimes certain intellectual adjustments have to be made or disaster will follow. For instance, Americans can't get hold of the difference between England and the UK. So, when Whitney Houston played a big hall in Glasgow, she came on stage and said, 'Hey, England!' You can imagine how that went down.

Bon Jovi's first big hit album, *Slippery When Wet*, had to have its title changed for Japan because, with no 'l' sound in their native language, the Japanese couldn't order it. And Judas Priest's album *Killing Machine* became *Hell Bent For Leather* in America because they have a tendency to shoot one another over there and the label didn't want to be seen to be making a contribution to that.

And, just to illustrate the potential for embarrassment and confusion when working with disparate cultures, let me point out that the words 'U kunt' in Dutch mean something along the lines of: 'Of course you can, you've very welcome.' Oh, and one more: in Japanese, the salute to a fellow drinker of 'chin chin' means 'dick'.

Sometimes different cultural sensibilities mean that artwork has to be altered to be more in keeping with the local tastes, sometimes tracks on the album are reordered and sometimes new tracks are added and others omitted. The advantage a global company has is that its labels on the ground in any given country know the local market and understand the national mores. This level of knowledge stops the original label making a complete chin chin of itself when its artists' albums are released by its sister company in an overseas market; with its intimate familiarity with local customs and sensitivities, the domestic company in that foreign territory will advise on any changes it deems necessary to sell more copies and maintain the global operation's good standing.

Of course, in this effort to sell the most copies possible, it is hoped that the labels will be helped by the artist. Good, professional stars work hard to have international hits, but this means not just going to the countries where the album is out but also doing the small oh-so-telling things. For example, nobody expects a star to learn Japanese on a fourteen-hour pan-Pacific flight, but picking up the words for 'hello', 'please', 'thank you' or even 'you're the best audience in the world' is going to go down a storm when he or she appears on Tokyo television or in concert. I remember a heavy metal man by the name of Gary Barden singing with the Michael Schenker Group at the massive Budokan arena in Tokyo. The only word in Japanese he had learned for the gig was 'ariga to' ('thank you'), but it got the biggest cheer of the night when he said it. One word, massive response. Worth doing, I'd say.

OK, that is major labels' global workings in a nutshell. But what, I hear you ask, about the indies?

Most indies, as we have seen, tend to be domestic only:

they are based in and operate in just one country. So how do they create international hits? In practice, by working together in networks of mutual assistance.

As we noted earlier, indies tend to operate in tandem with one another to give each of them an international reach. That is, they come together like the pieces of a jigsaw, each company bringing with it an expertise and infrastructure in its local market, to make up the global picture.

While indies buy and sell rights to ensure their music crosses borders, their relationship generally goes further than just that of buyer and seller – and it is this human connection that adds something important to their ability to do business effectively.

Indies are loosely bound, but bound nonetheless, by a philosophy. People working in the sector often feel a close connection with the indie ideology (whatever that happens to mean to them), so they have common cause and common ground when they talk to other indie labels. This fosters a camaraderie that smoothes the road to good relationships, in both a human and a commercial sense.

For instance, when A US indie label first signed Metallica, it needed somebody to try to break the band in Europe. It got into bed with Music For Nations, a London-based rock and metal specialist label. This, then, was not just a cold business partnership but a meeting of minds, enthusiasms and musical passions, all of which brought much mutual benefit.

Both sides of this liaison had an indie mentality, a penchant for the noisier end of the rock market and a commercial desire to sell as many records as possible. In this way they were true partners: like a marriage, at least part of their souls were invested in this communion (and, I'm sure, just like a marriage, there were probably a few rows, too).

Now, to make this relationship work properly and to help it produce as much money as possible for all concerned, Music For Nations needed the co-operation of the band in the marketing. In the purely commercial aspects of this

THE GLOBAL BUSINESS

relationship, the needs and requirements of Music For Nations were absolutely no different to those of a major-label affiliate company.

Just as a visit from Madonna would assist Warner Music Suomi, it eased Music For Nations' task enormously when Metallica, prompted by the US label, came to Europe to play gigs and do interviews and other promotional work. Had they not done so, it would have taken them a damn sight longer to break into the market here than it did.

Indies, then, co-operate – and they do so on many levels, from the purely financial to the completely human. Because of this co-operation, each good-size indie in the world can claim to have a truly global reach. That's important, because without such a claim, a lot of acts would be reluctant to sign to an indie and would concentrate solely on getting a deal with a major. The global indie network is, of course, much looser and made up of more components than a major label's operation, but a network it is nonetheless.

OK, now let's move on to publishers and what they do to spread music across national boundaries.

Major publishers are organised much like major labels and are very often part of the same group of companies. EMI Music Publishing is part of the same group as EMI's record division, BMG Music Publishing with BMG records and so on.

The major publishing affiliates – for example, EMI Music Publishing UK, EMI Music Publishing France, EMI Music Publishing Australia – talk to one another daily and get together regularly, just as their label counterparts do. Again, just like the record company execs, they exchange information, ideas, concepts for new projects and ways of making the most of the copyrights they own.

But publishers, remember, handle only rights to music, not the recording of it, and therefore, because they are not inhibited by having to shift large numbers of discs, they are more able to take music across national borders than the record companies.

So, when publishers get together, they will discuss what each of them administers and whether there are opportunities for those copyrights in another country. For instance, EMI Music Publishing Australia might mention it has signed a brilliant new writer of deep turbo nutter bastard folk. The man from EMI Music Germany might then say, 'Oh, there's an advertising agency in Cologne that needs plenty of that stuff for a new radio campaign they are putting together. I'll give you their number.'

Music publishers are crossing borders in this way every day and each major music publisher administers a catalogue of songs created by songwriters of many nationalities. And, because the publisher is constantly marketing this catalogue to film companies, advertising agencies, record companies and anybody else who uses music, a lot of people who can bring new talent to an international audience hear loads of new material every day. Film companies in particular help songs to cross from one nation to others, but each significant user of music is making a contribution to that, too.

And, of course, in that list of music users who can cross national boundaries, record companies feature very highly. Why so in this context of music publishers? Well ...

In this age of modern communications and the single European market, there are few barriers to a publisher from one European Union country selling its copyrights to a record company in another nation. If Sloterdijk Music in Amsterdam has a highly talented young composer of pop songs, it may get in touch with a UK record company to sell these to the UK label's hot new boy band. The UK label will pay its royalties to Sloterdijk Music in just the same way as it would to a publisher based just around the corner. On top of that, if Sloterdijk Music has a brilliant composition that has just been a big hit in the Netherlands but is sung in Dutch, it might well offer that song to a UK act but with new English lyrics. (This concept was pioneered long ago when the French song 'Comme d'Habitude' became the English-language classic 'My Way'.)

Now, Sloterdijk Music may have a UK office through which it handles the songs it sells in Britain, but there is no reason why it really needs one. Fifteen nations of Europe are one market and it is illegal to hinder or impede the flow of trade across that trading bloc. There is, then, no legal or practical barrier to Sloterdijk Music doing all its European business from one office above a bookie's in Amsterdam. The only real obstacle is that, even now, some Brits can't rise above the island-nation concept and get this cross-border thing into their heads.

Mind you, they are not alone. Back in the late nineties, the two French guys who write and play music as Daft Punk registered their copyrights with the PRS in the UK instead of their domestic collection society, SACEM. Though what they did was highly legal and in keeping with the free-trade precepts that underpin the European Union, the stink that SACEM raised was terrible. SACEM didn't have a leg to stand on, of course, but there was a part of that organisation's consciousness that couldn't assimilate that it was no longer number one in a field of one.

For a hundred years SACEM had had a monopoly on collecting royalties for French composers. With the advent of the single European market, suddenly there were fourteen other collecting societies all capable of doing that work. SACEM knew it but wouldn't admit to itself that it was happening. The brave boys from Daft Punk, because of their determination and refusal to be dissuaded, made them understand.

That brings us on to retailers and their role in the international business. Like the boys from Daft Punk, the retail chains have shown the potential of a single European market – much to the distress of the labels.

The retailers have invented a thing that has become known as trans-shipments. They work like this. Take a big retailer, like World Of Music (WOM) in Germany. Along with the purely domestic German stock, WOM sells a lot of international albums. Before the advent of the single European market, if it wanted, say, Michael Jackson's *Thriller*, it had to buy its copies of the album from the appropriate domestic record company, Sony Germany.

Now, the European Union opened up trade and allows WOM to buy its Michael Jackson albums from any of the Sony companies across the fifteen nations of the EU. So, it can go to Sony Portugal, Sony Greece, Sony Finland or any of those affiliates to get its albums.

Why is this significant? Well, economic conditions are not the same across Europe. Rents in Portugal are lower than those in Finland, staff costs are lower and so on, which means that an album coming out of Sony Portugal should be cheaper than the same album coming out of Sony Finland (and if it isn't, the EU's competition people are going to want to know why).

Further, before the euro, each nation's currency fluctuated in value against all the others. So, if the Greek drachma was weak against the German mark, WOM might buy its Jacko albums from Sony in Athens. If the arse fell out of the value of the franc, WOM would go to Sony France.

Now, all this is great for the retailers but a nightmare for the record companies. For the retailers, it means they have a choice for the first time in their trading lives. For the record companies, though, it means they are effectively competing against themselves.

And there ain't much they can do about it. As we noted in Chapter 13, the competition people watch the music industry like hawks. If every Jacko album from every Sony company in the euro zone was suddenly exactly the same number of euros, the EU's fair-trade department would be round there sharpish with a big stick (or whatever it is these financial people take with them on a raid).

The labels, though, have done all they can to resist this trans-shipment concept – and in that resistance they have used all legal and one or two only slightly illegal means.

Legal means include stopping co-operation with a retailer buying records from abroad. That happened in the Netherlands when one significant retail group told Universal Netherlands that it was buying its international albums from one of the other Universal companies around Europe. Theo Roos, boss at Universal Netherlands, was not best pleased and told the retailer that sales reps would no longer call at the stores, Universal artists would not be available for in-store signing sessions and other promotion work and there would be no co-operation between label and retailer.

The retailer said, 'Go on, then. Come and have a go if you think you're hard enough.'

Universal Netherlands stood its ground, the retailer stood his. And, in the end, it wasn't the retailer who had to back down. That hurt Theo. He's a real gentleman of rock but he had been forced to realise that you can't hold back the tide of progress.

Now on to the illegal methods of stopping trans-shipments, including simply declining to complete the order. This, however, is an unlawful restraint of trade as a major record company cannot refuse to supply any legitimate customer. If WOM orders all its Jacko albums from Sony Portugal, Sony Portugal must sell those albums. WOM is a known and respected operator and Sony Portugal – no matter what the president of Sony Europe in London says – must fill the order or face action in the courts. It is, though, only obliged to deliver those albums within Portugal's national borders, but that just means WOM has to get a cheap warehouse somewhere in Lisbon and transport the albums from there to Germany.

Sony UK once tried to block an order from another country – but only the once. When it was pointed out that the company could be both sued and charged under criminal law for such an action, it changed its mind rather rapidly.

Why do record companies hate trans-shipments so much? First of all, profits are cut if retailers are buying all their

European stock from the cheapest source. Secondly, it makes it impossible to account properly.

If Sony UK is suddenly the most expensive source for records of all the Sony companies in Europe, it might find its sales dropping despite having huge hits. Imagine that Michael Jackson is number one in the UK album chart, Oasis are number two and a re-released *Bat Out Of Hell* is number three. If it is cheaper to buy all those albums from Sony France rather than Sony UK, the UK company may have the chart to itself but not be selling a single record. Sony France, on the other hand, will find sales going through the roof with no additional effort on its part.

The lifeblood of the music industry is, of course, music and record companies argue that, if they are unable to account properly, they have no idea how much money they can invest in music through their A&R budgets. In the worst-case scenario, that would mean there were no new acts emerging from Europe at all and all we would be left with would be American rockers and the old stuff.

By and large, though, internationalism has been more of an advantage to the music industry than a handicap. Indeed, music is one of the few truly global commodities: a CD bought in London will give you exactly the same sound on a player bought in Tokyo as one bought in New York. A CD is a CD the world over. This one format is universal. The same is not true of video (American video cassettes are not the same size as European ones and don't fit our machines) and is not true of DVD. Only CD is truly universal.

This truism is a factor which helps retailers make their own positive contribution to the international business. A big retail chain will stock material from around the globe, often under the heading of 'world music' (whatever that means). Through the presence in the store's racks of records from Argentina or Cameroon or wherever, some buyers will give one or more of them a try. This may only give that overseas artist a tiny foothold in a European or American market, but it is at least a foothold that he or she would not have had were it not for the eclectic stocking policies of a big retailer.

Smaller stores also make their contribution, of course, and there are indies that specialise in world music. Their stocking policies and the knowledge and enthusiasm of their staff help to create additional demand and interest.

Music, then, is truly universal. It requires no translation (pretty much the whole world is prepared to sing along in English, whether they understand the words or not) and the tunes and melodies are a common thread among all humanity.

For this reason, the industry is organised globally, works globally, thinks globally and acts globally.

In a world where globalisation is increasingly unpopular, at least music is showing the positive sides of a world market.

Chapter 21

AND A FINAL WORD ON NEW TECHNOLOGY

SOME NEW PIECE OF music-playing technology has been produced since I wrote this.

Some new piece of music-playing technology has been produced since you read this.

I've no idea what it is or what it does. You're on your own.

But just remember that music is property and whoever uses it has to pay for it – and that holds true no matter what system they are using to play it.